高职高专"十三五"规划教材

# 船舶电子电气专业英语

## （项目化教程）

王欣 主编　管旭 王丽琴 副主编

化学工业出版社

·北京·

本书内容深入浅出，便于自学。全书共分10个单元（20个学习任务）和2个实训环节，主要内容包括船舶电站、船舶电力拖动、船舶信号系统、船舶电气安装、船舶通信与导航、船电工程师文档写作，以及船舶电气设备名称、调试专业术语等。

本书在内容选编和结构安排上均有创新。书中内容节选自某造船企业的电气说明书和相关文档，这些内容都是企业工作岗位需要的；结构上以造船典型的工作任务为核心，结合船舶电气技术专业的特点，安排相关的教学与技能培养环节，重在培养学生阅读电气说明书等英文材料和口语交流职业能力。

本书是高职高专船舶电气类专业教材，也可供造船企业、船舶维修及船务公司等相关单位的工程技术人员阅读参考。

### 图书在版编目（CIP）数据

船舶电子电气专业英语（项目化教程）/王欣主编.
北京：化学工业出版社，2016.3（2025.1重印）
高职高专"十三五"规划教材
ISBN 978-7-122-26286-8

Ⅰ.①船…　Ⅱ.①王…　Ⅲ.①船用电气设备-英语-高等职业教育-教材　Ⅳ.①H31

中国版本图书馆 CIP 数据核字（2016）第 028696 号

---

责任编辑：王听讲　　　　　　　　　　装帧设计：韩　飞
责任校对：边　涛

---

出版发行：化学工业出版社（北京市东城区青年湖南街 13 号　邮政编码 100011）
印　　装：北京天宇星印刷厂
787mm×1092mm　1/16　印张 13½　字数 349 千字　2025 年 1 月北京第 1 版第 3 次印刷

---

购书咨询：010-64518888（传真：010-64519686）　　售后服务：010-64518899
网　　址：http://www.cip.com.cn
凡购买本书，如有缺损质量问题，本社销售中心负责调换。

---

定　价：35.00 元　　　　　　　　　　　　　　　　　　　　　版权所有　违者必究

# 前　言

　　船舶电子电气专业英语是船舶电气类专业的一门专业必修课程，通过本课程的学习，学生将掌握船舶电气专业英语常用词汇、英文术语、缩写和特殊表达方式，并能阅读船舶电气设备英文操作面板及英文版操作手册；阅读、编写船舶电气设备订购单等船电生产管理中常用英文文件；学会造船和修船工作场所日常生活会话和日常业务会话方式和技巧，增强英语口语交流沟通能力。

　　本书是船舶电气类专业三年制高职或五年制高职教学教材。全书共分 10 个单元（20 个学习任务）和 2 个实训环节，主要内容包括船舶电气设备、船舶电站、船舶电力拖动、船舶信号系统、船舶电气安装、船舶通信与导航、船电工程师文档写作等内容。本书通过典型任务引领的项目活动，使学生具备从事本职业的高素质劳动者和高级技术应用型人才所必需的专业英语知识与技能。

　　本教材在内容编写和结构安排上力求有所创新。部分内容节选自某造船企业的英文电气说明书和相关文档，重点突出，难度适中，教材的内容都是企业工作岗位需求的；编写方法上以具体的工作任务为核心，结合船舶电气技术专业的特点安排相关的教学与技能培养环节，突出培养学生阅读电气说明书等英文材料和口语交流等相关的职业能力。

　　我们将为教师提供电子版的《教师参考书》，以及每个单元的教案、练习题答案和课文参考译文。我们还将为使用本书的教师免费提供电子教案等教学资源，需要者可以到化学工业出版社教学资源网站 http://www.cipedu.com.cn 免费下载使用。

　　本教材由渤海船舶职业学院电气工程系王欣担任主编，管旭和王丽琴担任副主编。王欣负责编写第 1、4、6、9 单元以及实训 1 和实训 2；管旭负责编写第 2、8、10 单元和语法部分；王丽琴负责编写第 3、5、7 单元；渤海船舶重工孙睿也参与了本教材的设计和编写工作。

　　本书的编写得到了渤海船舶职业学院教务处，特别是电气工程系各位同仁的支持与帮助，以及骨干校建设项目"电气工程系课程建设项目"的支持，在此表示由衷的感谢。

　　在本书的编写过程中，我们得到了大连中远、舟山中远造船企业、金陵造船厂及渤海船舶重工等单位多位同志的大力支持和帮助，在此一并致以衷心的感谢。

　　由于编者水平有限和时间仓促，疏漏之处在所难免，恳请广大同仁批评斧正。

编　者

2016 年 1 月

# Contents

## Unit 1　Ship's Bridge and Engine Control Room

Task 1　Ship's Bridge ········································································································· 1
Task 2　Engine Control Room ························································································· 8
【Unit Evaluation】············································································································ 14

## Unit 2　Marine Electric Drive System

Task 1　Deck Machinery ································································································· 15
Task 2　Marine Auxiliary System ················································································· 22
【Unit Evaluation】············································································································ 31

## Unit 3　Three-phase Asynchronous Motors and Electrical Control

Task 1　Three-phase Asynchronous Motors ······························································· 33
Task 2　Motor and Electrical Control ········································································· 40
【Unit Evaluation】············································································································ 47

## Unit 4　Marine Power Station

Task 1　Marine Electrical System ················································································· 48
Task 2　Marine Power Management System (PMS) ················································· 57
【Unit Evaluation】············································································································ 64

## Unit 5　Marine Electric Installation

Task 1　Introduction of Shipboard Cables ································································· 66
Task 2　Shipping Electric Installation ········································································· 72
【Unit Evaluation】············································································································ 77

## Unit 6　Marine Signal System

Task 1　Marine Alarm System ······················································································· 79
Task 2　Marine Automation System ············································································· 87
【Unit Evaluation】············································································································ 92

## Unit 7　Marine Communication and Navigation System

Task 1　GMDSS ·········93
Task 2　Marine Communication System and Navigation Equipment ·········100
【Unit Evaluation】·········108

## Unit 8　Marine Electrical Maintenance and Trouble Shooting

Task 1　Marine Electrical Maintenance ·········109
Task 2　Electrical Trouble Shooting ·········117
【Unit Evaluation】·········125

## Unit 9　Marine Electrical Test

Task　Marine Electrical Test ·········126
【Unit Evaluation】·········138

## Unit 10　Lists and Documents for Electrical Engineer's Profession

Task 1　Documents for Repairs ·········140
Task 2　Certificates, Letters, Telegram & Telex ·········152
Task 3　Business Writing Relating to Electro-technical Officer ·········160
【Unit Evaluation】·········168

## Practical Training 1

【Training Content】·········169
【Training Evaluation】·········178

## Practical Training 2

【Training Content】·········180
【Training Evaluation】·········191

## Grammar ·········192
## Appendix　New Words and Expressions ·········197
参考文献 ·········208

# Unit 1

# Ship's Bridge and Engine Control Room

【Unit Goals】

1. Get to know the function of ship's bridge and engine control room; Be familiar with the electrical equipment equipment in ship's bridge and engine control room: chronometer, compass, gyroscope, main switchboard(MSB), emergency switchboard(ESB) etc.

2. Students can introduce ship's bridge and engine control room to others in English.They can talk to each other about ship's bridge and engine control room fluently.

## Task 1  Ship's Bridge

【Task goals】

1. Get to know the function of ship's bridge. Be familiar with the electrical equipment in ship's bridge: telegraph, steering wheel, tachometer, compass etc.

2. Students can introduce the marine electrical equipment in bridge to others in English and talk to each other about equipment fluently.

【Knowledge linking】

What do ship's bridge include in your mind?
Please look at the following pictures carefully and try to learn the terms.
(1) Ship's bridge (Fig. 1-1)
(2) Bridge control console (BCC) (Fig. 1-2)

### Ship's Bridge

The bridge is also called the "wheelhouse". The bridge or the wheelhouse is headquarter of a ship, where much of the ship's navigational equipment and meters for maneuvering the ship are installed, for example: telegraph, radar, steering wheel, tachometer and so on, It can be said that the bridge is the command center on board.[1]

# Unit 1　Ship's Bridge and Engine Control Room

Fig.1-1　Ship's bridge

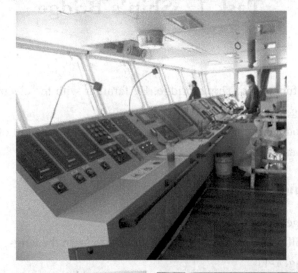

Fig. 1-2　Bridge control console (BCC)

When the ship is underway(航行中), the bridge, from which the navigation and control of the ship is exercised, is the control center for all operations. The officers, the helmsman, and the quartermaster of the watch stand their watches here.

The bridge includes the pilothouse or wheelhouse so called, because it contains the ship's steering wheel, and the charthouse where the navigator and his staff chart the course of the ship. Due to their responsibilities, both the captain and the navigator are required to be in this area frequency when the ship is at sea. The charthouse is a part of the bridge. The ship's course or route is laid out here on large nautical charts. The ship's position is frequently determined and plotted on the chart.[2] The stacks of drawers contain nautical charts for various areas of the entire world. The official ship's logbook is also put here. And on the bulkhead are the radio direction finder, a pair of global positioning system receivers, a NAVTEX receiver and a loran-C receiver. All of the units are used to help establish the ship's position (Fig. 1-3).[3]

(a) Charthouse

(b) Radio room

Fig.1-3　Charthouse and radio room

The outside platforms, called the bridge wings, permit greater overall visibility for the officers than the pilothouse, which simply looks forward. The navigator and quartermaster also take visual readings from the wings using gyrocompass bearings to known objects or sextant elevations to the stars, planets and sun to determine the ship's position. At sea during hours of darkness, the lookout stands his watch in this area, scanning the horizon for other ships or hazards to navigation. When he stops something unusual, he reports the information to the mate on watch, who is the officer in charge of safely navigating the ship. The mate reports to the captain or master who is the ultimate authority and responsible for the overall operation of the ship.

【 New Words and Expressions 】

| wheelhouse | [ˈwiːlhaʊs] | n. | 驾驶室，操舵室 |
| bridge | [brɪdʒ] | n. | 驾驶室，桥楼 |
| telegraph | [ˈtelɪɡrɑːf] | n. | 电报 |
| bulkhead | [ˈbʌlkhed] | n. | 隔离壁,堵墙,岸壁 |
| charthouse | [ˈtʃɑːthaʊs] | n. | 海图室 |
| fathometer | [fæˈðɒmɪtə] | n. | 回声探测仪 |
| gyrocompass | [ˈdʒaɪərəʊˌkʌmpəs] | n. | 陀螺罗经,电罗经 |
| gyroscope | [ˈdʒaɪrəskəʊp] | n. | 陀螺仪 |

| | | | |
|---|---|---|---|
| helmsman | [ˈhelmzmən] | n. | 舵手 |
| landmark | [ˈlændmɑːk] | n. | [航]陆标 |
| pilothouse | [ˈpaɪlət.haʊs] | n. | 操舵室 |
| quartermaster | [ˈkwɔːtəmɑːstə(r)] | n. | 舵手 |
| steering | [ˈstɪərɪŋ] | n. | 转向装置；掌舵；操作；指导 |
|    steering wheel | | | 方向盘；驾驶盘 |
|    steering gear | | | 操舵装置，舵机， |
| platform | [ˈplætfɔːm] | n. | 台；站台；平台 |
| tachometer | [tæˈkɒmɪtə] | n | 转速计；测速计；旋速计；速度计 |
| bridge wings | | | 驾驶台两侧的翼台 |
|    port bridge wing | | | 左翼（PORT WING） |
|    starboard bridge wing | | | 右翼(经常缩写为 STBD. WING) |
| (bridge control console)BCC | | | 驾控台 |
| Global Positioning System(GPS) Receiver | | | 全球定位系统接收机 |
| Loran-C receiver | | | 罗兰 C，接收机 |
| NAVTEX | | | 航行警告电传系统 |

## 【Notes】

(1) The bridge or the wheelhouse is headquarter of a ship, where much of the ship's navigational equipment and meters for maneuvering the ship are installed,for example: telegraph,radar, steering wheel,tachometer and so on, It can be said that the bridge is the command center on board.

驾驶室是一艘船舶的指挥总部，里面装备一艘船舶大多数的导航设备和驾驶船舶的各种仪表，如电报，雷达，舵机，测深仪等，它是一艘船舶的命令指挥中心。

注意：对专业英语翻译要求有三个层次，即信、达、雅。所谓"信"，是指翻译要忠实原文；所谓"达"，是指翻译通顺。所谓"雅"，要求翻译在修辞上加以润色，这要求翻译人员有较高的中文造诣。专业英语的句子一般都比较长，会有一些从句，翻译的时候可以按照两个步骤进行：先直译，后按照中文的习惯（中文句子一般是：时间、地点、人物、事件）调整语序。本句中就有 where 引导的从句。

(2) The chartroom is a part of the bridge. The ship's course or route is laid out here on large nautical charts. The ship's position is frequently determined and plotted on the chart.

海图室是驾驶室的一部分。大的航海图，可以显示船舶的航程和航线。在海图上通常可以确定和绘制船舶的位置。

lay out 设计；展示；安排

(3) And on the bulkhead are the radio direction finder, a pair of global positioning system receivers, a NAVTEX receiver and a Loran-C receiver. All of the units are used to help establish the ship's position.

隔壁是无线电测向仪、双套 GPS 接收、一台航行警告电传系统和双曲线无线电导航系统接收机。所有这些设备用来帮助确定船舶位置。

# Task 1 Ship's Bridge

【Task Implement】

## PART A  Reading Practice

### Navigation equipment(Table 1-1)

(SELECTED FROM ELECTRICAL SPECIFICATION FOR 165,000 DWT CRUDE OIL TANKER)

Table 1-1  Navigation equipment

| No. | Name | Number |
|---|---|---|
| 1 | gyro compass/ autopilot | One (1) set of gyro compass shall be installed in wheelhouse. |
| 2 | magnetic compass | One (1) set of reflect type magnetic standard compass of 165mm card dia(卡径), shall be installed on the compass deck (罗经甲板), and the repeater shall be extended through the deck to the Wheel House.[1]<br>One (1) set of spare (备用) compass bowl shall be provided in the wooden storage box.<br>Magnetic compass shall be adjusted at sea trials (航海试验).<br>One (1) piece of azimuth (航向) signal shall be provided with the gyro compass & auto pilot. |
| 3. | echo sounder | One (1) set of echo sounder with shallow water alarm shall be installed, it's transducer shall be installed at bottom on forward.[2]<br>One (1) recorder shall be installed in wheel house.<br>One (1) set of digital depth indicator shall be provided on measuring instrument panel.<br>The shallow water alarm shall be provided. |
| 4. | speed log | One (1) set of two axial Doppler speed log shall be installed in the wheel house and equipped with distance and speed indication.<br>One (1) repeater shall be installed in engine room control console.<br>One (1) speed indicator with a dimmer shall be installed in wheelhouse.<br>One (1) transducer shall be installed on forward. |
| 5. | radar plant | Two (2) sets of raster scan type marine radar shall be provided |
| 6. | horn | One (1) set of air horn on the radar mast (雷达桅) and one (1) set of electric horn on the foremast shall be provided.[3]<br>One (1) set of horn controller shall be fitted on bridge control console and shall be capable of operating horns and providing automatic for signaling.<br>Each one (1) set of push button shall be provided in the wheelhouse and both bridge wings.<br>The equipment shall be fed from emergency supply system.<br>The horn light shall be commonly used with morse signal light. |
| 7. | weather facsimile receiver | One (1) set of weather facsimile recorder shall be provided in the chart space and a whip antenna (鞭状天线) on the wheelhouse top. |
| 8. | NAVTEX receiver | One (1) set of 518 kHz NAVTEX receiver with printer shall be installed in wheel house.[4] |
| 9. | anemometer and anemoscope | One (1) set of anemometer for continuous measurement of wind speed and wind direction with illumination shall be provided. A combined anemometer transmitter shall be installed at radar mast. |
| 10. | DGPS | Two (2) set of DGPS satellite navigator shall be provided in wheelhouse and antenna on the radar mast. |
| 11. | window wiper | Five (5) sets of window wipers with glass heater shall be provided, the controller to be installed on wheelhouse console |

Ship's Bridge and Engine Control Room

## 【New Words and Expressions】

| | | | |
|---|---|---|---|
| autopilot | [ˈɔːtoʊpaɪlət] | n. | 自动驾驶仪 |
| echo | [ˈekoʊ] | n. | 回声 |
| echo sounder | | | 回声测深仪 |
| transducer | [trænzˈduːsər] | n. | 传感器 |
| facsimile | [fækˈsɪməli] | n. | 传真 |
| anemometer | [ænɪˈmɑːmɪtə(r)] | n. | 风速计 |
| anemoscope | [əneˈməskoʊp] | n. | 风速计 |
| horn | [hɔːn] | n. | 号角，喇叭 |
| transmitter | [trænsˈmɪtə, trænz-] | n. | 发射机 发报机 |
| receiver | [rɪˈsivə] | n. | 接收器 无线电接收机 |
| repeater | [rɪˈpitə] | n. | 复示器 |

## 【Notes】

(1) One (1) set of reflect type magnetic standard compass of 165mm card dia, shall be installed on the compass deck（罗经甲板）, and the repeater shall be extended through the deck to the Wheel House.

罗经甲板上安装一台反映式 165mm 卡径标准磁罗经，能将罗经卡读数投射到驾驶室内。

(2) One (1) set of echo sounder with shallow water alarm shall be installed, it's transducer shall be installed at bottom on forward.

安装一台带有浅水报警的回声测深仪，它的传感器安装在船舶的前方底部。

(3) One (1) set of air horn on the radar mast（雷达桅）and one (1) set of electric horn on the foremast shall be provided.

在雷达桅装汽笛，前桅上装备电笛。

(4) One (1) set of 518 kHz NAVTEX receiver with printer shall be installed in wheel house.

驾驶室装备一台 518kHz 带有打印机的航行警告电传接收机。

### PART B   Role Playing

#### Visit the Bridge

(A: cadet who comes on board for the first time; B: captain)

A: What is this one?

B: It is a gyroscope. The instrument provides an accurate indication of the ship's heading, or direction.

A: What is that on the bulkhead?

B: That is a recording fathometer. It displays and records the distance from the bottom of the ship to the ocean floor.

A: Is this the recorder?

B: You are right. It can plot the steering direction, the wind direction.

A: Where is the chronometer?

B: It is inside the glass case on the left end of the chart table.

A: It must be used together with a sextant and nautical almanac to calculate the position by observing stars and the sun.

B: Very correct.

## 【Task Evaluation】

### (一) Choice

1. What is also called the wheelhouse?
   A.chartroom　　　　　　　　B.bridge　　　　　　　　C.the console
2. Gyro,called gyroscope,provides_____.
   A.the distance from the bottom of the ship to the ocean floor
   B.the wind direction
   C.an accurate indication of the ship's direction.
3. What is the commanding center on board?
   A.the wheelhouse　　　　　　B.bridge wing　　　　　　C.engine control room
4. Where much of the ship's navigational equipment and meters for maneuvering the ship are installed?
   bridge wing　　　　　　　　B.the wheelhouse　　　　　C.engine control room
5. What called the bridge wings?
   A.upper deck　　　　　　　　B.the outside platforms　　C.engine control room

### (二) Translation.

1. Translate new words and expressions into Chinese (Table 1-2).

Table 1-2　Translation

| | |
|---|---|
| 1.gyro compass | |
| 2.magnetic compass | |
| 3.echo sounder | |
| 4.speed log | |
| 5.radar plant | |
| 6.fog horn | |
| 7.weather facsimile receiver | |
| 8.NAVTEX receiver | |
| 9.anemometer and anemoscope | |
| 10.GPS | |
| 11.BCC | |
| 12.autopilot | |
| 13.charthouse | |
| 14.bridge/wheelhouse | |
| 15.port wing | |

A. 回声测深仪；B. 电罗经、陀螺罗经；C. 磁罗经；D. 计程仪；E. 雾号；F. 气象传真机；G. 操舵仪；H. 全球定位系统；I. 航行警告电传系统；J. 驾控台；K. 海图室；L. 集控台；M. 驾驶室；N. 驾驶室左翼；O. 风速计。

2. Translate the following sentences into Chinese.

The bridge includes the pilothouse or wheelhouse so called, because it contains the ship's steering wheel, and the charthouse where the navigator and his staff chart the course of the ship. Due to their responsibilities, both the captain and the navigator are required to be in this area frequency when the ship is at sea. The chartroom is a part of the bridge. The ship's course or route is laid out here on large nautical charts. The ship's position is frequently determined and plotted on the chart.The stacks of drawers contain nautical charts for various areas of the entire world. The official ship's logbook is also put here. And on the bulkhead are the radio direction finder, a pair of global positioning system receivers, a NAVTEX receiver and a loran-C receiver. All of the units are used to help establish the ship's position.

(三) **Speaking Practice**

1. Group discussion

Work in groups. Look at the statements in the language bank task. Which of them are important aspects for general-cargo ships and container ships respectively? Why?

2. Short talk

Now it is your chance to practice what you have learned from this unit. Put your textbook away and give a short talk on the following topics. You should talk at least one minute. Don't be discouraged if you cannot make it. Review the lesson and try again. You are sure to do it better next time.

- bridge on the ship

3. Role playing

Work in groups or pairs and discuss the following topics. Then, you are advised to talk at least three minutes for each topic.

- A is a cadet visiting the ship. B is the captain.
- Prompts: Introducing the bridge control console.
- Bridge (its function and related equipment).

## Task 2  Engine Control Room

**【 Task goals 】**

1. Get to know engine control room. Be familiar with the marine electrical equipment in ECR: main switchboard(MSB),emergency switchboard(ESM) etc.

2. Students can introduce the marine electrical equipment in engine control room to others in English and talk to each other about equipment fluently.

**【 Knowledge linking 】**

What do ship's engine control room(ECR) include in your mind?
Please look at the following pictures carefully and try to learn the terms:

(1) Engine control room(ECR) (Fig.1-4)

Task 2 Engine Control Room

Fig.1-4 Engine control room(ECR)

(2) Engine control console(ECC) (Fig.1-5)

Fig.1-5 Engine control console(ECC)

## Engine Control Room(ECR)

The engine control room(ECR) is the workplace for marine engine operation and is equipped with appropriate equipment, many control panels, indicators, buttons are distributed over consoles and switch cabinets in such a way that all essential conditions of the main propulsion unit can be observed and controlled at the same time.[1] The main engine control station is the central point for main engine and auxiliary diesel generators, shaft generator, turbo generator, emergency diesel generator and the main switch cabinet are lined up face-to-face with the main engine control station. The engine diagnosis system permits a display of the cylinder and injection pressure curves and rotational uniformity and with the values obtained, and it is possible to visualize the engine status. Moreover,

9

there is a ship's control console serving as secondary control and monitoring station and allowing remote control of ship speed and direction in emergency situations.

The engine control room is the place where engine control room crews carry out instructions from the bridge by means of operating the various kind of machinery equipment.[2] Good cooperation between the bridge and engine control room is key for the ship's sailing at sea. With the rapid development of technology, Unattended Machinery Space（UMS） appears. That is to say, no one needs to work in the engine control room and the ship can be remotely controlled from the bridge. We are sure that the great change will certainly take place in the future.

## 【New Words and Expressions】

| | | | |
|---|---|---|---|
| Engine Control Room(ECR) | | | 集控室 |
| Engine Control Console(ECC) | | | 集控台 |
| switch | [swɪtʃ] | n. & v. | 开关 转换 |
| propulsion | [prəˈpʌlʃən] | n. | 推进 推进力 |
| engine | [ˈɛndʒɪn] | n. | 发动机，引擎 |
| main engine(ME) | | n. | 主机 |
| generator | [ˈdʒɛnəˌreɪtɚ] | n. | 发电机 |
| diesel generator(D.G) | | | 柴油发动机 |
| shaft generator | | | 轴带发电机 |
| turbo generator | | | 涡轮发电机 |
| Unattended Machinery Space（UMS） | | | 无人机舱 |

## 【Notes】

(1) The engine control room(ECR) is the workplace for marine engine operation and is equipped with appropriate equipment, many control panels, indicators, buttons are distributed over consoles and switch cabinets in such a way that all essential conditions of the main propulsion unit can be observed and controlled at the same time.

集控室是操纵船机的工作场所，这里有适当的设备、许多控制屏、指示器、按钮安装在控制台上，能够通过配电盘同时去观测和控制主推进单元的基本参数。

(2) The engine control room is the place where engine control room crews carry out instructions from the bridge by means of operating the various kind of machinery equipment.

集控室是这样的地方，它里面的船员通过操作各种机器设备执行从驾驶室发出的指令。

## 【Task Implement】

### PART A　Reading Practice

**Switchboard in ECR(Table 1-3)**

(SELECTED FROM ELECTRICAL SPECIFICATION FOR 165,000 DWT CRUDE OIL TANKER)

## Table 1-3  Switchboard in ECR

| No. | Name | Number |
|---|---|---|
| 1. | Main Switchboard (MSB) | The main switchboard shall be installed in the engine control room and consist of following panels:<br>Panel Arrangement<br>The main switchboard shall be installed in the engine control room and consist of following panels:<br>No.1 group starter panel<br>No.1 440V feeder panel<br>No.1 diesel generator panel<br>Synchronizing panel<br>No.2 diesel generator panel<br>No.3 diesel generator panel<br>No.2 440V feeder panel<br>No.2 group starter panel<br>220V feeder panel<br><br>Generator Panel — Shaft Generator Panel<br>400 Volt Feeder Panel — Group Starter Pane<br>220V Feeder Panel — Synchronizing Panel |
| 2. | Emergency Switchboard (ESB) | The emergency switchboard shall consist of one emergency generator panel, one AC 440V feeder panel and one 220V feeder panel. The emergency switchboard shall be installed in the emergency generator room.[1]<br>An emergency diesel generator engine automatic start device shall be installed in the emergency generator room, but not in the emergency switchboard. |
| 3. | Shore Connection | One (1) set of shore connection for receiving AC 440V volts, 400 amperes, 3 phase, 60Hz, shore source shall be provided with three (3) pole moulded case type circuit breaker and phase sequence indicator that shall be installed in the ESB. |

| No. | Name | Number |
|---|---|---|
| 4. | Charging and Discharging Boards | One (1) charging equipment for the battery for starting emergency generator shall be provided and shall be arranged in emergency generator room, which feed DC 24V power supply to ESB.<br>Each one (1) charging & discharging board for the battery for general use and E/R use shall be provided and shall be arranged in the electric equipment room or suitable location and E/R, with AC440 V power source from MSB & ESB. Battery charger alarm shall be provided in W/H and E/R monitoring system.<br>DC voltmeter, DC Ammeter for charging and discharging, indicating lamp for floating and equalizing charge, source pilot lamp, insulation resistance meter, change over switch and suitable voltage regulator shall be provided on them. |

【New Words and Expressions】

| | | | |
|---|---|---|---|
| switchboard | [ˈswɪtʃbɔːd] | n. | 配电板 |
| main switchboard(MSB) | | | 主配电板 |
| emergency switchboard (ESB) | | | 应急配电板 |
| voltage | [ˈvoʊltɪdʒ] | n. | 电压 |
| current | [ˈkɜːrənt] | n. | 电流 |
| circuit | [ˈsɜːrkɪt] | n. | 电路 |
| breaker | [ˈbreɪkɚ] | n. | 断路器 |
| phase | [feɪz] | n. | 相位 |
| phase sequence | | | 相序 |
| charge | [tʃɑːdʒ] | v. | 充电 |
| discharge | [dɪsˈtʃɑːdʒ] | v. | 放电 |
| charger | [ˈtʃɑːrdʒə(r)] | n. | 充电器 |
| battery | [ˈbætəri] | n. | 电池, 蓄电池 |

【Notes】

The emergency switchboard shall consist of one emergency generator panel, one AC 440V feeder panel and one 220V feeder panel. The emergency switchboard shall be installed in the emergency generator room.

由一组应急发电机屏、一组交流440V负载屏和220V负载屏组成。应急配电板应该安装在应急发电机室。

### PART B    Role Playing

#### Visit Engine Control Room

(A: cadet who comes on board for the first time; B: electrician)

A: Could you let me look around this ship?

B: OK, let's go to visit the engine control room and marine power station of this ship.

A: What can the main switchboards consist of ?

B: Usually the main switchboards consist of several panels: group starter panels, consumer panels, lighting panel, diesel generator panels etc.

A: Is the alarm system included in the above panels?

B: Yes, and there can also be the power interchange between shore supply and ship supply.

A: Can some controlling be done automatically?

B: Certainly!

## 【Task Evaluation】

### (一) Choice

1. What is the workplace for marine engine operation?
   A. engine control room(ECR)　　　B. bridge　　　C. the console

2. Where is crews carry out instructions from the bridge by means of operating the various kind of machinery equipment?
   A. engine control room(ECR)　　　B. bridge　　　C. the console

3. What can the main switchboard consist of ?
   A. charging and Discharging Boards
   B. group starter panels,consumer panels, lighting panel, diesel generator panels etc.
   C. emergency generator pane,emergency group starter panels,emergency consumer panels etc.

4. _____ is a box which can lead the shore power source to the ship power net .
   A. main switch board
   B. shore connection box
   C. charging & discharging panel

5. What is included in ECR?
   A. engine control console(ECC)　　　B. emergency switchboard　　　C. A and B

### (二) Translation

1. Translate new words and expressions into Chinese (Table 1-4).

Table 1-4　Translation

| | |
|---|---|
| 1.group starter panel | |
| 2. feeder panel | |
| 3.diesel generator panel | |
| 4.Synchronizing panel | |
| 5.main switchboard | |
| 6.emergency switchboard | |
| 7.engine control console(ECC) | |
| 8.engine control room(ECR) | |
| 9.shore connection box | |
| 10.charging & discharging panel | |
| 11.Unattended Machinery Space（UMS） | |
| 12.phase sequence | |
| 13.shaft generator | |
| 14.turbo generator | |
| 15.battery | |

A. 电池，蓄电池；B. 相序；C. 轴带发电机；D. 涡轮发电机；E. 无人机舱；F. 组合启动屏；G. 充电/放电屏；H. 岸接线箱；I. 控室；J. 集控台；K. 应急配电板；L. 主配电板；M. 同步屏；N. 柴油发动机屏；O. 负载屏。

2.Translate the following sentences into Chinese.

The engine control room is the place where engine control room crews carry out instructions from the bridge by means of operating the various kind of machinery equipment.Good cooperation between the bridge and engine control room is key for the ship's sailing at sea. With the rapid development of technology, Unattended Machinery Space（UMS） appears. That is to say, no one needs to work in the engine control room and the ship can be remotely controlled from the bridge.We are sure that the great change will certainly take place in the future.

（三）**Speaking Practice**

1. Group discussion

Work in groups. Look at the statements in the language bank task. Which of them are important aspects for general-cargo ships and container ships respectively? Why?

2. Short talk

Now it is your chance to practice what you have learned from this unit. Put your textbook away and give a short talk on the following topics. You should talk at least one minute. Don't be discouraged if you cannot make it. Review the lesson and try again. You are sure to do it better next time.

- ECR on the ship

3. Role playing

Work in groups or pairs and discuss the following topics. Then, you are advised to talk at least three minutes for each topic.
- A is a cadet visiting the ship. B is the captain.
- Prompts: Introducing the engine control console.
- ECR (its function and related equipment).

## 【 Unit Evaluation 】

The teacher evaluates the students on their performance and mutual evaluation results, the results in Table 1-5.

Table 1-5  Task Evaluation

| EVALUATION CONTENT | | | | DISTRIBUTION SCORE | SCORE |
|---|---|---|---|---|---|
| Unit1 Ship's Bridge and Engine Control Room<br>Task1 Ship's Bridge (50%)<br>Task2 Engine Control Room(50%) | | | | | |
| KNOWLEDGE EVALUATION | | | | | |
| Ⅰ.Choice | | | | 20 | |
| Ⅱ.Translation | 1.Translate new words and expressions into Chinese. | | | 20 | |
| | 2.Translate the following sentences into English. | | | 20 | |
| TIME: 30' | STUDENT SIGN: | | TEACHER SIGN: | TOTAL: | |
| SKILL EVALUATION | | | | | |
| Ⅲ. Speaking Practice<br>    Role playing | | | | 20<br>20 | |
| TIME: 30' | STUDENT SIGN: | | TEACHER SIGN: | TOTAL: | |

# Unit 2

# Marine Electric Drive System

【Unit Goals】

1. Get to know marine deck machinery and marine auxiliary system.Familiar with the basic equipment: marine electric steering gear, marine air compressor, marine boiler, marine air conditioning, marine Turbulo separators, marine incinerator, marine low sulfur oil, marine pump, etc.

2. Students can introduce marine electric drive equipment to others in English and talk to each other about marine deck machinery and marine auxiliary system fluently.

## Task 1　　Deck Machinery

【Task Goals】

1. Get to know different kinds of marine deck machinery.

2. Students can introduce marine electric drive equipment to others in English and talk to each other about marine deck machinery fluently.

【Knowledge linking】

What do you know about deck machinery on board?

Please look at pictures carefully and make sure what are they.

(1) Marine anchor windlass (Fig.2-1)

(2) Marine winch (Fig.2-2)

(3) Life boat (Fig.2-3)

The electrical-hydraulic, high pressure driven without auto-tension deck machinery shall be provided as shown on the General Arrangement. All mooring drums shall be split type.

Fig.2-1　Marine anchor windlass

Fig.2-2　Marine winch

Fig.2-3　Life boat

Gear for cable lifter part shall be open type with protector and closed type for that of winch part.The mooring capacity on the first layer of the drum shall be about 20 tones at average mooring line speed of 15 m/min at operation of single drum. That of the warping head should be as per manufacturer's standard.

The mooring drum shall be large enough to wind 200 meters of 72 mm diameter polyamide multifilament rope. Each deck machinery shall be fitted with hand-operated friction band brake and clutch, operated locally.[1] The brake holding force for cable lifters shall be in compliance with the requirements of the Classification Society.

The warping head shall be of cast iron as smooth barrel tube type and shall be directly connected to driving shaft without clutching device.[2] The control handle combined with a control valve shall be provided near the driving motor of each windlass and mooring winch for the local control at each machine side.

The mooring winch in the midship shall be operated by local and ship side remote control. The seat of deck machinery shall be of open type steel construction with steel lining for cable lifter, and its height as low as possible, and, the resin chock shall be used for the foundation/installation of winch only.

Hydraulic oil coaming of steel flat bar construction (8×100) with drain plug shall be provided in way of hydraulic motor of each mooring winch and windlass.[3] Open area of foundation (seats), which are not enclosed by the equipment, etc., shall be reasonably accessible for maintenance.

All swivels, pins, bushes, etc., for deck machinery shall have the grease nipples for greasing.

Material, construction, spare parts, etc. shall be in accordance with the Manufacturer's standard to comply with the Rule/Regulations where otherwise specified in the Specification.[4]

## 【 Windlass 】

Two (2) sets of separate type windlass, each combined with a mooring winch shall be installed on upper deck, and each windlass/mooring winch shall be equipped with one (1) cable lifter, two (2) mooring drums and one (1) warping head.

Each windlass shall be designed to obtain a rated line pull in compliance with the requirement of the Classification Society at average hoisting speed of 9 m/min. at individual operation of either cable lifter. The cable lifter and mooring drum shall be operated independently by a manual mechanical clutch.[5]

## 【Anchors and Anchor Chains】

Two (2) sets of 12075kg high holding power type stockless bow anchors cast steel construction shall be supplied.

Two (2) sets of stud welded steel chain cables for bower anchors, 97mm in diameter, grade 3 type with total length 742.5m shall be in accordance with the Class. The anchors shall be stowed on the bellmouth of the cast steel construction at the end of the hawse pipes.

Steps for observing anchor shall be fitted.

No spare anchor shall be provided for each vessel.Chain cables shall be of unit length of 27.5m jointed with Kenter shackles. <u>Swivel pieces shall be fitted at the extreme outboard ends of chain cables and connected to anchor shackles. Inboard ends of chain cables shall be fastened or released by the cable clench fitted at upper part of the chain lockers.</u>[(6)]

Releasing devices of the chains shall be possible from outside of the chain lockers in Bosun's store in each side. One rope ladder shall be provided for access into the chain locker.

Lifeboat

Two (2) F.R.P. totally enclosed type 30 persons, with hinged gravity type davits elec.-motor driven.

Engine: Diesel engine with possibility of emergency starting device

Dimension: Manufacturer's standard

<u>The lifeboat shall be supplied with inventory, accessories and spare parts required by the Rules.The name, call sign, boat No and port of registry of the Vessel shall be marked in position approved by the Regulation.</u>[(7)]The dimension, capacity and certified date, etc., shall be marked on the boats. The outside surface of the boats shall be of orange colour. All equipment and fittings required by SOLAS requirement for the lifeboat shall be completely supplied.

## 【New Words and Expressions】

| | | | |
|---|---|---|---|
| electrical-hydraulic | | adj. | 电动液压 |
| auto-tension | | n. | 自动张力 |
| general arrangement | | n. | 总布置图 |
| split type | | | 分体式 |
| manufacturer's standard | | | 制造商标准 |
| polyamide | | n. | 聚酰胺 |
| holding force | [ˈhəʊldɪŋ fɔːs] | n. | 矫顽力，自持力 |
| warping head | [ˈwɔːpɪŋˌhed] | n. | 绞缆筒 |
| midship | [ˈmɪdʃɪp] | n. / adj. | 船体中央部； 船体中央的；（航海用舵令）正舵； |
| coaming | [ˈkəʊmɪŋ] | n. | 舱口栏板，边材；围板 |
| drain plug | [ˈdreɪnˌplʌg] | n. | 排污螺塞，放油塞 |
| swivel | [ˈswɪvəl] | n. | 转节；转环；旋轴； |

| | | | |
|---|---|---|---|
| windlass | [ˈwindləs] | n. | 卷扬机，辘轳，绞盘； |
| hawse pipe | [ˈhɔːzˌpaip] | | 锚链孔衬管，锚链筒 |
| shackle | [ˈʃækəl] | n. | [机]钩环；[电]绝缘器 |
| chain locker | | | [船] 锚链舱；锚链房；链锁 |
| emergency starting device | | | 应急启动装置 |

## 【Notes】

(1) Each deck machinery shall be fitted with hand-operated friction band brake and clutch, operated locally.

每个甲板机械应配备手动摩擦制动器和离合器，本地操作。

(2) The warping head shall be of cast iron as smooth barrel tube type and shall be directly connected to driving shaft without clutching device.

绞缆筒应为铸铁件，为光滑管式，应直接连接在驱动轴上而不需离合装置。

(3) Hydraulic oil coaming of steel flat bar construction (8×100) with drain plug shall be provided in way of hydraulic motor of each mooring winch and windlass.

每个系泊绞车、锚机液压马达应该被提供带有排污螺塞的钢扁条结构(8×100)的液压油围板。

(4) Material, construction, spare parts, etc. shall be in accordance with the Manufacturer's standard to comply with the Rule/Regulations where otherwise specified in the Specification.

材料、建筑、零部件等，应符合制造商的标准，以符合规范中规定的规则/法规。

(5) The cable lifter and mooring drum shall be operated independently by a manual mechanical clutch.

锚链轮和系泊卷筒应通过手动机械离合器独立操作。

(6) Swivel pieces shall be fitted at the extreme outboard ends of chain cables and connected to anchor shackles. Inboard ends of chain cables shall be fastened or released by the cable clench fitted at upper part of the chain lockers.

旋转件应安装在锚链极外侧端并与锚栓连接。锚链舱内的两端应固定或由装在锚链舱上部的系链扣座释放。

(7) the lifeboat shall be supplied with inventory, accessories and spare parts required by the rules.The name, call sign, boat no and port of registry of the vessel shall be marked in position approved by the regulation.

救生艇须按规定提供存货、配件及备件，其名称、呼叫标志、船籍及船舶登记处的位置须在规定的位置上标明。

## 【Task Implement】

### PART A  Reading Practice

#### Deck machines

The various items of machinery and equipment can be found outside of the machinery space. These include deck machinery such as mooring equipment, anchor handling equipment, cargo handling equipment and hatch covers. The deck machines will be described briefly now.

The duty of a deck winch or crane is to lift and lower a load. Cranes have replaced derricks on many modern ships. Every crane has at least three motors: one hoisting motor for lifting the load, one luffing motor for topping the jib and one slewing motor for rotating the crane. [1]The motors can be hydraulic, electric or electric-hydraulic. In case of hydraulic power, the hoisting and the slewing both require revolving hydraulic motors, the topping of the jib is done using one or two hydraulic cylinders.

The purpose of anchor handling device (shown in Fig. 2-4) is to fix the position of the ship in water. The anchor winches are to heave and drop the anchor and anchor chains in a controlled way. Anchor winches are normally provided with a mooring drum via a separate clutch. [2]Then the same winch can be used to operate a mooring drum. In most cases the main shaft is horizontal, however in rare cases it can be vertical, like a capstan. The winches can powered by hydraulic system, electricity or electric-hydraulic system.

Winches with various arrangements of barrels are the usual mooring equipment used on board ships. It usually consists of a driving motor, a reduction gear, a winch barrel or drum and one or two warp ends. [3] The mooring equipment is designed to moor a ship with bollards ashore at regular distances.

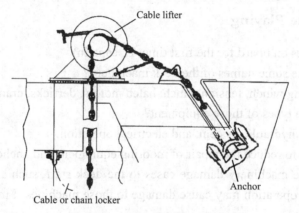

Fig.2-4 Anchor handling device

## 【 New Words and Expressions 】

| | | | |
|---|---|---|---|
| cargo handling equipment | | | 货物装卸设备 |
| hatch cover | | | 舱盖 |
| deck machinery | | | 甲板机械 |
| mooring equipment | | | 绞缆设备 |
| anchor handling equipment | | | 起锚设备 |
| crane | [kreɪn] | n. | 吊车，起重机 |
| jib | [dʒɪb] | n. | 吊臂 |
| derrick | ['derɪk] | n. | 起重机；（油井的）井架； |
| mooring drum | | n. | 绞缆筒 |
| drum | [drʌm] | n. | 卷筒 |
| clutch | [klʌtʃ] | n. | 离合器 |
| warp | [wɔːp] | n. | [航]绞船索 |

## 【Notes】

(1) Every crane has at least three motors: one hoisting motor for lifting the load, one luffing motor for topping the jib and one slewing motor for rotating the crane.

每台吊车至少 3 台电动机：用于起吊货物的起升电动机一台，用于升降吊臂的变幅电动机一台和用于旋转吊车的旋转电动机一台。

(2) The anchor winches are to heave and drop the anchor and anchor chains in a controlled way. Anchor winches are normally provided with a mooring drum via a separate clutch.

起锚绞车以一种控制方式把锚和锚链举起或抛下。锚机通常通过一个单独的离合器设有绞缆筒。

(3) Winches with various arrangements of barrels are the usual mooring equipment used on board ships. It usually consists of a driving motor, a reduction gear, a winch barrel or drum and one or two warp ends.

带有各种圆筒的绞车是常见的船用系泊设备。它通常由一个驱动电动机，减速齿轮，绞车圆筒或卷筒和一个或两个绞船索末端组成。

## PART B　Role Playing

(A: cadet who comes on board for the first time; B: captain)

A: Could you tell me some names of the deck machinery?

B: Windlass, mooring winch, tension winch, hatch motors, derricks, crane, etc.

A: Do you know the types of those equipment?

B: Yes, I do. Steam, hydraulic system, and electrical operation.

A: What will we do to reduce the repair of mooring equipment and anchor-handling equipment?

B: I will discuss the machinery damage cases to the deck staff, such as the carpenter or bosun and tell them that rough operation may cause damage to those machines. I may help them to create a safe operational manual.

A: Do you know the safe operation of cargo handling equipment?

B: The lifting load is not permitted to exceed to S.W.L. When operating the cargo winch, it is required to start it slowly and operate it steadily. We will remind the duty officer to strictly observe the operation of the winch during cargo handling. The electrical engineer or electrician if any are on board instructed to maintain and repair the motors frequently. In winter, it is necessary to warm them up when the ambient temperature is below 15℃.

A: Do you know the hull equipment?

B: Stabilizing systems-fin stabilizer and tank stabilizer, watertight doors, bow thrusters, etc.

A: Do you know who takes charge of deck machinery?

B: The deck department takes charge of safety operations and the fourth engineer takes charge of maintenance and repair of the mechanical section. In general, the chief engineer is the general technical manager of the ship, if the fourth engineer is unable to make repairations, the chief engineer will deal with that personally.

A: How often do you test various crane limits?

B: Prior to loading, the crane limits must be checked, since the stevedore company requires it. Normally, it is checked monthly.

Task 1  Deck Machinery

# 【Task Evaluation】

## (一) Choice

1. The _____ is used for hauling in or letting out the wires or ropes.
   A. windlass          B. anchor capstan          C. turning gear          D. winch drum
2. On an anchor windlass, the wheel over which the anchor chain passes is called a _____.
   A. brake compressor wheel                        B. devil's claw
   C. wildcat                                        D. winchhead
3. The _____ takes charge of safety operations and the fourth engineer takes charge of maintenance and repair of the mechanical section.
   A. deck department                                B. machinery department
   C. deck machinery                                 D. electrical engineer
4. Every crane has at least _____ motors.
   A. two              B. three                     C. three              D. four
5. The purpose of _____ (shown in Fig. 2-4) is to fix the position of the ship in water.
   A. cargo handling equipment                       B. deck machinery
   C. mooring equipment                              D. anchor handling device

## (二) Translation.

1. Translate new words and expressions into Chinese (Table 2-1).

Table 2-1   Translation

| | |
|---|---|
| 1. electrical-hydraulic | |
| 2. auto-tension | |
| 3. general arrangement | |
| 4. split type | |
| 5. manufacturer's standard | |
| 6. polyamide | |
| 7. holding force | |
| 8. warping head | |
| 9. drain plug | |
| 10. hawse pipe | |
| 11. chain locker | |
| 12. emergency starting device | |
| 13. cargo handling equipment | |
| 14. hatch cover | |
| 15. deck machinery | |
| 16. mooring equipment | |
| 17. anchor handling equipment | |
| 18. mooring drum | |

A.[船] 锚链舱，锚链房，链锁；B.甲板机械；C.货物装卸设备；D.绞缆设备；E.聚酰胺；F.制造商标准；G.总布置图；H.自动张力；I.电动液压；J.矫顽力，自持；K.绞缆筒；L.排污螺塞，放油塞；M.起锚设备；N.应急启动装置；O.舱盖；P.绞缆筒；Q.锚链孔衬管；锚链筒；R.分体式。

2.Translate the following sentences into Chinese.

As the power system works smoothly, the power supply of illumination comes from the normal lighting circuit through lighting distribution boxes that it can be easily cut off from the wheelhouse for the sake of convenient night voyage. When the main power station breaks down, the power supply of emergency lighting to be got from the emergency generating set through the emergency lighting circuit.Whereas the temporary emergency lighting will be supplied with power by battery units, and its circuit can be closed automatically if the main network or emergency networks fails, or their voltage drops to 40% of the rated value. On the contrary, the circuit will be open automatically as well when the main network or emergency network restores their voltage. The temporary emergency lighting serves as a supplemental means to instantaneous shortage of electricity when normal power supply is switched over to emergency power supply.

(三) Speaking Practice

1. Group discussion

Work in groups. Look at the statements in the language bank task. Do you know what is the starting current and how to reduce the starting current?

2. Short talk

Now it is your chance to practice what you have learned from this task. Put your textbook away and give a short talk on the following topics. You should talk at least one minute. Don't be discouraged if you cannot make it. Review the task and try again. You are sure to do it better next time.

- Deck machinery

3. Role playing

Work in groups or pairs and discuss the following topics. Then, you are advised to talk at least three minutes for each topic.

- A is a cadet visiting the ship. B is the captain.
- Prompts: Introducing the deck machinery.
- Deck machinery.

# Task 2　Marine Auxiliary System

【Task Goals】

1. Get to know marine auxiliary system. Familiar with the basic equipment: marine electric steering gear, marine air compressor, marine boiler, marine air conditioning, marine turbulo separators, marine incinerator, marine low sulfur oil, marine pump, etc.

2. Students can introduce marine electrical elements to others in English and talk to each other about electrical equipment fluently.

## 【Knowledge linking】

(1) Marine electric steering gear (Fig.2-5)
(2) Marine air compressor (Fig.2-6)

Fig.2-5  Marine electric steering gear

Fig.2-6  Marine air compressor

(3) Marine boiler (Fig.2-7)
(4) Marine air conditioning(Fig.2-8)

Fig.2-7  Marine boiler

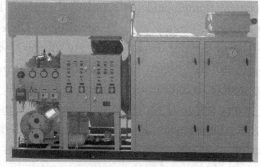

Fig.2-8  Marine air conditioning

(5) Marine turbulo separators(Fig.2-9)
(6) Marine incinerator(Fig.2-10)

Fig.2-9  Marine turbulo separators

Fig.2-10  Marine incinerator

(7) Marine low sulfur oil (Fig.2-11)

(8) Marine pump (Fig.2-12)

Fig.2-11　Marine low sulfur oil

Fig.2-12　Marine pump

## Marine Auxiliary System

The pumps employed on board ship can be divided into two main categories: (i) positive displacement pumps, and (ii) centrifugal pumps. They can be broken down into three classes; (1) reciprocating, (2) rotary and (3) centrifugal. Under reciprocating are the direct acting, power, and crank-fly wheel types. Under rotary are the gear, vane, crew and piston types. Under centrifugal are the volute, diffuser, mixed-flow, axial flow and turbine or regenerative types.

In general, reciprocating pumps are suitable for delivering small quantities at high pressure, rotary pumps are used for moderate quantities at moderate pressure, and centrifugal pumps are more suitable for large quantities at low pressure[1]. Centrifugal pumps, however, can be designed with a number of impellers in series to attain a high final delivery pressure. They are popular because they are very simple in construction, and can produce smooth, constant, non-pulsating discharge.

There are two distinct types of marine boilers in use on hoard ship, the fire-tube boiler in which the hot gases from the furnaces pass through the tubes while the water is on the outside, and the water-tube boiler in which the water through the inside of the tubes while the hot furnace gases pass around the outside[2]. The water tube boiler is employed for high pressure, high temperature, high capacity steam applications, e.g. providing steam for main propulsion turbines or cargo pump turbines. Fire tube boilers are used for auxiliary purposes to provide smaller quantities of low-pressure steam on diesel engine powered ships.

Fire tube boilers were commonly used with steam reciprocating engines on board ship, but because of their comparative poor efficiency and low power / weight ratio, these systems are no longer installed for propulsion plant.

A steering engine is a device used to aid in moving the rudder of a large ship. First used in the mid 1800s, the first steering engine was a steam-operated unit used to improve the steering speed of the steam ship Great Eastern in 1866. The steering engine acts as a type of power steering for a large slip. The enormous size of the rudders used in the manufacture of the largest ocean and river-going ships created a problem when the crew was required to quickly turn the ship's wheel. Some of the first steering engines worked so effectively that the ship's wheels were said to turn like the blades of a fall.

A typical steering engine used a steam cylinder that ran across the axis of the ship's rudder arm, forcing the arm to the port and starboard sides as a mechanical valve was actuated. The power the cylinder applied to the rudder arm made turning the ship an easier task[3]. Many ships went from having several men in the wheel house to having only one to steer the ship. In foul weather, some ships would actually employ several men with block-and-cackle equipment. It was placed from the ship's wheel to the ship's inner steel structure to aid in turning the vessel in rough water.

## 【New Words and Expressions】

| | | | |
|---|---|---|---|
| displacement | [dɪsˈpleɪsmənt] | n. | 位移，排水量 |
| centrifugal | [ˌsentrɪˈfjuːgl] | adj. | 离心的 |
| rotary | [ˈrəʊtəri] | adj. | 旋转的 |
| reciprocating | [rɪˈsɪprəkeɪtɪŋ] | adj. | 往复的 |
| volute | [vəˈljuːt] | adj. n. | 涡形的，蜗壳 |
| turbine | [ˈtɜːbaɪn] | n. | 涡轮，涡轮机 |
| boiler | [ˈbɔɪlə(r)] | n. | 锅炉 |
| distinct | [dɪˈstɪŋkt] | adj. | 截然不同的 |
| furnace | [ˈfɜːnɪs] | n. | 炉子，炉膛 |
| bent | [bent] | adj. | 弯的 |
| drum | [drʌm] | n. | 鼓，锅筒 |
| header | [ˈhedə(r)] | n. | 联箱 |
| generate | [ˈdʒenəreɪt] | v. | 产生 |
| downcomer | [ˈdaʊnˌkʌmə] | n. | 下降管 |
| donkey | [ˈdɒŋki] | adj. | 辅助的 |
| installation | [ˌɪnstəˈleɪʃn] | n. | 装置 |
| steam ship | [stiːm ʃɪp] | n. | 蒸汽机船 |
| motor ship | [ˈməʊtəʃɪp] | n. | 内燃机船 |
| composite | [ˈkɒmpəzɪt] | adj. | 混合的，复合的 |
| cylinder | [ˈsɪlɪndə(r)] | n. | 汽缸 |

## 【Notes】

(1) In general, reciprocating pumps are suitable for delivering small quantities at high pressure, rotary pumps are used for moderate quantities at moderate pressure, and centrifugal pumps are more suitable for large quantities at low pressure.

在一般情况下，往复泵适用于少量高压，旋转泵适用于中量中压，离心泵更适合大量低压。

(2) There are two distinct types of marine boilers in use on hoard ship, the fire-tube boiler in

which the hot gases from the furnaces pass through the tubes while the water is on the outside, and the water-tube boiler in which the water through the inside of the tubes while the hot furnace gases pass around the outside.

船舶上使用两种不同型号的锅炉，火管式锅炉热气来自火炉，通过管内流动，管外是水。而水管锅炉中的水通过管内流动，而热风炉的气体通过管外。

(3) The power the cylinder applied to the rudder arm made turning the ship an easier task.

汽缸的能量作用在舵臂上，船只就比较容易转向。该句主语是 the power，谓语是 made。宾语是 turning the ship。the cylinder applied to the rudder arm 为 the power 的后置定语，an easy task 是补语。注意"make+宾语+宾+补"这种用法，如 We made him monitor of our class. 我们选他当班长。

## 【Task Implement】

### PART A    Reading Practice

#### Automatic Control and Pollution Prevention System of Marine Auxiliary Machinery

<u>The natural transfer of heat is from a hot body to a cold body, the function of a refrigeration plant is to act as a heat pump and reverse this process so that rooms can be maintained at low temperatures for the preservation of foodstuffs, or air can be cooled for the air conditioning.</u>[(1)]

Air conditioning systems fall into two main classes: individual unit system, in which each room contains its own small refrigeration plant and fan and air cooler; and central systems, where larger refrigeration machinery units are installed and their output distributed about the ship by a variety of means. <u>Self-contained units are noisier than central systems, require more maintenance and have been found to have a relatively short life (about 7 years).</u>[(2)]

Turbulo separators with the 'Turbulo' filter are used for the separation of oil from bilge and ballast water. The complete plant consists of a separator for the preliminary separation, and for the remaining separation a filter with inserts for stopping dirt and for coalescence and an HDW eccentric helical rotor pump with an output precisely suited to the plant. Designed in accordance with the International Convention for the Prevention of Pollution from Ships, 1973, and with the IMCO Test Rules for separators and filtering equipment, the plant enables a degree of purity better than 15 ppm to be attained.

To incinerate solid waste, stop the auxiliary and waste oil burners and then charge it through the solid waste dump chute. To incinerate water cloths, charge 1 to 2 kg at a time as a standard and avoid charging them excessively (When the dump chute is opened during burner combustion, the burner interlock functions to make the burners off).

After charging solid waste, close the dump chute, and ignite it with the auxiliary burner. Burn solid waste with the auxiliary burner only without using the waste oil burner. <u>This is because, when solid waste is changed during waste oil burning, the waste oil burner may be turned off owing to the pressure charge in the combustion chamber.</u>[(3)]Even if things go well for a moment, the incinerator is bound to be shut down by the flue gas temperature indicator/regulator as the flue gas temperature will rise excessively.

A number of biological sewage treatment plant types are in use at sea but nearly all work on what is called the extended aeration process. Basically this consists of oxygenating the liquor either by bubbling air through it or by agitating the surface. By so doing a family of bacteria is propagated which thrives on the oxygen content and digests the sewage to produce an innocuous sludge. The impression that bubbling air through the sewage serves to oxidize it thus reducing BOD is not strictly the case. It is the bacteria that reduce the BOD by inverting the organic content of the sewage to a chemically and organically inert sludge.

## 【New Words and Expressions】

| | | | |
|---|---|---|---|
| refrigeration | [rɪˌfrɪdʒəˈreɪʃn] | n. | 制冷 |
| preservation | [ˌprezəˈveɪʃn] | n. | 保存，储藏 |
| foodstuff | [ˈfuːdstʌf] | n. | 食品 |
| self-contained | [ˌselfkənˈteɪnd] | | 自带的，整装的 |
| individual unit | [ˌɪndɪˈvɪdjuəlˈjuːnɪt] | | 单体式 |
| incineration | [ɪnˌsɪnəˈreɪʃn] | n. | 焚烧 |
| incinerate | [ɪnˈsɪnəreɪt] | v. | 焚烧 |
| dump | [dʌmp] | | 倾斜，门 |
| chute | [ʃuːt] | n. | (斜、划)槽 |
| biological | [ˌbaɪəˈlɒdʒɪkl] | a. | 生物学的 |
| sewage | [ˈsuːɪdʒ] | n. | 污水 |
| aeration | [eəˈreɪʃn] | n. | 充气，曝气 |
| oxygenate | [ˈɒksɪdʒəneɪt] | v. | 用氧处理，氧化，充氧 |
| liquor | [ˈlɪkə(r)] | n. | 液体，溶液 |
| agitate | [ˈædʒɪteɪt] | v. | 搅动 |
| propagate | [ˈprɒpəgeɪt] | v. | 繁殖，传播 |
| digest | [daɪˈdʒest] | v. | 消化 |
| innocuous | [ɪˈnɒkjuəs] | a. | 无毒（害）的 |
| BOD | | | 生化需氧量 |
| IMCO | | | 国际海事协调组织 |

## 【Notes】

(1) The natural transfer of heat is from a hot body to a cold body, the function of a refrigeration plant is to act as a heat pump and reverse this process so that rooms can be maintained at low temperatures for the preservation of foodstuffs, or air can be cooled for the air conditioning.

热的自然传递是从热的物体传到一个冰冷的物体，一个制冷设备的功能是作为热泵并逆转这一过程，因此为了保存食品可以使房间保持低温，或用空调冷却空气。

(2) Self-contained units are noisier than central systems, require more maintenance and have been found to have a relatively short life (about 7 years).

独立单元比中央系统需要更多的维护，并已发现使用寿命相对较短（约 7 年）。

(3) This is because, when solid waste is changed during waste oil burning, the waste oil burner may be turned off owing to the pressure charge in the combustion chamber.

这是因为，在废油燃烧过程中固体废物被改变，由于燃烧室中的压力负荷，废油燃烧器可能会被关闭。

## PART B　　Role Playing

1. (A: cadet who comes on board for the first time; B: captain)

A: What are functions of a steering gear?

B: The steering gear provides a rudder movement in response to a rudder signal from the conning bridge. The total system is made up of three parts: control equipment, a power unit, and a transmission to the rudderstock.

A: Could you tell us the rules of the control of the steering gear?

B: The transmission system is the means by which the movement of the rudder is accomplished. There should be two independent means of steering, automatic steering and manual steering. The power torque capacity must be such that the rudder can be swung from 35 degrees on one side to 35 degrees on the other side with the ship at the maximum speed. It is not allowed to exceed 28 seconds to swing from 35 degrees from one side to 30 degrees to the other side. The system will be protected from shock loading and have its own pipework. There are two independent steering gear control systems for tanks of 10,000 tons and upwards. The steering gear itself must include two independent systems where a failure of one results in an automatic changeover to the other within 45 seconds.

A: Do you know the types of basic power systems?

B: Hydraulic control equipment and electrical control equipment.

A: Do you know the types of pumps used to obtain the displacement of fluid and produce movement of the rudder?

B: Variable delivery pump, radial cylinder pump, swash plate type pump.

A: What is the emergency steering gear?

B: It is a method of steering the ship alternative to the steam engine gear which must be be provided. It can be used in an emergency. In the event of total failure of the telemotor system, the ship is still steered directly from a position aft. A direct gear from the aft steering wheel station to the power unit control is used for this purpose.

A: What kind of steering gear have you managed?

B: I have managed a hydraulic steering gear made by Kawasaki.

A: Could you show us examples of trouble shooting?

B: In general,I referred to the trouble shooting part in the operational manual. The troubles I met are:(1)slow rudder turning speed. (2)Unstable working of the rudder. (3)abnormal noise in a voyage. For symptom(1), the possible reasons are problems with the hydraulic pump, trouble and mis-operation of valves, or external oil leakage. For symptom(2), the possible reasons are accumulated air in the hydraulic circuits, over-tightening of ram V-packing, play between rudder stock and bearing. For symptom(3), the possible reasons are noises from the ram packing, noises from rudder carrier, abnormal noises from the pump.

2. (A: cadet; B: captain)

A: What test is required after the repair of the air compressor?

B: A pressure test is required.

A: Do you know some types of refrigerant?

B: Refrigerant 23, 22 and 502.

A: Do you know the types of compressors?

B: Three types, reciprocating compressor, centrifugal compressor, and screw compressor.

A: Do you know the components of the refrigeration plant?

B: The compressor, condenser, expansion valve and controlling sensor, the evaporator, the oil separator, the filter drier.

A: Do you know the major parts of a reciprocating compressor?

B: Yes, I do, such as cylinder head, crank shaft, piston and connecting rod, main bearing, shaft seal, oil pump, and suction strainer.

A: Do you know the use of brines in refrigeration plants?

B: Brines are usually used in marine refrigeration system on a reefer vessel where a large cold storage room or cargo hold is used to transport perishable cargoes.

3. (A: cadet; B: captain)

A: Who takes charge of the oily water separator?

B: The fourth engineer. As mentioned before, if the fourth engineer is unable to do it the chief engineer is required to deal with it personally. Everybody in the engine room is required to familiarize themselves with the O-W-S.

A: What is the limit of oil when we pump oily water outboard?

B: The control of oil in oily water should be within 15 ppm.

A: How do you maintain the 15 ppm alarm device?

B: I will test it frequently by flowing the oily water to observe whether the alarm is sounded or not.

A: How often are the O-W-S, the oil filtering equipment, 15 ppm alarm, and the auto-stop valve tested? Who takes charge of those?

B: The basic rules are that we must keep the oily water separator and the 15 ppm alarm in good order at all times. There are no specific rules for frequency of maintenance. The fourth engineer takes charge of those. The chief engineer may take charge of those in person.

A: What is permitted to be burnt in the incinerator? What is not permitted to be burnt in the incinerator?

B: Oily cotton yarn, sludge oil and oil waste are permitted to be burnt while at sea. But plastics or any other material liable to cause toxic gases are not permitted to be burnt any place or at any time.

A: Who takes charge of the incinerator?

B: The fourth engineer or the chief engineer takes charge of it in person.

A: What should be born in mind when burning garbage?

B: We must contact the bridge to know which areas are restricted according to the annex VI of MARPOL 73/78. We separate the plastics or synthetic fibre from the garbage, since they may pollute the air.

A: How often is the incinerator operation training executed? Who is in charge of that?

B: The chief engineer takes charge of that quarterly.

# Unit 2　Marine Electric Drive System

## 【Task Evaluation】

### (一) Choice

1. The _____ is a device used to aid in moving the rudder of a large ship.
   A. Carge　　　　　B. compressor　　　　C. refrigerator　　　　D. steering engine

2. The primary function of a waste heat boiler is to _____.
   A. reduce engine exhaust noise　　　　　B. reduce engine back pressure
   C. recover heat which otherwise would be lost　　D. increase turbocharger efficiency

3. Cylinders of marine diesel engineers are normally cooled by _____.
   A. sea water　　　B. fine mineral oil　　C. sanitary water　　D. fresh water

4. _____ is not permitted to be burnt in the incinerator.
   A. plastics or any other material liable to cause toxic gases
   B. oily cotton yarn
   C. sludge oil
   D. oil waste

5. _____ takes charge of the oily water separator?
   A. The fourth engineer　　　　　　B. The third engineer
   C. The chief engineer　　　　　　　D. The fifth engineer

### (二) Translation.

1. Translate new words and expressions into Chinese (Table 2-2).

Table 2-2　Translation

| | |
|---|---|
| 1. refrigeration | |
| 2. preservation | |
| 3. self-contained | |
| 4. individual unit | |
| 5. incineration | |
| 6. sewage | |
| 7. oxygenate | |
| 8. BOD | |
| 9. IMCO | |
| 10. displacement | |
| 11. centrifugal | |
| 12. rotary | |
| 13. reciprocating | |
| 14. volute | |
| 15. turbine | |
| 16. boiler | |

| | 续表 |
|---|---|
| 17.downcomer | |
| 18.installation | |
| 19.steam ship | |
| 20.motor ship | |

A.内燃机船；B.下降管；C.涡轮，涡轮机；D.往复的；E.用氧处理，氧化，充氧；F.单体式；G.自带的，整装的；H.旋转的；I.保存，储藏；J.制冷；K.焚烧；L.位移，排水量；M.离心的；N.国际海事协调组织；O.蜗形的，蜗壳；P.锅炉；Q.装置；R.蒸汽机船；S.生化需氧量；T.污水。

2.Translate the following sentences into Chinese.

The principal feature of the internal construction of the separator consists of the coarse separating compartment in the upper part and the fine separating compartment arranged below it. After the separation of relatively large quantities of oil in the upper part, the fine separation takes place in the fine separating compartment, which is fitted with a number of chambers with catch-plates with equal flow-through. The oil to be separated collects on the undersides of the catch-plates. After the oil has formed larger drops it detaches itself from the edges of the catch-plates and rises into the oil collecting space in the upper part of the separator. From there it is automatically drained into the used-oil tank. The air brought along with the oil/water mixture when pumping the bilge is constantly let out of the separator through an air-vent valve.

### (三) Speaking Practice

1. Group discussion

Work in groups. Look at the statements in the language bank task. What have you learned in this task?

2. Short talk

Now it is your chance to practice what you have learned from this task. Put your textbook away and give a short talk on the following topics. You should talk at least one minute. Don't be discouraged if you cannot make it. Review the task and try again. You are sure to do it better next time.

- the steering gear
- marine pumps
- marine boilers
- automatic control and pollution prevention system of marine auxiliary machinery

3. Role playing

Work in groups or pairs and discuss the following topics. Then, you are advised to talk at least three minutes for each topic.

- A is a cadet visiting the ship. B is the captain.
- Prompts: Introducing the marine auxiliary system.
- the steering gear
- marine pumps
- marine boilers
- automatic control and pollution prevention system of marine auxiliary machinery

# Unit 2 Marine Electric Drive System

## 【 Unit Evaluation 】

The teacher evaluates the students on their performance and mutual evaluation results, the results in Table 2-3.

Table 2-3  Task Evaluation

| EVALUATION CONTENT | | | DISTRIBUTION SCORE | SCORE |
|---|---|---|---|---|
| Unit3 Marine Electric Drive System and Equipment<br>Task1 Deck Machinery (50%)<br>Task2 Marine Auxiliary System(50%) | | | | |
| KNOWLEDGE EVALUATION | | | | |
| I . Choice | | | 20 | |
| II .Translation | 1.Translate new words and expressions into Chinese. | | 20 | |
| | 2.Translate the following sentences into English. | | 20 | |
| TIME: 30' | STUDENT SIGN: | TEACHER SIGN: | TOTAL: | |
| SKILL EVALUATION | | | | |
| III. Speaking Practice<br>    Role playing | | | 20<br>20 | |
| TIME: 30' | STUDENT SIGN: | TEACHER SIGN: | TOTAL: | |

# Unit 3

# Three-phase Asynchronous Motors and Electrical Control

【 Unit Goals 】

1. Get to know construction of asynchronous motors and electrical control. Be familiar with the parameter information of nameplate and low-voltage electrical apparatus like relay, contact, air breaker, etc.

2. Students can introduce both the basic information of the motors and electrical control to the others in English. Furthermore, they can talk to each other about the motor and its control circuits fluently.

## Task 1　Three-phase Asynchronous Motors

【 Task goals 】

1. Get to know electric motor and familiar with the parameter information of its nameplate.

2. Students can introduce the basic information of the motor to the others in English fluently.

【 Knowledge linking 】

Which kind of motor is the most commonly used in a ship?
What are the two basic components of the three-phase cage motor?
Please look at the following pictures carefully and try to learn the terms:
(1) Three-phase squirrel cage motor (Fig. 3-1)
(2) Stator of motor(Fig. 3-2)
(3) Wound rotor (Fig. 3-3)
(4) Squirrel-cage rotor (Fig. 3-4)

Fig. 3-1  Three-phase squirrel cage motor

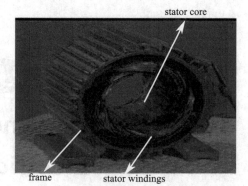

Fig. 3-2  Stator of motor

Fig. 3-3  Wound rotor

Fig. 3-4  Squirrel-cage rotor

## Three-phase Asynchronous Motors

Motor is an machine that converts electrical energy into mechanical energy, which main types are AC motors and DC motors. An AC motor which is also called induction motor is driven by alternating current.

As far as AC motor is concerned, it is either synchronous or asynchronous. Because of rugged, reliable and economical performance of three-phase squirrel-cage induction motor, also called cage motor, which is the most widely used motor in a ship.[1] It is suitable for driving various machines on ship such as pumps, blowers, separators, hydraulic engines and other auxiliary equipment.[2] Special type of motor can also be found on board ship, for example the single-phase motor. Single-phase induction motors are used extensively for small loads, such as household appliances like fans and galley equipment. Following, we mainly learn three-phase squirrel-cage motor.

## 【Motor Construction】

Three-phase squirrel-cage motor has two main components, an outside stationary stator and an inside rotor.

Stator supplied by AC power creates a magnetic field that rotates in time with the AC oscillations. Synchronous motor's rotor turns at the same rate as the stator field, whereas an asynchronous motor's rotor at a slower speed than the stator field. The main components of the stator are frame, stator core and stator windings. Stator core is made up of many thin metal sheets, called laminations. Three separate insulated phase stator windings are spaced 120° (electrical) apart. There are two possible connections among the three-phase stator windings, star-connected and delta-connected. This can be achieved with motors equipped with terminal box with 6 terminals, so that it is possible to feed the same motor with different three-phase network voltages. (3)

Rotor is the moving part of a motor, which is positioned inside the stator and constitutes the induced circuit of the motor. It turns the shaft of the motor to deliver the mechanical power. Rotor of squirrel-cage motors is made up of solid bars, usually aluminum or copper, joined by rings at the ends of the rotor, which is much like an animal's rotating exercise cage. The conductors of the rotor carry currents that interact with the magnetic field of the stator to generate the forces that turn the shaft(Fig.3-5).

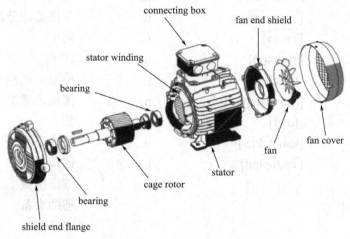

Fig. 3-5　Motor construction

## 【Nameplates】

A motor is characterized by different electrical and constructional parameters which identify its correct application field. The main parameters of a motor is reported on a nameplate positioned on the motor itself. The motor parameter details are shown as in the example in Fig. 3-6.

| 3 phase asynchronous motor | | | |
| --- | --- | --- | --- |
| Type:Y100L-2 | | | |
| KW:2.2 | V:380 | A:6.4 | Conn:Y |
| r/min:2870 | LW 79 dB（A） | | Ins.Class:B |
| IP:44 | Hz:50 | Duty:S1 | kg: |
| Ser.No. ZBK22007-88 | | | Date: |

Fig. 3-6　Nameplate of 3 phase asynchronous motor

Motor nameplate definitions including rated voltage, rated frequency, power rating, rated speed, IP number, weight, duty type, etc. IP(Ingress Protection) number indicates the degree of protection given by motor enclosure, which is defined in terms of its opposition to the ingress of solid particles and liquids. (4) By temperature and temperature rise of insulation material used on motor, insulation is divided into different classes. An adequate life-span for insulation material is based on the assumption that the maximum temperature limit is not exceeded.

## Unit 3  Three-phase Asynchronous Motors and Electrical Control

### 【New Words and Expressions】

| | | | |
|---|---|---|---|
| induction | [ɪnˈdʌkʃən] | n. | （电或磁的）感应 |
| synchronous | [ˈsɪŋkrənəs, ˈsɪn-] | adj. | 同步的 |
| asynchronous | [eˈsɪŋkrənəs] | adj. | 异步的 |
| squirrel-cage | [skˈwɪrəlk ˈeɪdʒ] | n. | 笼型 |
| pump | [pʌmp] | n. | 泵 |
| blower | [ˈbloʊə(r)] | n. | 送风机，通风机 |
| separator | [ˈsɛpəˌretə] | n. | 分离器，分离装置 |
| stator | [ˈsteɪtə] | n. | 定子 |
| rotor | [ˈroʊtə(r)] | n. | 转子 |
| frame | [frem] | n. | 框架，机座 |
| lamination | [ˌlæməˈneɪʃən] | n. | 薄板，薄层，层状体 |
| shaft | [ʃɑːft] | n. | 轴 |
| conductor | [kənˈdʌktə] | n. | 导体 |
| nameplate | [ˈnemˌpleɪt] | n. | 铭牌 |
| hydraulic engine | | | 液压机械 |
| auxiliary equipment | | | 辅助设备 |
| stator core | | | 定子铁芯 |
| stator winding | | | 定子绕组 |
| Ingress Protection | | | 防护 |
| insulation material | | | 绝缘材料 |

### 【Notes】

(1) Because of rugged, reliable and economical performance of three-phase squirrel-cage induction motor, also called cage motor, which is the most widely used motor in a ship.
由于三相笼型感应电动机的坚固性、可靠性和经济性，它是船上应用最广的电动机。

(2) It is suitable for driving various machines on ship such ad pumps, blowers, separators, hydraulic engines and other auxiliary equipment.
它适用于船舶上作驱动各种机械，如泵类、通风机、分离器、液压机械及其他辅助设备等之用.

(3) There are two possible connections among the three-phase stator windings, star-connected and delta-connected. This can be achieved with motors equipped with terminal box with 6 terminals, so that it is possible to feed the same motor with different three-phase network voltages.
(电动机)三相定子绕组有星形连接和三角形连接 2 种方式。接线盒有 6 个端子的电动机可以实现这两种接法，从而使一台电动机可以有两种供电电压。

(4) IP(Ingress Protection) number indicates the degree of protection given by motor enclosure, which is defined in terms of its opposition to the ingress of solid particles and liquids.
IP 数字指出了电动机外壳的防护等级，它是按照防尘防湿气来定义的。

## 【Task Implement】

### Part A　　Reading Practice

#### Methods of staring cage motors

**Direct-on-Line Staring**

Directing-on-line (DOL) is a very simple starting arrangement which is used for the majority of 3 phase induction motor drives.

In the example circuit shown in Fig.3-7, the 3 phase motor is directly switched onto the three-phase A.C. power supply lines. The typical application are relevant to small power motors also with full load starting. The switching sequence for DOL starter circuit is as follows: manual closing of knife switch QS, control circuit voltage available, press start button SB2, closing of main contact KM and auxiliary contact KM self-locking, motor start, press stop button SB1,KM contactor drops out, motor stop.

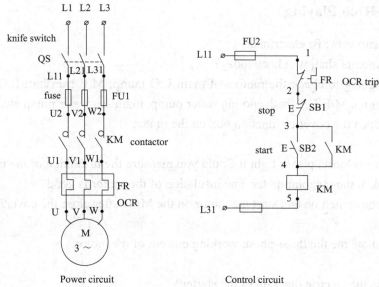

Fig. 3-7　　DOL starter

**Star-delta starting**

During the run-up period the size of motor starting current can be limited by applying a reduced supply voltage. <u>If a motor is direct-on-line started with the stator winding star connected, it will take one-third of the starting current that it would take if the windings were delta connected.</u>[1] The most common arrangement is to apply reduce voltage is the methods of star-delta switching. <u>For star-delta starting, to begin with, the windings of the motor are connected in star, then, when the speed of motor approaches its running value, the windings are switched to delta connection.</u>[2]

## 【New Words and Expressions】

| | | | |
|---|---|---|---|
| contact | ['kɒn,tækt] | n. | 触点 |
| contactor | ['kɒn,tæktə] | n. | 接触器 |

directing-on-line staring 直接启动
knife switch 刀开关
start button 启动按钮
self-locking 自锁

【Notes】

(1) If a motor is direct-on-line started with the stator winding star connected, it will take one-third of the starting current that it would take if the windings were delta connected.

在电动机的直接启动电路中，定子绕组星形连接的启动电流是角形连接启动电流的 1/3。

(2) For star-delta starting, to begin with, the windings of the motor are connected in star, then, when the speed of motor approaches its running value, the windings are switched to delta connection.

对于△-Y 降压启动，开始时电动机绕组连接成星形的，然后当电动机速度接近运行速度时，绕组连接变成三角形的。

**Part B   Role Playing**

(A:　ship surveyor; B: electrician)

A: Which motors shall we check today?

B: We are going to check the motors of main L.O pump, M/E camshaft L.O pump, M/E jacket cooling water pump, M/E L.T fresh cooling water pump, main sea water pump etc.

A: Please open the cover of junction box on the motor.

B: OK.

A: This wire is loose. please tight it.Could you measure the insulation of the motor?

B: You look at the megohmmeter. The insulation of the motor is good.

A: Could you switch on and start the motor on the MSB after close the cover?

B: All right.

A: Please show me the three-phase working current of the motor.

B: Yes.

A: Where is the electric diagram of the starter?

B: Here you are.

A: Thank you !you'd better put this drawing in the starter. it's more convenient for working.

B: OK.

【Task Evaluation】

(一) Choice

1. The primary function of an electric motor is to _____.
   A. develop torque　　　　　　　　B. generate high voltages
   C. produce a magnetic field　　　　D. generate high electrical resistance

2. _____ is a machine by which electrical energy is transformed into mechanical energy.
   A. An alternator　　　　　　　　　B. An electric motor

C. A diesel engine  D. A main switchboard

3. Electrical leads and insulation on a motor should be painted with _____.
   A. heat-resisting acrylic  B. heat-resisting aluminum
   C. insulating varnish  D. insulating white lead

4. AC motor is _____ into single-phase motor and three-phase motor.
   A. dividing  B. divide  C. divided  D. divid

5. Generally, three-phase asynchronous motor, the direct starting current is rated current of the _____ times.
   A. 10  B. 1~3  C. 5~7  D. 1/3

6. Ship three-phase asynchronous motor is often used to _____.
   A. transformer start-up way  B. start-up mode of resistance
   C. step-down start way  D. direct starting way

**(二) Translation.**

1. Translate new words and expressions into Chinese (Table 3-1).

**Table 3-1　Translation**

| | |
|---|---|
| 1.induction motor | |
| 2.asynchronous motor | |
| 3.squirrel-cage motor | |
| 4.pump | |
| 5.insulation material | |
| 6.stator core | |
| 7.stator winding | |
| 8.frame | |
| 9.hydraulic engine | |
| 10.auxiliary equipment | |
| 11.rotor | |
| 12.knife switch | |
| 13.starting current | |
| 14.self-locking | |
| 15.wound rotor | |

A. 定子铁芯；B. 机座；C. 辅助设备；D. 定子绕组；E. 转子；F. 泵；G. 感应电动机；H.异步电动机；I. 液压机械；J.笼型电动机；K. 绝缘材料；L. 启动电流；M. 自锁；N. 刀开关；O. 绕线式转子。

2. Translate the following sentences into Chinese.

As far as AC motor is concerned, it is either synchronous or asynchronous. Because of rugged, reliable and economical performance of three-phase squirrel-cage induction motor, also called cage motor, which is the most widely used motor in a ship. It is suitable for driving various machines on ship such ad pumps, blowers, separators, hydraulic engines and other auxiliary equipment. Special type of motor can also be found on board ship, for example the single-phase motor. Single-phase induction motors are used extensively for small loads, such as household appliances like fans and galley equipment. Following, we mainly learn three-phase squirrel-cage motor.

(三) **Speaking Practice**

1. Group discussion

Work in groups. Look at the introduction of motors. Which type of them are most commonly used on board?Why?

2. Short talk

Now it is your chance to practice what you have learned from this unit. Put your textbook away and give a short talk on the following topics. You should talk at least one minute. Don't be discouraged if you cannot do it. Review the lesson and try again. You are sure to do it better next time.

 • Three-phase asynchronous motor.

3. Role playing

Work in groups or pairs and discuss the following topics. Then, you are advised to talk at least three minutes for each topic.

 • A is ship surveyor. B is an electrician.
 • Prompts: Introducing three-phase asynchronous motor and its staring.
 • Three-phase asynchronous motor (its construction and nameplate).
 • Starting(Direct-on-Line Staring and Star-delta starting).

## Task 2　Motor and Electrical Control

**【 Task Goals 】**

1. Get to know motor and electrical control. Familiar with the basic elements: fuse, circuit breaker, over current and short circuit protection etc.

2. Students can describe components' function in English.

**【 Knowledge linking 】**

(1) Fuse (Fig.3-8)
(2) Circuit breaker (Fig.3-9)

Fig.3-8　Fuse

Fig.3-9　Circuit breaker

(3) Contactor (Fig.3-10)
(4) Relay (Fig.3-11)

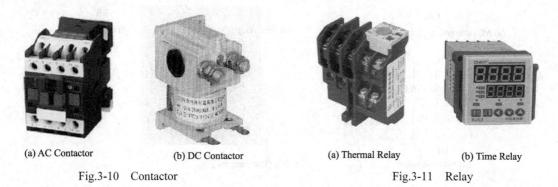

(a) AC Contactor  (b) DC Contactor  (a) Thermal Relay  (b) Time Relay

Fig.3-10   Contactor                Fig.3-11   Relay

## Motor and Electrical Control

There are active contact control and passive contact control in electrical control. Active contact control system is also called relay-contactor control system. Passive contact control system is digital control system with PLC and CPU, but finally it need contact system to act on the object. This passage introduces the composing of active contact control system and typical control circuit.

1. Commonly low-voltage electrical apparatus

Control circuit is make up of many low-voltage electrical apparatus, like is automatic air-break switch, fuse, contactor (KM), relay, push button, over travel-limit switch (SQ) and so on. The form of relay or contactor is various, but the circuit symbol is disciplinary, it is all made up of coil and contact.

Diagram symbols for components is shown in Fig.3-12 (a) (b) (c), with rare expect, the coil is in the left, the normally closed contact is in the right and the middle is normally open contact. The current flowing through the coil excites the contact to work on.

Using these electrical implement people should know their conformation principle and the parameters, for example rated voltage and rated current of winding.

2. Designation for electrical control system

Electrical control systems can accomplish many control requirement. Take the example, using time relay can realize time control; using travel switch can realize travel control, using two group contacts can control electromotor forward/reversal rotation.

• The panel of the Worktable (Fig.3-13).
• Control requirement.

When you press the start-button, electromotor could rotate continuously, five minutes late, the machine reverse direction. But once the travel switch is touched, the motor changes again.

Essentially, it is also called electric motor revolution and counter revolution control.

• Electrical schematic diagram (Fig 3-14).
• Components and their function.

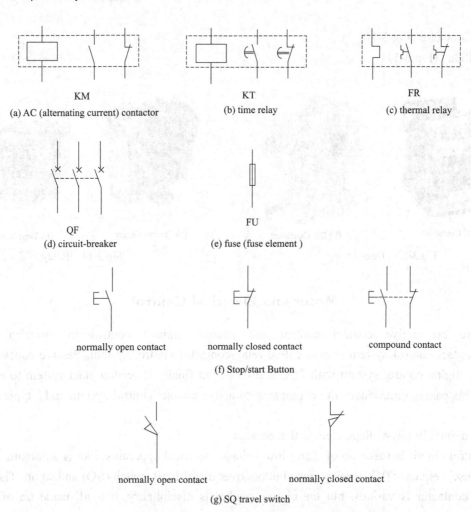

Fig.3-12　Diagram symbols for components

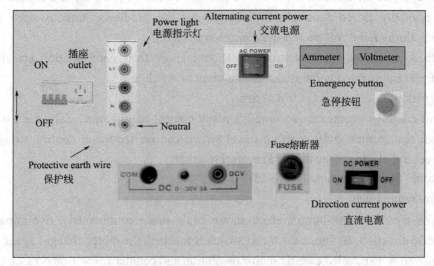

Fig. 3-13　The panel of the worktable

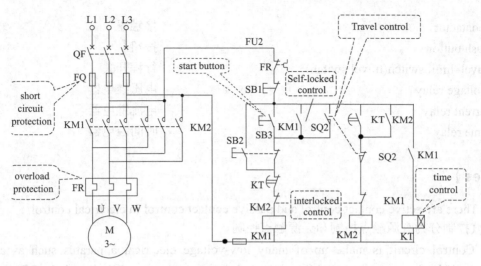

Fig. 3-14　Electrical schematic diagram

**Table 3-2　List of components**

| Letter symbol | Chinese name | English name | function |
|---|---|---|---|
| QF | 自动开关 | automatic air-break switch | Short-circuit protection |
| FU | 熔断器 | Fuse | Short-circuit protection |
| KM | 接触器 | contactor | Receive control signal and close the main circuit |
| KT | 时间继电器 | time relay | Close the circuit in time delay |
| FR | 热继电器 | thermal relay | Over-load protection |
| SB | 按钮 | Button | Turn on /cutoff the circuit |
| SQ | 行程开关 | travel switch | Detect and control location |

## 【New Words and Expressions】

| | | | |
|---|---|---|---|
| relay | [ˈriːleɪ] | n. | 继电器 |
| protector | [prəˈtektə] | n. | 保护装置，保护器 |
| performance | [pəˈfɔːməns] | n. | 性能，工作情况 |
| mechanism | [ˈmekənɪzəm] | n. | 构造；机理 |
| phase | [feɪz] | n. | 相，相位 |
| phase sequence | | | 相序 |
| active contact | | | 有源触点 |
| passive contact | | | 无源触点 |
| relay-contactor | | | 继电器-接触器 |
| electrical schematic diagram | | | 电气原理图 |
| element symbol | | | 元件符号 |
| forward/reversal rotation | | | 正/反转 |
| thermal relay | | | 热继电器 |
| low-voltage electrical apparatus | | | 低压控制电器 |
| (QF)automatic air-break switch | | | 自动开关 |
| (FU)fuse | | | 熔断器 |

| | |
|---|---|
| (KM)contactor | 接触器 |
| (SB)push button | 按钮 |
| overtravel–limit switch(travel switch) | 行程开关 |
| (KV)voltage relay | 电压继电器 |
| (KI)current relay | 电流继电器 |
| (KT)time relay | 时间继电器 |

【Notes】

(1) There are active contact control and passive contact control in electrical control.
电气控制分为有源触点控制和无源触点控制。

(2) Control circuit is make up of many low-voltage electrical apparatus such as automatic air-break switch, fuse, contactor (KM), relay, push button, over travel-limit switch (SQ) and so on. The form of relay or contactor is various, but the circuit symbol is disciplinary, it is all made up of coil and contact.
控制电路是由许多低压电器比如空气开关、熔断器、接触器、继电器、按钮开关、限位开关等组成。继电器和接触器的形式是多种多样的，但是电路符号是一致的，由线圈和触电构成。

(3) 单词巧记忆——巧识前缀，事半功倍

| 前缀 | 词意 |
|---|---|
| semi-(半) | Semiconductor(半导体)；semiautomatic（半自动的） |
| Mal-(不良，坏了) | Malfunction(故障) |
| in/im-(里、内) | Internal(内部的)；import（进口） |
| ex-(out，外) | external(外部的)；export（出口） |
| a-(向) | stern(船尾)——astern（向后） |
| | head(船艏)——ahead（向前） |
| a-(not 否定) | normal(正常)——abnormal(反常的) |
| uni-(一个，一边，单一) | unidirectional（单向的，单向性的）；uniform（同一）； |
| | unique(独一无二的)；unify（统一） |
| un- 表示否定 | Unfavorable |
| de-(离开……、除去……、解除……) | activate(触发)——deactivate（使不活动） |
| | Magnetize(磁化)——demagnetize（去磁）excitation（励磁） |

【Task Implement】

### PART A  Reading Practice

#### Marine Motor and Protection

Generally, on board all motors shall be marine type squirrel cage induction motor and shall conform to International Electro-technical Commission (IEC) standard.

Motors, in general shall be rated AC 440V, 3 Ph except motors less than 0.5 kW output, which are rated AC 440V & 220V, 3 Ph or 1 Ph.

Insulation of cargo hose handling crane shall be class B or F (unless otherwise specified or with the equipment).

In general, motors shall be of semi-enclosed drip-proof type 〔IP(Ingress Protection) 23〕. However, the protection degree for motor in Engine room shall be totally enclosed type IP44, motor on exposed deck shall be weather tight type IP56 and motor for steering gear shall be IP44. Motors installed in dangerous area shall be of explosion proof type according to the requirement of the Class.

The design of motor protection relay must be adequate protection to cater for the protection needs of any one of the vast range of motor designs in service, many of the designs having no permissible allowance for overloads. A relay offering comprehensive protection will have the following set of features:

(1) Thermal(overload) protection.
(2) start protection.
(3) short-circuit protection.
(4) earth fault protection.
(5) negative phase sequence protection.
(6) undervoltage protection.
(7) loss-of-load protection.

### Part B  Role Playing

**Trouble shooting**

(A: cadet ,B:electrician)

A: I have made a simple control circuit (unidirectional start-up), but when I turned on, the contactor would be electrified or turn-off, and have abuzz noise, why is it?

B: Maybe the normally closed contact is connected for self-locked control. If the coil is connected with normally closed contact in series, it would occur, causing the damage without elimination.

A: I known, thank you. Can I avoid it?

B: Of course. We could find it by checking up the circuit before power-on.

A: I known. We can't turn-on blindly. It is important to check up the circuit before power-on test.

B: Oh yes. Teachers have also told us that it could ensure whether the circuit is short and the requirement is achieved by checking.

A: I really regret that fooling around so much in school. Thank you very much.

B: That's OK.

## 【Task Evaluation】

### (一) Choice

1. There are active contact control and passive contact control in electrical control. Active contact control system is also called_____.
 A.control system             B.safety system
 C.relay--contactor control system   D.digital control system with PLC and CPU

2.Using_____can realize time control; using_____can realize travel control.
A.thermal relay, time relay            B.time relay, travel switch
C. travel switch, time relay           D.thermal relay, travel switch

3.Control circuit is make up of many low-voltage electrical apparatus such as_____and so on
A.automatic air-break switch, fuse, push button.
B.contactor, relay
C.over travel-limit switch
D.A+B+C

4.A relay offering comprehensive protection will have the following set of features.
A. thermal(overload) protection,start protection
B. short-circuit protection,earth fault protection
C. negative phase sequence protection,undervoltage protection, loss-of-load protection
D. A+B+C

5._____receive control signal and close the main circuit.
A. contactor            B. contact            C. fuse            D. relay

(二) Translation

1. Translate new words and expressions (Table 3-3).

Table 3-3   Translation

| | |
|---|---|
| 1.circuit breaker | |
| 2.relay--contactor control system | |
| 3.active contact control | |
| 4.low-voltage electrical apparatus | |
| 5.air-break switch | |
| 6.normally closed contact | |
| 7.normally open contact | |
| 8.rated current of winding | |
| 9.time relay | |
| 10. press the start-button | |
| 11.control electromotor forward/reversal rotation | |
| 12.electrical schematic diagram | |
| 13.short circuit protection | |
| 14.interlocked control | |
| 15.undervoltage protection | |

A. 短路保护；B. 互锁控制；C. 控制电动机正反转；D. 有源触点控制；E. 时间继电气；F. 断路器；G. 继电接触器控制系统；H. 低压电器；I. 空气开关；J. 按下启按钮；K. 电气原理图；L. 线圈的额定电流；M. 欠电压保护；N. 常闭触点；O. 常开触点。

2.Translate the following sentences into Chinese.

Control circuit is make up of many low-voltage electrical apparatus, like is automatic air-break switch, fuse, contactor (KM), relay, push button, over travel-limit switch (SQ) and so on. The form of relay or contactor is various, but the circuit symbol is disciplinary, it is all made up of coil and contact.

Diagram symbols for components is shown in Fig.3-12 (a) (b) (c), with rare expect, the coil is in the left, the normally closed contact is in the right and the middle is normally open contact. The current flowing through the coil excites the contact to work on.

Using these electrical implement people should know their conformation principle and the parameters, for example rated voltage and rated current of winding.

(三) Speaking Practice

1. Group discussion

Work in groups. Look at the statements in the language bank task. Which of them are important aspects for electrical protection system? Why?

2. Short talk

Now it is your chance to practice what you have learned from this unit. Put your textbook away and give a short talk on the following topics. You should talk at least one minute. Don't be discouraged if you cannot make it. Review the task and try again. You are sure to do it better next time.

- relay contactor control
- trouble shooting

3. Role play

Work in groups or pairs and discuss the following topics. Then, you are advised to talk at least three minutes for each topic.

- relay contactor control
- motor and electrical control

## 【 Unit Evaluation 】

The teacher evaluates the students on their performance and mutual evaluation results, the results in Table 3-4.

**Table 3-4　Task Evaluation**

| EVALUATION CONTENT | | | DISTRIBUTION SCORE | SCORE |
|---|---|---|---|---|
| Unit 3 Three-phase Asynchronous Motors and Electrical Control<br>Task1 Three-phase Asynchronous Motors (50%)<br>Task2 Motor and Electrical Control(50%) | | | | |
| KNOWLEDGE EVALUATION | | | | |
| Ⅰ. Choice | | | 20 | |
| Ⅱ.Translation | 1.Translate new words and expressions into Chinese. | | 20 | |
| | 2.Translate the following sentences into English. | | 20 | |
| TIME: 30′ | STUDENT SIGN: | TEACHER SIGN: | TOTAL: | |
| SKILL EVALUATION | | | | |
| Ⅲ. Speaking Practice<br>　　Role playing | | | 20<br>20 | |
| TIME: 30′ | STUDENT SIGN: | TEACHER SIGN: | TOTAL: | |

# Unit 4

# Marine Power Station

【 Unit Goals 】

1. Get to know different parts of the marine electrical system and Power Management System (PMS). Familiar with the basic equipment: generator, power station, cables and wires, switchboard, parallel operation, blackout, air compressor, steering gear, etc.

2. Students can introduce different parts of the marine electrical system and PMS in English. They can talk to each other about the marine electrical system and PMS fluently.

## Task 1  Marine Electrical System

【 Task goals 】

1. Get to know different parts of the marine electrical system. Familiar with the basic equipment: generator, cables and wires, switchboard, motors, etc.

2. Students can introduce different parts of the marine electrical system in English. They can talk to each other about the marine electrical system fluently.

【 Knowledge linking 】

What does the marine electrical system include in your mind?
Please look at the following pictures carefully and try to learn the terms:
(1)Marine generator (Fig.4-1).

Fig. 4-1  Marine generator

(2) Main switchboard (Fig.4-2).

Fig. 4-2　Main switchboard

(3) Marine generator set (Fig.4-3).

Fig. 4-3　Marine generator set

## Marine Electrical System

　　The marine electrical(power) system consists of devices for generation (production),transmission and distribution of electric energy, as well as its consumers.[1] It mainly includes these components: (a) energy sources-in the basic configuration three electric generating sets are usually applied, sometimes shaft generators are also installed ; (b) main switchboard together with protective system, switches as well as main bus-bars, measurement and control systems of the processes realized within the electric power systems; (c) emergency switchboard; (d) power cable lines and (e) electric energy consumers(Fig.4-4).

# Unit 4 Marine Power Station

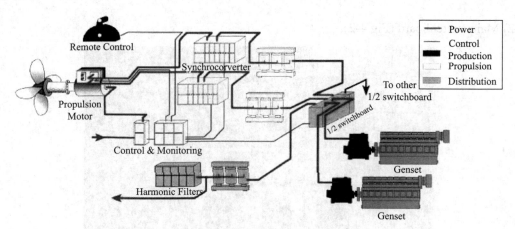

Fig. 4-4   Marine electrical system

1. The working principle to produce electricity

The shaft is driven by the generator engine and the shaft drives the rotation of a rotor.The Emf will be produced in the process of the rotation. The current will be thereafter produced, so the conversion of the energy from mechanical energy into the electric energy is completed.

2. Components of a marine power system

The marine power system is consisted of power generators, consumers and distribution system. It could also be deemed as three stages, namely a generator or generators in parallel operation in which produces electricity,switchboard which is treated as a relay to connect the load and the power supply or to regulate the voltage, the load which is considered as an electric consumer.[2]

3. Electric load on board

The electric load on board is the terminal of the shipboard electric power system.The electric load includes a lot machines driven by electricity. Examples are lighting system, radio communication, deck machinery, machinery concentrated in the engine room, steering gear system,main propulsive plant, etc.

4. Emergency power distribution

To ensure a dependable independent power source with the capacity to supply all those services necessary in an emergency, an emergency power distribution system is incorporated in all vessel. For all cargo vessel over 1,600 tons and certain passenger vessels with restricted operation, an automatically connected storage battery bank or automatically stared generator is required as a final emergency power source. For passenger vessels operating on oceans or the Great Lakes,on international or coastwise voyages,a temporary emergency source of limited capacity is required in addition to the final source described above.

Special sensitive equipment should be fed back by means of an Uninterruptible Power Supply (UPS). To Supply all those services necessary for the safety of passengers, crew, and other persons in an emergency, an emergency power distribution system is incorporated into the marine power system on board all ships.[3] An automatically connected storage battery bank or automatically started generator is required as a final emergency power source.

Fig.4-5 is Battery charging and discharging board; Fig.4-6 is Emergency switchboard.

## Task 1  Marine Electrical System

Fig. 4-5  Battery charging and discharging board

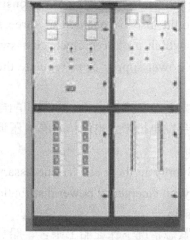

Fig.4-6  Emergency switchboard

Main switchboard would automatically start the emergency generator and simultaneously connected the emergency bus to the final emergency power source. The feedback breaker is designed to open automatically upon overload of the emergency power source before the emergency generator is tripped off the line from overload.[(4)]

## 【New Words and Expressions】

| generate | ['dʒenəreɪt] | v. | 发生，产生 |
| distribute | [dɪ'strɪbjuːt] | v. | 分配，分给 |
| consume | [kən'sjuːm] | v. | 消耗，分配 |
| consumer | [kən'sjuːmə(r)] | n. | 消费者，顾客 |
| parallel | ['pærəlɛl] | adj. &adv. | 并联的,并行的 并联地,并行地 |
| electricity | [ɪlɛk'trɪsɪti] | n. | 电力 |
| Uninterruptible Power Supply（UPS） | | | 不间断电源 |
| propel | [prə'pel] | v. | 推进；驱动；驱使 |
| propeller | [prə'pelə(r)] | n. | 螺旋桨，推进器 |
| propulsion | [prə'pʌlʃn] | n. | 推进 |
| prime mover | | n. | 原动机 |
| marine power system | | | 船舶电力系统 |
| power source | | | 电源 |

## 【Notes】

(1) The marine electrical(power) system consists of devices for generation (production),transmission and distribution of electric energy,as well as its consumers.

船舶电力系统由发电、输电、配电和负载组成。

(2) The marine power system is consisted of power generators, consumers and distribution system. It could also be deemed as three stages, namely a generator or generators in parallel operation in which produces electricity, switchboard which is treated as a relay to connect the load and the power supply or to regulate the voltage, the load which is considered as an electric consumer.

船舶电力系统包括发电机、负载和配电系统。也可以视其为3个部分，即一台发电机或并联运行的多台发电机产生电能；具有电压调节或传递作用的配电盘连接负载和电源；最后电力被负载消耗。

(3) To Supply all those services necessary for the safety of passengers, crew, and other persons in an emergency, an emergency power distribution system is incorporated into the marine power system on board all ships.

为了在紧急情况下保证船上乘客、船员和其他人的安全服务所需的（设备）供电，所有船上的电力系统中需要设置应急供电系统。

(4) The feedback breaker is designed to open automatically upon overload of the emergency power source before the emergency generator is tripped off the line from overload.

回馈断路器的设计是用来在应急电源过载时，在应急发电机跳闸之前自动断开。

(5) 单词巧记忆之构词法

① 有些动词，在词尾直接或经过变换后加上 or/er，意思变成相应的 ~人/器件、设备 (Table 4-1)

**Table 4-1　词尾变化**

| 规则 | 动词 | | 名词 | |
| --- | --- | --- | --- | --- |
| 在词尾后直接加上 or/er | transform | 改变；变换 | transformer | 变压器 |
| | print | 打印 | printer | 打印机 |
| | contact | 联系，接触 | contactor | 接触器；触点 |
| | survey | 检验，测量 | surveyor | 验船师 |
| | detect | 侦测 | detector | 探测器 |
| 把 e 去掉，加 or | generate | 造成；产生（能量）；发（电） | generator AC generator DC generator | 发电机 交流发电机 直流发电机 |
| | sense | 感到；检测出 | sensor | 传感器，灵敏元件 |
| | transduce | 转换 | transducer | 传感器 |
| | alternate | 交替，轮流 | alternator | 交流发电机 |
| | commutate | 使方向转换，整流 | commutator | 换向器；整流器 |
| | receive | 接收 | receiver | 接收器 |
| 词尾双写辅音字母 | transmit | 发射 | transmitter | 发射机 发报机 |
| 以辅音字母加 y 结尾，把 y 去掉，加 er/or | rectify | 改正，校正；[电]整流 | rectifier | 整流器 |

② 对照记忆(Table 4-2)。

## Task 1　Marine Electrical System

**Table 4-2　对照记忆**

| 人员职位 | master 船长(正式称谓)、captain (尊称) officer | chief engineer 轮机长 engineer |
|---|---|---|
| | chief(first) officer 大副<br>second officer 二副<br>third officer 三副<br><br>assistant officer 驾助 | second engineer 大管轮<br>third engineer 二管轮<br>fourth engineer 三管轮<br>engineer 轮机员<br>assistant engineer 轮助 |
| 意思相反 | forward (正转) | reverse (反转) |
| 物理名词与器件对照 | 物理名词<br>电阻 resistance<br>电容 capacitance<br>电感 Inductance<br>电抗 reactance　　阻抗 impedance | 器件<br>电阻器 resistor<br>电容器 capacitor<br>电感器 inductor |

③ 巧识前缀，事半功倍(Table 4-3)。

**Table 4-3　前缀**

| 前缀 | 词意 |
|---|---|
| in/im-(里、内)<br>ex-(out，外) | internal 内部的　　import 进口<br>external　　　　　export |
| a-(向) | stern(船尾)——astern（向后）<br>head(船艏)——ahead （向前） |
| uni-唯一，单向 | unidirectional （单向的，单向性的） |
| un- 表示否定 | Unfavorable |

④ 熟词新义。
dead　　原意:死的　　新意:微速
ahead full　　　　正车全速
ahead half　　　　正车半速
ahead slow　　　　正车慢速
ahead dead　　　　正车微速
astern full　　　　倒车全速
astern half　　　　倒车半速
astern slow　　　　倒车慢速
astern dead　　　　倒车微速

⑤ 合成词构成的新词意思，跟合成部分意思有关。
wheel（轮子）+house（住宅）　→　wheelhouse 驾驶室
switch（开关）+board（板）　→　switchboard 配电板
main switchboard (MSB)　　　emergency switchboard(ESB)

⑥ 联想记忆。
contact（接触，触点）
normally open contact 　（常开触点）
normally closed contact（常闭触点）

53

⑦ 重要的缩写。
M/E(Main Engine) 主机
DG(Diesel Generator) 柴油发电机
SG(Steering Gear) 舵机
ECR (Engine Control Room) 集控室
STBD(Starboard) 右舷
UPS( Uninterruptible Power System) 不间断电源
UMS (Unattended Machinery Space) 无人机舱

【Task Implement】

PART A　　Reading Practice

### Switchboard

The control and distribution of the electrical energy generated by generators are effected by power distribution equipment, i.e. switchboards. Switchboards are either (a) Main switchboards, to which the main generators are connected, (b) Emergency switchboards, to which the emergency generator or emergency battery is connected, (c) Section boards(sub-boards) or (d) Distribution boards.[1] In small equipment, particularly in small cargo ships, most of motors can be fed directly from the main switchboard, but as the size and multiplicity of services increase, it becomes necessary to reduce the number of outgoing circuits on the main board. This is done by grouping some services on one or more section boards (sometimes referred to as sub-boards), supplied by a feeder from the main board.

For DC switch boards, there are ammeters, voltmeters, circuit breakers, tipping devices and so on, but AC requires additional equipment as compared with DC, such as frequency meters, synchroscopes, wattmeters, voltage and current transformers, ammeter switches, voltage regulators, etc. circuit breakers and switches will be three-pole as compared with two-pole for DC. However, in spite of the additional equipment, an AC switchboard is usually smaller and lighter than the corresponding DC board because of the higher voltage and lower current and smaller bus-bars, etc.

Electrical supply is always needed, even if only for lighting. So after a ship goes into service it is extremely rare for the main bus-bars to be made dead, it therefore follows that the bus-bars are continuously alive throughout the life the ship. Even when in a shipyard for repair, a shore supply will usually be taken.

【New Words and Expressions】

| | | | |
|---|---|---|---|
| ammeter | [ˈæmˌmitə] | n. | 电流表 |
| voltmeter | [ˈvoʊltmiːtə(r)] | n. | 电压表 |
| synchroscope | [ˈsɪŋkrəˌskoʊp] | n. | 同步表 |
| wattmeter | [ˈwɒtˌmiːtə] | n. | 功率表 |
| transformer | [trænsˈfɔːrmə(r)] | n. | 变压器 |
| regulator | [ˈregjəˌletə] | n. | 调整器 |

voltage regulators　　　　　　　　　　　　　　　　　　　电压调制器
bus-bar　　　　　　　　　　　　　　　　　　　　　　　　汇流排

【Notes】

The control and distribution of the electrical energy generated by generators are effected by power distribution equipment, i.e. switchboards. Switchboards are either (a) Main switchboards, to which the main generators are connected, (b) Emergency switchboards, to which the emergency generator or emergency battery is connected, (c)Section boards(sub-boards) or (d)Distribution boards.

配电板控制和分配发电机发出的电能，配电板分为：（a）主配电板，和主发电机相连；（b）应急配电板，和应急发电机和应急电池相连；（c）区配电板；（d）分配电板。

### PART B　　Role Playing

(A: Cadet;　　B: Electrician)

A：Nice to meet you!

B：Nice to meet you,too!

A：Your ship seems to be a new ship.

B：Yes. She's just gone into service for 2 years.

A：Oh! You must have a lot of modern equipment.

B：Certainly! We have many advanced instruments and devices, especially our electrical power station.

A：What's the power station?

B：It is one of the most important parts of the marine power system. It is composed of the primer mover, generators and some main distributing devices.

A：I know the generator is used to supply the power for all equipment.

B：Yes, but it is not very accurately. In fact, there are different kinds of generators used on board. The equipment can get the power from main station, auxiliary station,and emergency station respectively.The first station works for the main propulsion motor, the second station works for lighting and auxiliary machinery, and the last one serves only in the emergency condition.

A：Could you let me look around this ship?

B：OK, let's go to visit the engine room and marine power station of this ship.

A：I think the main engine control is the most complicated.

B：You are quite right. There are three control modes for the main engine: bridge maneuvering, controlling in the machinery control compartment and local maneuvering which is also called emergency maneuvering.

A：Oh! Today I have learned a lot of knowledge. Thank you very much!

B：You are welcome!

【Task Evaluation】

(一) Choice

1. Ship power system is composed by the _____.

A. main power, emergency power, power grids, the load
B. power supply, voltage regulator, power grid
C. power supply, power distribution equipment, power grid, the load
D. power supply, load

2. Which can not serve as the marine main power supply _____.
A. shaft generator          B. battery
C. diesel generator sets    D. turbine

3. The following is a direct power supply from the main distribution board equipment is _____.
A. steering gear, windlass         B. navigation lights, radio power supply board
C. electric navigation instrument power box    D. A and B and C

4. Power distribution equipment is the device which can _____ the power, power grids and load
A. protect                  B. monitoring, measure
C. control                  D. A and B and C

5. _____ is a machine by which mechanical energy is transformed into electrical energy.
A. A motor                  B. An alternator
C. A diesel engine          D. A main switchboard

### (二) Translation.

1. Translate new words and expressions into Chinese.

Table 4-4  Translation

| | |
|---|---|
| 1.Uninterruptible Power Supply（UPS） | |
| 2.marine generator set | |
| 3.voltage regulators | |
| 4.lighting system | |
| 5.deck machinery | |
| 6.steering gear | |
| 7.bus-bar | |
| 8. battery charging and discharging board | |
| 9.three-phase transformer | |
| 10.voltage regulator | |
| 11.half-wave rectifier | |
| 12.overload | |
| 13.power source | |
| 14.power supply | |
| 15.power station | |

A. 电源；B. 供电；C. 船舶电站；D. 照明系统；E. 不间断电源；F. 舵机；G. 甲板机械；H. 蓄电池充放电板；I. 过载；J. 半波整流器；K. 船用发电机组；L. 电压调整器；M. 三相变压器；N. 汇流排；O. 电压调整器。

2.Translate the following sentences into Chinese.

The marine power system is consisted of power generators, consumers and distribution system. It could also be deemed as three stages, namely a generator or generators in parallel operation in which produces electricity, switchboard which is treated as a relay to connect the load and the power supply or to regulate the voltage, the load which is considered as an electric consumer.

The electric load on board is the terminal of the shipboard electric power system. The electric load includes a lot machines driven by electricity. Examples are lighting system, radio communication, deck machinery, machinery concentrated in the engine room, steering gear system, main propulsive plant, etc.

(三) Speaking Practice

1. Group discussion

Work in groups. Look at the statements in the language bank task. Which of them are important aspects for marine electrical system? Why?

2. Short talk

Now it is your chance to practice what you have learned from this unit. Put your textbook away and give a short talk on the following topics. You should talk at least one minute. Don't be discouraged if you cannot make it. Review the lesson and try again. You are sure to do it better next time.
- marine electrical system.
- generating system.
- main switchboard.

3. Role play

Work in groups or pairs and discuss the following topics. Then, you are advised to talk at least three minutes for each topic.
- A is a cadet visiting the ship. B is an electrician.
- Prompts: Introduce marine electrical system.
- marine electrical system (its function and related equipment).

# Task 2　Marine Power Management System (PMS)

【Task goals】

1. Get to know PMS.Familiar with the basic words and expressions: power station, parallel operation, Power Management System (PMS), blackout, air compressor, steering gear, captain, third engineer etc.

2. Students can introduce marine Power Management System (PMS) in English.They can talk to each other about PMS fluently.

【Knowledge linking】

What functions does power station include in your mind?
Please look at the following pictures carefully and try to learn the terms（Fig.4-7）.

(a) Combination Starter Panel

(b) Distribution Board

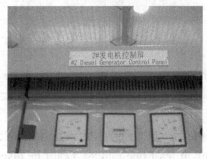
(c) Diesel generator control panel

(d) The primary side of lighting transformer

Fig.4-7　Panel

## **Ship Automatic Electric Power Station**[1]

The composition of marine automatic electric power station is also called marine Power Management System (PMS), which achieves the automation of engine room. So far, the marine automatic electric power station develops and reaches maturity with the function be perfect, work credibility, operation convenience, maintain easy. [2]

With the requirements of ship construction standards and CCS, the marine power station must achieve that:

1. The spare generator must be rated to start and provide power for the power net quickly (no more than 45s) and automatically at any time (when there are two parallel operation of generators , it can be paralleled in automatically).[3]

2. The master switches of generators should be able to stop repetitive working if the short circuit happens.

3. When the voltage and frequency continued become low and more overload than the maximum of scheduled in the net, or running unit is at fault, the power station should raise the alarm from the control panel of main and auxiliary machine in the engine room, and sent out the starting instructions to let the spare generator to start and provide power for the power net quickly and automatically. [4]

4. When the marine power station is overload, it should be able to unloaded secondary load automatically.

5. The sets of power generator-units, automatic starting, should be fitted with program starting system or manual selection switch. In case of the program starting system in a certain generator-unit is failure or not switching on, the power station should be able to send the starting instructions to another spare generator-unit automatically. [5]

6. When the automatic control or remote control of marine power station is failure, it should be able to be manually control or local control.

7. A reflect signal in transient conditions (such as the starting current from motor) should not start the spare generator-unit.

8. The main switchboards should be able to start and stop the generator, connect or cut off bridging connection of bus-bars, control two independent ways of power supply conversion, and have either the measurement and display unit about the performance of the generator-units, or alarm equipment, and control the motor load according to procedures starting to avoid the main switches tripped because of high impulse current.

【 New Words and Expressions 】

| | | | |
|---|---|---|---|
| maintain | [meɪnˈteɪn] | vt. | 保持；维护；维持 |
| maintenance | [ˈmentənəns] | n. | 保持；维护；维持 |
| maturity | [məˈtʃʊərɪti] | n. | 成熟；完备 |
| credibility | [ˌkredəˈbɪləti] | n. | 可靠性，可信性；确实性 |
| spare | [speə] | adj.&n. | 多余的，备用的；备件 |
| auxiliary | [ɔːgˈzɪliəri] | adj. | 辅助的；备用的， |
| repetitive | [rɪˈpetətɪv] | adj. n. | 重复的（是学过的动词 repeat 的形容词的形式，repeat 的意思是：复述、重复） |
| manual | [ˈmænjuəl] | adj. | 手动的；手制的，手工的；体力的 |
| | | n. | 手册；指南 |
| instruction | [ɪnˈstrʌkʃn] | n. | 授课；[计算机科学]指令 |
| procedure | [prəˈsiːdʒə] | n. | 步骤、程序 |
| forego | [fɔːˈgəʊ] | vt. | 走在……之前，居先 |
| power station | | | 电站 |
| auxiliary machine | | | 辅机 |
| short circuit | | | 短路 |
| switch on | | | 闭合，接通 |
| switch off | | | 断开 |
| indicator lights | | | 指示灯 |
| manual control buttons | | | 手动控制按钮 |
| reset buttons | | | 复位开关 |
| change-over switch | | | 转换开关 |
| split up | | | 分成……份，分配 |

【 Notes 】

(1) The Basic Function of Ship Automatic Electric Power Station
船舶自动化电站

(2) So far, the marine automatic electric power station develops and reaches maturity with the

function be perfect, work credibility, operation convenience, maintain easy.

到目前为止，船舶自动化电站发展并达到成熟，其功能完善，运行可靠，操作方便，容易维护。the function be perfect, work credibility, operation convenience, maintain easy 几个短语的结构虽不尽相同，但可知其要表达的汉语意思为并列结构，理解和翻译时要注意协调。

(3) The spare generator must be rated to start and provide power for the power net quickly (no more than 45s) and automatically at any time (when there are two parallel operation of generators, it can be paralleled in automatically).

备用发电机必须处在分级启动，并能在任何时候快速（45s 内）和自动地向电网供电（当有两台发电机并联运行的时，可以自动并网）。

(4) When the voltage and frequency continued become low and more overload than the maximum of scheduled in the net, or running unit is at fault, the power station should raise the alarm from the control panel of main and auxiliary machine in the engine room, and sent out the starting instructions to let the spare generator to start and provide power for the power net quickly and automatically.

当电压和频率持续变低，超过电网既定的最大负荷，或者运行中的机组出现故障，电站应该从机舱内主机和辅助机械的控制面板发出警报，并发出启动指令，令备用发电机启动，并迅速自动地向电网供电。句子主干为 the power station should raise the alarm … and sent out the starting instructions. when 引导的部分为状语从句。

(5) In case of the program starting system in a certain generator-unit is failure or not switching on, the power station should be able to send the starting instructions to another spare generator-unit automatically.

假设某个发电机单元的程序启动系统失灵或无法接通，电站应当能够自动地向另一备用发电机单元发送启动指令。in case of 意为"假设，万一"。

# 【Task Implement】

## PART A  Reading Practice

### Parallel Operation of Generators

Three phase alternators arranged for parallel operation require a considerable amount of instrumentation. This will include ammeters, wattmeters, voltmeters, frequency meters and a synchronizing device.[1] Reverse power protection is provided to alternators since current protection cannot be used. Alternatively various trips may be provided in the event of prime mover failure to that the alternator does not act as a motor.

The operation of paralleling two alternators requires the voltages to be equal and also in phase.[2] The alternating current output of any machines is always changing, so for two machines to operate together their voltages must be changing at the same rate for frequency , and must be reaching their maximum (or any other value) together. They are then said to be "in phase". Use is nowadays made of a synchroscope when paralleling two AC machines. The synchroscope has two windings which are connected one to each side of the paralleling switch. A pointer is free to rotate and is moved by the magnetic effect of the two windings. When the two voltage supplies are in phase the pointer is stationary in the 12 o'clock position. If the pointer is rotating then a frequency difference exists and the dial is marked for clockwise rotation FAST and anti- clockwise rotation SLOW, the reference being to the incoming machine frequency.

To parallel an incoming machine to a running machine therefore it is necessary to ensure firstly both voltages are equal. Voltmeters are provided for this purpose. Secondly the frequencies must be brought into phase. In practice the synchroscope usually moves slowly in the FAST direction and the paralleling switch is closed as the pointer reached the 11 o'clock position. This results in the incoming machine immediately accepting a small amount of load.

A set of three lamps may also be provided to enable synchronising. The sequence method of lamp connection has a key lamp connected across one phase with two other lamps cross connected over the other two phases. If the frequencies of the machines are different the lamps will brighten and darken in rotation, depending upon the incoming frequency being FAST or SLOW. The correct moment for synchronizing is when the key lamp is dark and the other two are equally bright.

【 New Words and Expressions 】

| | | | |
|---|---|---|---|
| alternator | [ˈɔːltərneɪtə(r)] | n. | 交流发电机 |
| trip | [trɪp] | n. | 脱扣机构 |
| winding | [ˈwaɪndɪŋ] | n. | 绕组 |
| pointer | [ˈpɔɪntə-] | n. | 指针 |
| parallel operation | | | 并车操作 |
| reverse power protection | | | 逆功率保护 |

【 Notes 】

(1) Three phase alternators arranged for parallel operation require a considerable amount of instrumentation. This will include ammeters, wattmeters, voltmeters, frequency meters and a synchronizing device.

三相发电机并车需要相当数量的仪器仪表。包括电流表、功率表、电压表、频率计和同步表。

(2) The operation of paralleling two alternators requires the voltages to be equal and also in phase.

两台发动机电压相等和同相位才能够并车。

## PART B  Role Playing

**Blackout**

（A: navigator　B: third engineer　C: chief engineer　D: captain）

A：Hello, is that the duty engineer?
B：Yes, this is the third engineer.
A：Is the chief engineer there?
B：Yes, but he is engaged in the blackout.
A：Will you ask him to answer the call?

B: OK.
C: Hello, this is the chief engineer.
A: I'd like to know that what's wrong with the power supply now, when can it be restored?
C: No.1 and No.3 generators stopped for no reason. We're trying to start No.2 now.
A: Our ship is in a narrow channel and the ship ahead is quite close to us. Although I've dropped anchor, the ship is still hard to be controlled. Please restore the running of the main engine as quick as possible.
C: Yes, I will.
C: Third engineer, why can't No.2 generator be started?
B: It was all right yesterday, but we failed to start it just now. The lube oil pressure can't be built up and the motorman now is pumping the lube oil by hand pumping.
C: Try to prolong the starting period and see.
B: OK. All depends on the last time. No starting air is left for more start.
C: Isn't the emergency air compressor started?
B: Yes. But the emergency air compressor can't supply enough starting air to the air receiver for the auxiliary engine.
C: I wish it would be a success this time.
B: It's started, chief.
C: Supply the power, electrical engineer. Provide the pumps for the main engine and the steering gear with power supply first to ensure the proper running of the main engine.
B: OK. The power supply is finished and the pumps for the main engine have been started.
C: Well done. Third engineer, check the oil and water pressures to see if everything is all right, start the main engine if no problem.
B: All right.
C: Hello, is it the captain?
D: Yes, how is the main engine now?
C: It's ready for use.
D: That's great! Thank you very much.
C: We're detecting the defects of the two generators. Now we can provide power supply only for the main engine. Others won't be put into normal operation until either of the two generators is repaired.
D: When you put right the NO.2 generators, please measure their output, temperature, voltage, current and frequency, and so on. And see, during the test, whether they can run smoothly. They must run continuously at full load for one hour.
C: No problem. We'll do that exactly as you required.

## 【Task Evaluation】

### (一) Choice

1. The main functions of automation power station are_____.
① the fault of Short circuit to be automatic repair
② under-voltage protection fault setting value to be automatic adjustment

③ standby generator to be automatic starting
④ the generator to be automatic decompose
⑤ the frequency and load to be automatic adjustment
⑥ the ship power station to be comprehensive protection
A. ①②③④          B. ②③④⑤          C. ③④⑤⑥          D.①②⑤⑥

2. The main generators are connected to _____.
A. distribution board            B. section boards
C. emergency switchboards        D. main switchboards

3. In a general way, _____ do not belong to the functions of power station control system itself in the computer control system of the ship power station.
A. the generator to be automatic decompose
B. the power to be automatic assignment
C. power factor to be automatic adjustment
D. the ship power station to be comprehensive protection

4. When the ship power station _____, the secondary load should be able to automatic unloading.
A. underload          B. overload          C. undervoltage          D. overvoltage

5. In the parallel operation of generator sets, the ship power station should be set _____ to prevent synchronous ac generator into synchronous motor running.
A. overload protection device           B. reverse power protection device
C. short circuit protection device      D. over-voltage protection device

(二) **Translation.**

1. Translate new words and expressions into Chinese (Table 4-5).

Table 4-5   Translation

| | |
|---|---|
| 1.Power Management System(PMS) | |
| 2.marine automatic electric power station | |
| 3.spare generator | |
| 4.unloaded secondary load | |
| 5.manual selection switch | |
| 6.automatic control | |
| 7.manual control buttons | |
| 8.parallel operation of generators | |
| 9.three phase alternators | |
| 10.reverse power protection | |
| 11.alternating current | |
| 12.synchroscope | |
| 13.emergency air compressor | |
| 14.run continuously at full load | |
| 15.auxiliary engine | |

A. 手动控制按钮；B. 发电机并车；C. 逆功率保护；D. 三相交流发电机；E. 交流；F. 同步表；G. 应急空压机；H. 满载连续运行；I. 自动化船舶电站；J. 辅机；K. 手动选择开关；L. 卸载次级负载；M. 备用发电机；N. 电力管理系统；O. 自动控制。

2.Translate the following sentences into Chinese.

Yet, for all of those functions noted in the foregoing, the marine automatic electric power station also has the following operations:

(1) Starting any one generator automatically. When the diesel generator is in stopped status and the main switch is braked, the engine can be started the automatically with the starting signal.

(2) Automatical approximate synchronous switching. As a power supply units working in the net, the unit after the success of the automatic starting will be automatically thrown into the parallel operation with the help of automatical approximate synchronous equipment and automatic frequency or load adjustment.

(3) Automatic constant frequency and active power automatic distributed.

(4) To make a generator splitting up from the parallel operation of generator, firstly, the automatic equipment should transfer its load to the running-generator automatically, then accept the trip instruction and realize splitting up.

(5) Automatic constant voltage and reactive power automatic distributed.

(6) The power station has automatic classification unload device and procedures sequence starting device.

(7) There are supervisory instruments, indicator lights, alarm devices, manual control buttons, reset buttons, change-over switch, etc.

(三) Speaking Practice

1. Group discussion

Work in groups. Look at the statements in the language bank task. Which of them are important functions for PMS? Why?

2. Short talk

Now it is your chance to practice what you have learned from this unit. Put your textbook away and give a short talk on the following topics. You should talk at least one minute. Don't be discouraged if you cannot make it. Review the lesson and try again. You are sure to do it better next time.

- PMS.
- the basic function of ship automatic electric power station.

3. Role play

Work in groups or pairs and discuss the following topics. Then, you are advised to talk at least three minutes for each topic.

- A is a cadet visiting the ship. B is an electrician.
- Prompts: Introduce PMS.
- the basic function of ship automatic electric power station.

## 【Unit Evaluation】

The teacher evaluates the students on their performance and mutual evaluation results, the results in Table 4-6.

Marine Power Management System (PMS)

**Table 4-6  Task Evaluation**

| EVALUATION CONTENT | | | DISTRIBUTION SCORE | SCORE |
|---|---|---|---|---|
| Unit 4 Marine Power Station  marine electrical system (50%)  Task2 Marine Power Management System (PMS)(50%) | | | | |
| KNOWLEDGE EVALUATION | | | | |
| Ⅰ. Choice | | | 20 | |
| Ⅱ.Translation | 1.Translate new words and expressions into Chinese. | | 20 | |
| | 2.Translate the following sentences into English. | | 20 | |
| TIME: 30' | STUDENT SIGN: | TEACHER SIGN: | TOTAL: | |
| SKILL EVALUATION | | | | |
| Ⅲ. Speaking Practice  Role playing | | | 20  20 | |
| TIME: 30' | STUDENT SIGN: | TEACHER SIGN: | TOTAL: | |

# Unit 5

# Marine Electric Installation

【Unit Goals】

1. Get to know ship's electric installation and familiar with the construction of marine cable. Be familiar with the basic requirements of the cable's selection and its installation.

2. Students can introduce the basic information of the marine electric installation to the others in English. Furthermore, they can talk to each other about the cable and its selection requirements fluently.

## Task 1　　Introduction of Shipboard Cables

【Task goals】

1. Get to know ship's electric installation and familiar with the construction of marine cable.
2. Students can introduce the basic information of the marine electric installation to the others in English fluently.

【Knowledge linking】

How many types of marine cables do you know? Give some examples.
Please look at the following pictures carefully and try to learn the terms:
(1) Cables (Fig. 5-1).
(2) Cable ladders (Fig. 5-2).
(3) Cable tray(Fig.5-3).

Fig.5-1　Cables

Fig.5-2　Cable ladders

Fig.5-3　Cable tray

(4) Cable pipe (Fig. 5-4).
(5) Cable ties (Fig. 5-5).
(6) Multiple cable ladder(Fig.5-6).

Fig.5-4  Cable pipe    Fig.5-5  Cable ties    Fig.5-6  Multiple cable ladder

## Introduction of Shipboard cables

Cables are the means of transport of electricity between the various components. Due to the high quantity of man-hours involved in fitting them, it is the largest cost in a ship's electrical installation. The shipboard and ocean environments pose severe challenges to power cables with heat, vibration, salt corrosion, mud and mechanical stress. So, the cable must be selected to operate reliably in such harsh environments.

Shipboard cables including power, control, instrumentation, data transmission and communication cables. [1] Shipboard power cable is suitable for power transmission, lighting and control of offshore buildings, such as ship, petroleum-exploitation platform and so on. Shipboard control cable is applicable to control system of a ship. The telecommunication cable is intended for telecommunication, computer and information processing unit of shipboard and naval ship. The main parameters of the cables are model and type, number of cores, rated voltage, nominal cross-section areas, etc. [2]

Here, we will take a short overview of the main and the most typical cable construction of low voltage power and control cables(Fig.5-7).

The most ordinary cable is the PVC-insulated cable. However, PVC insulated cable is vulnerable in a fire: the insulation burns, a short circuit can be result, and/or dangerous and corrosive gasses are in large quantities produced, causing much more damage to the installation than the fire only. [3] Other, higher quality cables are: Higher temperature class, Non-smoke, Low-toxic, or fire-resistant.

1. Selection of Cables

All electric cables and the installation shall meet the requirements of the Classification societies and Regulatory

Fig.5-7  Construction of cable
1—conductor; 2—insulation; 3—filler; 4—tape;
5—inner sheath; 6—amour; 7—out sheath

Bodies. In general, all cable routing shall be located with due regards to fire hazards and mechanical damage. Cables for safety critical systems such as fire detection, PA/GA, and elevators shall be fire resistant. All control, measuring, alarm and communication cables shall be adequately screened against electrical noise.

Cable sizes shall be selected on the basis of current carrying capacity and voltage drop with due considerations given to cable grouping and ambient temperatures in areas of cableways[4]. The ambient temperatures on the open deck shall be 45°C for purpose of cable size selection; in engine room the ambient temperature for cable size selection shall be 50°C, and the appropriate correction shall be applied.

Three-phase circuits shall in general be supplied by three-core cables; two or more three-core cables in parallel may be used for larger capacities. The minimum conductor size is in general to be 1.5 mm$^2$ for power and 1.0mm$^2$ for signal/control cables. Smaller conductor sizes may be considered for special purposes, they have to be approved by the buyer in each case. Signal/control cables can be 0.75 mm$^2$ for more than 5 cores.

2. Installation of Cables

During cable installation operation on board, cable supports, cable fasteners and cable penetrations always be used.

Cable fastener (Fig.5-8 and Fig.5-9)

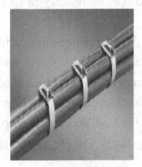 

Fig.5-8  Stainless steel cable ties            Fig.5-9  Nylon cable ties

Cable Penetration (Fig.5-10 and Fig.5-11).

  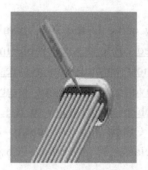 

Fig. 5-10  Cable gland            Fig.5-11 Cable frame

Cable support (Fig.5-12～Fig.5-15).

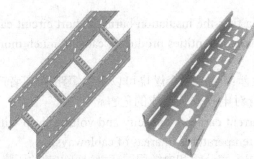 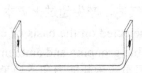 

Fig.5-12　Cable ladder　　Fig.5-13　Cable tray　　Fig.5-14　Cable hanger　　Fig.5-15　Multiple cable ladder

## 【New Words and Expressions】

| | | | |
|---|---|---|---|
| installation | [ˌɪnstəˈleɪʃn] | n. | 安装；装置 |
| vibration | [vaɪˈbreɪʃn] | n. | 摆动；振动 |
| corrosion | [kəˈrəʊʒən] | n. | 腐蚀，侵蚀，锈蚀 |
| mud | [mʌd] | n. | 污物 |
| telecommunication | [ˈtelikəˌmjuniˈkeɪʃn] | n. | 电信；电通信 |
| petroleum | [pɪˈtrəʊliəm] | n. | 石油 |
| exploitation | [ˌeksplɔɪˈteɪʃn] | n. | 开发；利用； |
| insulation | [ˌɪnsəˈleɪʃn] | n. | 绝缘；绝缘或隔热的材料 |
| conductor | [kənˈdʌktə] | n. | 导体 |
| braid | [breɪd] | n. | 编织物 |
| armour | [ˈaːmə(r)] | n. | 铠装 |
| cross-section areas | | | 横截面积 |
| open deck | | | 露天甲板 |
| rated voltage | | | 额定电压 |
| fire-resistant | | | 防火 |
| Classification societies | | | 船级社 |
| Regulatory Bodies | | | 监管机构 |
| PA/GA | | | 广播/通用报警系统 |
| engine room | | | 机舱 |
| ambient temperature | | | 环境温度 |

## 【Notes】

(1) Shipboard cables including power, control, instrumentation, data transmission and communication cables.

船舶电缆包括电力电缆、控制电缆、仪表电缆、数据传输电缆和通信电缆。

(2) The main parameters of the cables are model and type, number of cores, rated voltage, nominal cross-section areas, etc.

电缆的主要参数有电缆型号、芯数、额定电压、横截面积等。

(3) However, PVC insulated cable is vulnerable in a fire: the insulation burns, a short circuit can be result, and/or dangerous and corrosive gasses are in large quantities produced, causing much more damage to the installation than the fire only.

然而，聚氯乙烯 PVC 绝缘电缆在火灾中耐受性差：绝缘层会燃烧可以引起短路和/或者产生大量的危险气体和腐蚀性气体，产生超过火灾本身对电缆安装造成的危害。

(4) Cable sizes shall be selected on the basis of current carrying capacity and voltage drop with due considerations given to cable grouping and ambient temperatures in areas of cableways.

电缆尺寸的选择应该根据电流承载能力和适当考虑电缆分组和电缆周围环境温度引起的压降。

## 【Task Implement】

### PART A  Reading Practice

#### Cable

Colors (outer sheath)

All cables shall be colored on the outside according to the following:

- Instrument cables        :    Grey (other color than power and lighting)
- Lighting                 :    Black (other color can be agreed)
- Power (below 1 kV)       :    Black (other color can be agreed)
- Wire colors for earthing :
    - PE                   :    Yellow/green wire
    - Instrument earth     :    Black wire

All other cables and wires are to be agreed.

Cables with function-retention, have mica protection around the copper wires, and keep their function for at least one hour in accordance with SOLAS A-60 requirements. This type of cables need to be utilized for all systems which need to keep their function in case of fire, needed in fire-fighting systems which are not interfere with alarms or the function of fire-fighting in another fire zone. This problem can partly be dealt with by choosing another route for cables, and partly by using above type cables.

## 【New Words and Expressions】

| | | | |
|---|---|---|---|
| retention | [ri'tenʃən] | n. | 保留；保持力；滞留 |
| SOLAS( the Safety of Life at Sea ) | | | 海上人命安全公约 |
| fire-fighting systems | | | 灭火系统 |

### PART B  Role Playing

(A: ship surveyor，B: electrician)

A: You see here. These cables on the cable tray are out of order.

B: where?

A: Here, could you add some metal cable straps on the vertical cable tray?

B: OK

Introduction of Shipboard Cables

A: How do you fix a cable?

B: For example, Single cables may be fixed by clips welded to structures; cables in groups are supported by metal cable hangers.

A: What do you do if a cable passes through a watertight bulkhead?

B: In that case, special stuffing tube will be used to keep the watertightness.

A：OK，moreover, how to protect the cables from damage?

B: In places such as hatches, and open decks, we use removable metal coverings, in some hot or refrigerated places, we use insulated cables.

## 【Task Evaluation】

### (一) Choice

1. Which kind of cable on board is suitable for power transmission _____.
   A. power cables        B. control cables        C. telecommunication cables

2. Which one isn't the main parameters of the cables in the following options _____.
   A. number of cores              B. rated voltage
   C. nominal cross-section areas  D. length

3. which one of the following option is cable fastener? Which one is cable penetration? which one belongs to cable support _____.
   A. Cable ladder                 B. Stainless steel cable ties
   C. Cable gland                  D. Cable size

### (二) Translate the phrases and sentences.

1. Translate new words and expressions into Chinese (Table 5-1).

Table 5-1    Translation

| | |
|---|---|
| 1.cable | |
| 2.cable support | |
| 3.shipboard power cable | |
| 4.shipboard control cable | |
| 5.shipboard communication cable | |
| 6.number of cores | |
| 7.cross-section areas | |
| 8.fire-resistant | |
| 9.cable pipe | |
| 10.amour | |
| 11.PA/GA | |
| 12.Nylon cable ties | |
| 13.Feeder cable | |
| 14.rated voltage | |
| 15.Classification societies | |

A. 额定电压；B. 船级社；C. 广播/通用报警；D. 防火；E. 铠装；F. 电缆；G. 电缆支架；H. 船用控制电缆；I. 船用通信电缆；J. 船用电力电缆；K. 芯数；L. 横截面积；M. 电缆管；N. 尼龙电缆扎带；O. 馈电电缆。

2. Translate the following sentences into Chinese.

All electric cables and the installation shall meet the requirements of the Classification societies and Regulatory Bodies. In general, all cable routing shall be located with due regards to fire hazards and mechanical damage. Cables for safety critical systems such as fire detection, PA/GA, and elevators shall be fire resistant. All control, measuring, alarm and communication cables shall be adequately screened against electrical noise.

### (三) Speaking Practice

1. Group discussion

Work in groups. Look at the statements in the language bank task. What attentions should be paid when we fix the cable on board?

2. Short talk

Now it is your chance to practice what you have learned from this unit. Put your textbook away and give a short talk on the following topics. You should talk at least one minute. Don't be discouraged if you cannot make it. Review the lesson and try again. You are sure to do it better next time.

- cable selection.
- cable installation.

3. Role play

Work in groups or pairs and discuss the following topics. Then, you are advised to talk at least three minutes for each topic.

- Introducing construction of cable.
- Discussing the basic materials of cable installation.

## Task 2　Shipping Electric Installation

### 【Task goals】

1. Get to know the basic requirements of the shipping electric installation: package of equipment, the main electric equipment installation, some basic technical requirements of equipment installation.

2. Students can introduce the procedure of the electric installation to others in English and talk to each other about the technical requirements of equipment installation fluently.

### 【Knowledge linking】

How to install the electric equipment on board?

Please look at the following pictures carefully：

(1) Electric installation(Fig.5-16)

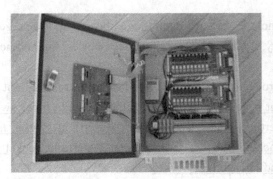

Fig.5-16　Electric installation

## Shipping Electric Installation

All electric equipment and machinery are to be designed and selected for marine use, in the consideration of vibration, heat and humidity. Furthermore, the design shall be in accordance with the design of the shipyard and Builders Electrical Installation Standard approved by Owner, as well as normal practice for a vessel of this type. All electrical equipment/fittings located in hazardous area to be ex-proof type.

1. Package of equipment

<u>Materials preparation is according to equipment list or material list and arrangement drawing and cable trays drawing.</u>[1] All electric equipment should have quality certificate from maker. Some important equipment should have class type approval certificate, equipment certificate or other necessary certificate, and pay attention to the effective date.

First, we should check whether equipment specification is accordance with equipment list and whether equipment has some defect and measure insulation resistance if necessary. <u>Then, we should check cable gland specification and quantities are in accordance with drawings and check the supports, foundation and ground accessories and so on to be prepared according to relative drawings.</u>[2] At last, we should remember to place electric equipment in the dry and clean environment.

2. Tools are commonly used for installation(Fig.5-17)

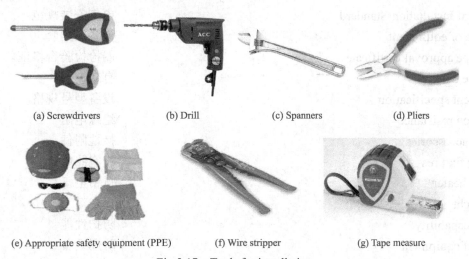

(a) Screwdrivers　　(b) Drill　　(c) Spanners　　(d) Pliers

(e) Appropriate safety equipment (PPE)　　(f) Wire stripper　　(g) Tape measure

Fig.5-17　Tools for installation

The main electric equipment on board include motor, main switchboard and emergency switchboard, control and distribution panel, battery, lighting fixtures, light accessories, fan and heater and internal communication and signal equipment.

For lighting fixtures, there are bed lamp, mirror lamp, wall lamp, flood light, searching light and navigation lights and signal lights. As far as light accessories concerned, they include inner switch and flush-mounted switch in corridor, inner watertight switch and corridor watertight switch, table lamp socket, table telephone socket, table fan socket, wall fan socket, inner watertight socket and socket with switch, lower flush-mounted socket and H/L voltage socket.[3]

3. Some basic technical requirements of equipment installation

For the equipment installation, the security and convenient for use and maintenance should been considered as far as possible. There should have enough lighting and good ventilation in installation site and should not break bulkhead or deck the defend capability and the intensity. The equipment should not direct install the shell under the main deck.

In dangerous space, prohibit installed non-safety equipment except needed ex-proof equipment. The equipment liable being machine damaged site, the protection degree should be accommodate to installation position. Otherwise, it should be adopted essential protection.

If the equipment has to be installed on the bulkhead of oil tank, the distance to the surface should be more than 50mm, and electric equipment (heart etc.) producing high temperature forbid installed on the mentioned place. Moreover, proper absorber should be adopted if shake of installation place can influence normal and reliable working.

## 【 New Words and Expressions 】

| | | | |
|---|---|---|---|
| humidity | [hjuːˈmiditi] | n. | 湿度；潮湿 |
| gland | [glænd] | n. | 填料函 |
| ventilation | [ˌventlˈeɪʃən] | n. | 空气流通；通风设备 |
| absorber | [əbˈsɔːbə] | n. | 减振器 |
| screwdriver | [ˈskruːˌdraɪvə] | n. | 螺钉旋具 |
| Electrical Installation Standard | | | 电气安装规范 |
| package of equipment | | | 设备的配套 |
| class type approval certificate | | | 船检检验合格证 |
| effective date | | | 有效期限 |
| equipment specification | | | 设备型号规格 |
| insulation resistance | | | 绝缘电阻 |
| ground accessories | | | 接地附件 |
| lighting fixtures | | | 舱室照明灯具 |
| fan and heater | | | 日用电气 |
| flood light | | | 投光灯 |
| defend capability | | | 防护性能 |
| ex-proof equipment | | | 防爆设备 |

## 【Notes】

(1) Materials preparation is according to equipment list or material list and arrangement drawing and cable trays drawing

按照设备明细表或电装图及电气设备布置图进行领料配套。

(2) Then, we should check cable gland specification and quantities are in accordance with drawings and check the supports, foundation and ground accessories and so on to be prepared according to relative drawings.

接下来，我们需要检查填料函的规格和数量是否与图样要求相符，并安装相关图样配齐好设备的底脚、支架及接地附件。

(3) As far as light accessories concerned, they include inner switch and flush-mounted switch in corridor, inner watertight switch and corridor watertight switch, table lamp socket, table telephone socket, table fan socket, wall fan socket, inner watertight socket and socket with switch, lower flush-mounted socket and H/L voltage socket.

照明附具包括室内开关及走道暗式开关、室内水密开关及走道防水开关、台灯插座、台式电话插座、台扇插座、壁扇插座、室内防水插座、开关插座、落地暗式插座盒高低压插座箱。

## 【Task Implement】

### PART A    Reading Practice

#### Some documentation necessary for maritime electrical installation

Material lists

One-line diagrams for the entire installation, which show the principal lay-out of the electric installation, indicating quantities and rating of generators. Electrical arrangement of main bus-bars, show also separation and the division over the bus-bar sections of the essential consumers, power supply to distribution boxes and panels throughout the ship.

Arrangement drawings showing the location of generators, transformers, main and emergency switchboards, important services, cable layout for main circuits and circuits for emergency power supply.

Complete diagram and arrangement drawings for main switchboard and major junctions etc.

Description of emergency power system.

Documentation of ship's lights system.

Overview diagram of steering engine system.

Special documentation for installations in hazardous areas (fie/explosion), including area classification and certificates for electrical equipment in hazardous areas.

Specifications showing arrangement and performance of the various protective devices and how they provide complete and coordinated automatic protection to ensure continuity of service through the discriminative action of the protective devices.

## Unit 5 Marine Electric Installation

### 【New Words and Expressions】

| | | | |
|---|---|---|---|
| transformer | [træns'fɔːmə(r)] | n. | 变压器 |
| hazardous | ['hæzədəs] | adj. | 危险的 |
| One-line diagrams | | | 一次电力系统图 |
| distribution boxes | | | 配电箱 |
| Complete diagram | | | 完工图 |

### PART B  Role Playing

(A: ship surveyor; B: electrician)

A: Good afternoon!
B: Good afternoon!
A: There is something wrong with the hatch cover. I would like to discuss it with you.
B: I'm sorry. I can't follow you. Can you speak slowly?
A: I mean I want to talk with you about the hatch cover.
B: Oh, I see. Let's go to my office and talk it cover in detail.
A: That couldn't be better. I would like a copy of this drawing.
B: I'm sorry. I can't help you. You may ask the technical department for it.
A: Do you know the telephone number?
B: It's 4557 extension.
A: Thank you.
B: My pleasure!

### 【Task Evaluation】

#### (一) Choice

1. The design of marine electric equipment shall be in accordance with the design of the folling except_____.
   A. shipyard electrical installation standard approved by owner.
   B. Builders Electrical Installation Standard approved by owner.
   C. normal practice for a vessel of this type.
   D. beauty.

2. For the equipment installation on board, what should been considered as far as possible_____.
   A. the security and convenient for use and maintenance.
   B. beauty.
   C. size.

3. If the equipment has to be installed on the bulkhead of oil tank, the distance to the surface should be more than _____.
   A.100mm      B.30mm      C.50mm      D.70mm

4. Electrical equipment/fittings located in hazardous area to be _____ type.
   A. waterproof      B.watertight      C.ex-proof      D.sealed

Shipping Electric Installation

(二) **Translation.**

1. Translate new words and expressions into Chinese (Table 5-2).

Table 5-2  Translation

| | |
|---|---|
| 1. Electrical Installation Standard | |
| 2. insulation resistance | |
| 3. effective date | |
| 4. ex-proof equipment | |
| 5. absorber | |
| 6. screwdriver | |
| 7. equipment specification | |

A. 电气安装规范；B. 防爆设备；C. 减震器；D. 螺钉旋具；E. 绝缘电阻；F. 设备型号规格；G. 有效期限。

2. Translate the following sentences into Chinese.

Materials preparation is according to equipment list or material list and arrangement drawing and cable trays drawing. All electric equipment should have quality certificate from maker. Some important equipment should have class type approval certificate, equipment certificate or other necessary certificate, and pay attention to the effective date.

First, we should check whether equipment specification is accordance with equipment list and whether equipment has some defect and measure insulation resistance if necessary. Then, we should check cable gland specification and quantities are in accordance with drawings and check the supports, foundation and ground accessories and so on to be prepared according to relative drawings. At last, we should remember to place electric equipment in the dry and clean environment.

(三) **Speaking Practice**

1. Group discussion

Work in groups. Look at the statements in the language bank task. Which of them are important aspects for Shipping Electric Installation? Why?

2. Short talk

Now it is your chance to practice what you have learned from this unit. Put your textbook away and give a short talk on the following topics. You should talk at least one minute. Don't be discouraged if you cannot make it. Review the lesson and try again. You are sure to do it better next time.

- package of equipment.
- basic technical requirement of equipment installation.

3. Role play

Work in groups or pairs and discuss the following topics. Then, you are advised to talk at least three minutes for each topic.

- Prompts: Introduce main electric equipment on board.
- Shipping Electric Installation.

## 【 Unit Evaluation 】

The teacher evaluates the students on their performance and mutual evaluation results, the results in Table 5-3.

Table 5-3  Task Evaluation

| EVALUATION CONTENT ||| DISTRIBUTION SCORE | SCORE |
|---|---|---|---|---|
| Unit 4 Marine Electric Installation<br>Task1 Cables (50%)<br>Task2 Shipping Electric Installation (50%) |||||
| KNOWLEDGE EVALUATION |||||
| Ⅰ. Choice ||| 20 | |
| Ⅱ.Translation | 1.Translate new words and expressions into Chinese. || 20 | |
|  | 2.Translate the following sentences into English. || 20 | |
| TIME: 30' | STUDENT SIGN: | TEACHER SIGN: | TOTAL: ||
| SKILL EVALUATION |||||
| Ⅲ. Speaking Practice<br>Role playing ||| 20<br>20 | |
| TIME: 30' | STUDENT SIGN: | TEACHER SIGN: | TOTAL: ||

# Unit 6

# Marine Signal System

【 Unit Goals 】

1. Get to know different parts of the marine alarm system and the marine automation system. Familiar with the new words and expressions: monitoring and alarm system, automation system, detector etc.

2. Students can introduce the marine alarm system and the marine automation system in English. They can talk to each other about them fluently.

## Task 1   Marine Alarm System

【 Task goals 】

1. Get to know different parts of the marine alarm system. Familiar with the basic units of the alarm system, etc.

2. Students can introduce the marine alarm system in English. They can talk to each other about it fluently.

【 Knowledge linking 】

What does marine signal system include in your mind?
Please look at the following pictures carefully and try to learn the terms:
(1) Several types of alarm devices (Fig.6-1)

(a) Alarm indicator column

(b) Fog horn

(c) Pushbutton(water-tight)

(d) Anchor light

(e) Port light

Fig.6-1　Alarm devices

(2) Detectors (Fig.6-2)

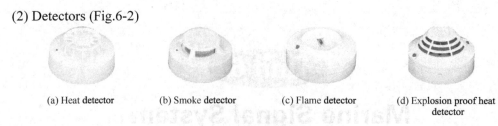

(a) Heat detector    (b) Smoke detector    (c) Flame detector    (d) Explosion proof heat detector

Fig.6-2   Detectors

## Monitoring System and Engine Room Alarm[1]

With the development of science and technology, automation of electric control has been widely applied in the UMS(Unattended Machinery Space).All ships have some degree of automation and instrumentation which is centered around a console. The alarm and monitoring system is the basic functionality of the marine engine automation system. The main purpose of the system is to give ship's officers all the basic alarm and status information they require to maintain safe and efficient operation of the machinery and other related equipment in the engine room.[2] It can display status and parameters of engine room equipment by different means such as indicating lights and color monitor, and give voice and light alarm in the engine room when an alarm occurs. For the ship of UMS, it also has extension alarms of bridge, public places & engineers' cabins (Fig.6-3).

The functions of alarm and monitoring system are as follows:

(1) Alarm detection with audible and visual alarm indication

The system can monitor the status and parameters of equipment in the engine room. There are lots of switching and analog values: for the former, the system can display the quantitative（数量的）value and alarm when necessary, there are upper limit alarm, lower limit alarm and deviation alarm such as the main engine exhaust gas temperature deviation alarm. Usually the audible and visual alarm will be sent out on the engine control console in the engine control room, and also in the whole engine room to notify the patrolling（巡逻）crew on duty.[3] There are silencing, flicker（闪烁）stop and alarm acknowledgement（确认） buttons for the crew on duty to press when an alarm occurs.

(2) Parameters and status display

There are different types of display modes used in the system. Indicating light are commonly adopted. For analogue values,the traditional indicating devices are electric meters with change over switches: but, nowadays the indicating devices are monitors of different types such as color CRT on LCD monitors , they can display text, numeric and graphic(图解的) information.[4]

(3) Setting adjustment counter and alarm logging functions(设定调整、计算和报警记录功能)

The system can record the status changes,such as alarm acknowledgements and alarm condition cleared. When all alarm conditions are cleared, the system returns to normal. Alarms and other information are presented either as lists or graphic displays on the monitor in the control station.[5] To record alarms and events a number of different logging options are available including complete log, alarm summary log , group log, etc.

(4) Delayed alarm

To avoid false alarm, the alarm can have a delay element, e.g. the level alarm device of an oil tank may give a wrong alarm when the ship rocks; so we can adopt a delay of about 2 to 30 seconds for this alarm.

Task 1　Marine Alarm System

Fig.6-3　Monitoring and alarm system

(5) Group alarm

The system will divide all alarms into several groups. Usually the alarms of the same equipment and properties will be in one alarm group such as alarm of the NO.1 generator diesel or the main engine exhaust gas.

(6) Alarm extension system of bridge cabins forums operation

For the ship of UMS, in the status of unattended mode. The alarm signals will be sent to the extension alarm panels in the bridge, public places and the duty engineer's cabin. The duty engineer change over switch on the control console can select the engineer on duty and send the alarm to his cabin The extension alarm panels can display the alarm group information and give sound and alarm signal: when the alarm occurs, the duty engineer must acknowledge it on the panel and go down to the engine room immediately.

① Inhibition of alarms (alarm block)
② Dereliction alarm（失职报警）

③ Function test
④ Self checking function
⑤ Standby power supply auto-switching when main power faults

## 【New Words Expressions】

| | | | |
|---|---|---|---|
| anchor | [ˈæŋkə] | n. | 锚 |
| detector | [dɪˈtɛktə] | n. | 探测器,探头 |
| detection | [dɪˈtekʃn] | n. | 侦查,检测 |
| UMS(Unattended Machinery Space) | | | 无人机舱 |
| monitor | [ˈmɒnɪtə(r)] | n/v. | 监控 |
| audible | [ˈɔːdəbl] | adj. | 听得见的 |
| visual | [ˈvɪʒuəl] | adj. | 视觉的，看得见的； |
| audible and visual alarm | | | 声光报警 |
| analog | [ˈænəlɔːg] | adj./n. | 模拟的 |
| digital | [ˈdɪdʒɪtl] | adj. | 数字的 |
| exhaust gas | [ɪgˈzɔːstˈgæs] | | 废气 |
| F.O.(Fuel Oil) | [ˈfjuəlˈɔɪl] | | 燃油 |
| L.O. (Lube Oil) | [ˈlubˈɔɪl] | | 滑油 |
| F.O.and L.O. system | | | 燃油和滑油系统 |
| false alarm | | | 误报警 |
| extension alarm | | | 延伸警报 |
| upper/lower limit | | | 上/下限 |

## 【Notes】

(1) monitoring system and engine room alarm
集中监视与报警系统

(2) The main purpose of the system is to give ship's officers all the basic alarm and status information they require to maintain safe and efficient operation of the machinery and other related equipment in the engine room.
该设备的目的是为船员提供所有状态信息和基本报警情况，以保持机舱内机械和其他相关设备安全高效运行。 They require to … 从句修饰 all the basic alarm and status information。

(3) Usually the audible and visual alarm will be sent out on the engine control console in the engine control room, and also in the whole engine room to notify the patrolling（巡逻）crew on duty.
在通常情况下，声光警报会被发送到集控室内的集控台上，也会发送到整个机舱以便引起在巡视的值班人员的注意。

(4) For analogue values,the traditional indicating devices are electric meters with change over switches: but, nowadays the indicating devices are monitors of different types such as color CRT on LCD monitors , they can display text, numeric and graphic(图解的) information.
对于模拟量来说，传统的指示设备是带转换开关的电表，但现在的指示设备是不同类型的监视器，例如 CRT 显示器和液晶显示器，它们可以显示文本、数字和图像信息。

(5) Alarms and other information are presented either as lists or graphic displays on the monitor in the control station.

报警及其他信息在控制站的显示器上以列表或图形的方式显示出来。Either…or 为"或者……，或者……"的意思，要两者择一。

【Task Implement】

PART A  Reading Practice

**Marine Alarm System**

(a) Audible and visual alarm　　(b) Fire alarm　　(c) BNWAS

Fig.6-4　Alarm devices

### 1. Engineer safety alarm system

One set of ER safety alarm system shall be provided for unattended engine room(Fig.6-4). The system shall be switched on when the engineer goes to the engine room, and has to reset in intervals of maximum 60 minutes, by using switches in the engine room. If the system is not reset, alarm shall be occurred in the engine room. If still not reset within 1 to 2 minute, alarm shall be come up on the bridge and accommodation area.

### 2. Fire & General Alarm

Fire and general alarm supply system is to be taken from 230V A.C. and the 24V D.C. supplies. Alarm push buttons are to be fitted in wheelhouse, forecastle deck, main deck, bow thruster compartment and engine room. Alarm bells are to be sited in wheelhouse, forecastle, and main deck lobby. An alarm horn is to be installed in the bow thruster compartment. In the engine room, an alarm horn complete with a red rotating beacon is also to be fitted. The installation shall meet SOLAS, Classification and relevant Authority requirements.

Fire alarm system shall be addressable type(寻址类型). On/off switch (inside ECR) C/W nine (9) sirens and yellow beacons and system (alarm & indicator light) linkage to engine room and bow thruster compartment. All alarm and siren can be heard in engine room and control room.

### 3. Engine room alarm and monitoring system

As usual, two sets of micro-processor based engine room alarm and monitoring system shall be installed inside the engine control console.[1] It can be composed of two LCD display with keyboard, an alarm/data printer and the required quantity of sensors such as thermoresistance, pressure transducers and level switches etc.[2] And one set for alarm, the other for monitoring and can be changed with each other as stand by. Input channels shall be continuously monitored and when any input of them deviates from the preset value, an alarm shall be issued with audible and visual signal by the annunciator unit.

The alarm system shall be arranged in separate groups for main engine and its auxiliary and when engine room is unattended the alarm shall be extended to the wheelhouse and engineer's cabin and other places specified in extension alarm system (Fig.6-5).

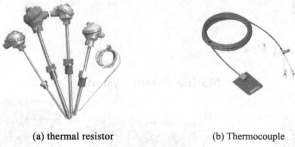

(a) thermal resistor        (b) Thermocouple

Fig.6-5   Sensors

### 4. Extension alarm system

One set of extension alarm for watch and responsibility shall be installed on ship. The selector switch for the duty engineer and engineer simultaneous call push button shall be included in the engine control console. The wheelhouse panel shall be installed with the indicating lamps to indicate who the duty engineer is.

## 【New Words and Expressions】

| | | | |
|---|---|---|---|
| malfunction | [mæl'fʌŋkʃən] | n. | 故障，功能障碍；失灵 |
| thermoresistance | [θɜːmriːˈsɪstəns] | n. | 热电阻 |
| thermocouple | [ˈθɜːməˌkʌpəl] | n. | 热电偶 |
| transducer | [trænzˈduːsər] | n. | 传感器，变频器，变换器 |
| stand by | | | 备用 |
| forecastle | [ˈfəuksl] | n. | 艏楼 |
| horn | [hɔːn] | n. | 号角，喇叭 |
| thruster | [ˈθrʌstə(r)] | n. | 推进器 |
| annunciator | [əˈnʌnsɪeɪtər] | n. | 信号器；通报者；信号机 |
| unattended | [ˌʌnəˈtɛndɪd] | adj. | 无人陪伴的；无人出席的； |

## 【Notes】

(1) As usual, two sets of micro-processor based engine room alarm and monitoring system shall be installed inside the engine control console.

通常，集控台里安装两台机舱监测报警系统微处理器。

(2) It can be composed of two LCD display with keyboard, an alarm/data printer and the required quantity of sensors such as thermoresistance, pressure transducers and level switches etc.

它由两个液晶显示器组成，还带有键盘，一台报警数字打印机和所需数量的传感器，比如热电阻传感器、压力变送器和液位开关等。

| | | | |
|---|---|---|---|
| thermal | 热的 | thermology | 热学 |
| thermoresistance | 热电阻 | thermometer | 温度计 |
| thermostat | 恒温器 | thermocouple | 热电偶 |
| thermoregulator | 温度调节器 | | |

## PART B　Role Playing

### Test of Automation

(O-owner; S-surveyor; Q-quality inspector)

S: Which one shall we start?

Q: At first, we want to test the temperature sensor of the A/E.

S: How are you going to do the test?

Q: We have two methods to do the test. one is heater, another is calibrator, I recommend the latter one, because it's more accurate and convenient. Which one do you prefer?

S: Could you show me the calibrator?

Q: OK

S: All right, Mr.XX(owner), what do you think about it?

O: OK, however, I want to check one of these sensors with heater for comparison no problem, do you have anything else shall we start the test?

Q: Certainly.

## 【Task Evaluation】

### (一) Choice

1. The alarm control unit of centralized monitoring and alarm system can be to achieve _____.
   A. outputting error parameters alarm signal
   B. controlling alarm lighting, Electric flute, and Buzzer rotating lights
   C. detecting self-failure of alarm device
   D. detecting self-failure of alarm device controlling the generation of flash signals

2. The core unit of Centralized monitoring and alarm system is_____.
   A. variety of sensors　　　　　　B. audible and visual alarm
   C. Power supply　　　　　　　　D. Alarm control unit

3. Ship monitoring and alarm system consist of: _____.Monitoring and alarm system consist of three major parts.
   A. sensors distributed in every monitoring points of engine room
   B. monitoring panel and control tank installed in ECR
   C. extension alarm installed the bridge, screw's rooms
   D. A+B+C

4. A _____ is a device that detects smoke and issues an alarm to alert nearby people that there is a potential fire.

A. smoke detector      B. heat detector
C. photoelectric detector      D. portable monitors

5. What are included in the functions of alarm and monitoring system?

A. Alarm detection with audible and visual alarm indication.

B. Group alarm

C. Parameters and status display

D. A+B+C

**(二) Translation**

1. Translate new words and expressions into Chinese(Table 6-1).

**Table 6-1  Translation**

| | |
|---|---|
| 1. Monitoring And Alarm System | |
| 2. marine engine automation system | |
| 3. voice and light alarm /audible and visual alarm | |
| 4. switching and analog values | |
| 5. upper/lower limit alarm | |
| 6. the main engine exhaust gas temperature | |
| 7. delayed alarm | |
| 8. extension alarm panels | |
| 9. the duty engineer's cabin | |
| 10. go down to the engine room | |
| 11. F.O.and L.O. system | |
| 12. engineer safety alarm system | |
| 13. fire & general alarm | |
| 14. pressure transducers | |
| 15. level switches | |

A. 声光报警；B. 开关量和模拟量；C. 主机排气温度；D. 延迟报警；E. 值班轮机员室；F. 上下限报警；G. 延伸报警板；H. 下机舱；I. 燃油和滑油系统；J. 轮机员安全报警系统；K. 火警和通用报警；L. 压力传感器；M. 机舱监测和报警系统； N. 船舶机舱自动化系统；O. 液位开关。

2. Translate the following sentences into Chinese.

With the development of science and technology，automation of electric control has been widely applied in the UMS(Unattended Machinery Space).All ships have some degree of automation and instrumentation which is centered around a console. The alarm and monitoring system is the basic functionality of the marine engine automation system. <u>The main purpose of the system is to give ship's officers all the basic alarm and status information they require to maintain safe and efficient operation of the machinery and other related equipment in the engine room.</u>[(2)] It can display status and parameters of engine room equipment by different means such as indicating lights and color monitor, and give voice and light alarm in the engine room when an alarm occurs. For the ship of UMS, it also has extension alarms of bridge, public places & engineers' cabins (Fig.6-3).

**(三) Speaking Practice**

1. Group discussion

Work in groups. Look at the statements in the language bank task. Which of them are important aspects for marine alarm system? Why?

2. Short talk

Now it is your chance to practice what you have learned from this unit. Put your textbook away and give a short talk on the following topics. You should talk at least one minute. Don't be discouraged if you cannot make it. Review the lesson and try again. You are sure to do it better next time.
- the functions of alarm and monitoring system.
- marine alarm system.

3. Role play

Work in groups or pairs and discuss the following topics. Then, you are advised to talk at least three minutes for each topic.
- prompts: introducing marine alarm system.
- the functions of alarm and monitoring system.

## Task 2　　Marine Automation System

### 【Task goals】

1. Get to know different parts of the marine automation system. Familiar with the basic units of marine automation system: automation system, detector, comparator, controller, regulator etc.

2. Students can introduce the marine automation system in English.they can talk to each other about it fluently.

### 【Knowledge linking】

（1）Main engine remote control system (Fig.6-6)
（2）Engine telegraph(车钟) (Fig.6-7)

Fig.6-6　Main engine remote control system　　　　Fig.6-7　Engine telegraph

87

## Marine Automation System

The automated systems consist of control, safety and alarm systems. Marine control systems are electric, hydraulic and pneumatic.(1) During UMS period overnight, when the ship is at sea, the bridge will control the engines. Then when the remote control system breaks down, the engine will be controlled locally. And when entering and leaving port, we also control it from local position. There are so many instruments and buttons. They are all connected with the main engine and auxiliary machines. The main engine and auxiliary machines can be operated and turned on and off here.(2) So that it's unnecessary for the engineer to keep watch on the engines.

Sufficient instruments, alarms and control equipment for safe operation of the main engine and all auxiliaries are very important. Just as what we know before, sometime we don't need to check machines in the engine room at all times. The duty engineer is assigned to take charge of the machines. And when the alarm sounds, the engineer on cabin duty has to go to the engine room and take remedies.

One examples for automation is engine control room, we can find many instruments and buttons on the control stand which are interconnected with the main engine and auxiliary equipment. It is convenient for the duty engineer to operate the machinery remotely there. Other examples for automation are the electricity control, fire detection and security system, emergency lighting system, automatic speed reduction and stopping system and so on. On the ship with UMS, automatic system plays a more important role.(3) Sometimes it can even work instead of the duty engineer. Thus he can keep watch in his cabin and is relieved from the hot and noisy environment. Furthermore, the automatic system also contributes to reduce the improper operation to the engine and improve the safety and reliability of the navigation.(4)

## 【 New Words and Expressions 】

| | | | |
|---|---|---|---|
| engine telegraph | | | 车钟 |
| automation | [ˌɔːtəˈmeɪʃən] | n. | 自动化（技术），自动操作 |
| button | [ˈbʌtn] | n. | 按钮 |
| instrument | [ˈɪnstrəmənt] | n. | 仪器 |
| connect | [kəˈnekt] | v. | 连接，联结；使……有联系；为……接通电话；插入插座 |

## 【 Notes 】

(1) The automated systems consist of control, safety and alarm systems. Marine control systems are electronic, hydraulic and pneumatic.

自动化系统由控制，安全和报警系统组成。船舶自动系统可以是电子的，液动的和气动的。

(2) There are so many instruments and buttons. They are all connected with the main engine and auxiliary machines. The main engine and auxiliary machines can be operated and turned on and off here.

有那么多仪器和按钮。它们都和主机和辅机相连。在这儿（集控室）可以操作主机和辅机。

(3) On the ship with UMS, automatic system plays a more important role.
自动化系统在带有无人机舱的船舶中起到非常重要的作用。
Play an more important role, 起到更重要的作用, 与 play a part 同义。
The computer has played more and more important role in the marine automation.
计算机在船用自动化系统中起到越来越重要的作用。

(4) Furthermore,the automatic system also contributes to reduce the improper operation to the engine and improve the safety and reliability of the navigation.
另外, 自动化系统还有助于减少机器的操作故障, 提高航行的安全性和可靠性。

# 【Task Implement】

## PART A  Reading Practice

### M/E Control System Test

(Excerpted from Mooring Test Scheme for Electrical Part)

The automation remote control system is designed for remote control of the main engine from the combined telegraph and maneuvering lever in the wheelhouse. By mover this lever, the system will automatically start, reverse, stop and control the speed set to the main engine(Table 6-2).

Table 6-2  Test items

| NO. | TEST ITEMS |
|---|---|
| 1. | Starting the main engine<br>　　Normal start<br>　　Start fail<br>　　Start block |
| 2. | Main Engine Speed setting |
| 3. | Stopping the Main Engine |
| 4. | Reversing the Main Engine |
| 5. | Control Transfer System<br>　　From Local control to bridge control<br>　　Forced Command take over<br>　　From ECR AUTO CONTROL to ECR MANUAL CONTROL<br>　　From ECR MANUAL CONTROL to ECR AUTO CONTROL in control room |
| 6. | Engine Protection<br>　　Emergency Stop Switches<br>　　Overspeed<br>　　Shut Down, none cancellable<br>　　Shut Down, cancellable<br>　　Slow Down, none cancellable<br>　　Slow Down, cancellable<br>　　RPM Detector System |

## PART B  Role Playing

(O- owner; S-surveyor; Q-quality inspector; E-electrician)

Q: Who will go to the A/E side with me ?
S: Let's go. Give me a talkie-talkie . What's the temperature for alarm?
Q: This is high temperature alarm of 80 degrees Centigrade. We will simulate to raise the

temperature slowly from 70 degrees with the calibrator and get the alarm

O: Hello , this is XXX. Are you ready ?

Q: Hello, this is YYY. We are ready now .

E: You see the calibrator on which 70 degrees now .

Q: Hello , Mr. XXX. Here is 70 degrees now.

O: Sorry! I can't catch it , repeat it please.

Q: 70 degrees.

O: All right! Here is 70.1 degrees on the monitor. Please raise the temperature slowly to 80 degrees.

Q: OK. go up to 80 degrees slowly please

E: Yes.

O: Hello ,Mr.YYY, what's the temperature exactly now?

Q: Hello, Mr.XXX, it is 80 degrees .Does the monitoring system give an alarm?

O: Yes ,it's coming

Q: OK. I have seen the light of alarm rotating light and heard the sound of the alarm horn . Shall we test the next one ?

O: It's time for lunch . I suggest we continue doing the test this afternoon

Q: OK. See you afternoon.

## 【Task Evaluation】

### (一) Choice

1. what does the automated system consist of _____.
   A.control system            B.safety system
   C.alarm system              D.A+B+C
2. During UMS period overnight, when the ship is at sea, _____ will control the engines?
   A.engine control room       B.the bridge
   C.local position            D.alarm control unit
3. What are examples for automation _____.
   A.engine control room,the electricity control,fire detection and security system,automatic speed reduction and stopping system
   B.engineer safety alarm system
   C.extension alarm
   D.emergency lighting system and general alarm
4. The automatic system also contributes to_____.
   A. engineer safety alarm system
   B. extension alarm
   C.reduce the improper operation to the engine and improve the safety and reliability of the navigation
   D.sensors
5. By mover this lever,the automation remote control system will automatically_____.

## Task 2 Marine Automation System

A. control the speed set to the main engine.　　B. Start, reverse the main engine
C. stop the main engine　　D. A+B+C

**(二) Translation.**

1. Translate new words and expressions (Table 6-3).

Table 6-3　Translation

| | |
|---|---|
| 1. marine automation system | |
| 2. many instruments and buttons | |
| 3. keep watch | |
| 4. fire detection and security system | |
| 5. emergency lighting system | |
| 6. automatic speed reduction and stopping system | |
| 7. Starting the main engine | |
| 8. Normal start | |
| 9. From Local control to bridge control | |
| 10. MANUAL CONTROL | |
| 11. Emergency Stop Switches | |
| 12. Shut Down(SHD) | |
| 13. Slow Down(SLD) | |
| 14. RPM Detector System | |
| 15. engine telegraph | |

A. 值守；B. 火警探测安全系统；C. 船舶自动化系统；D.应急照明系统；E. 许多仪表和按钮；F. 正常启动；G. 从机旁控制转到驾驶室控制；H. 手动控制；I. 应急停车开关；J. 停车；K. 减速；L. 转速监测系统；M. 车钟；N. 启动主机；O. 自动降速停车系统。

2. Translate the following sentences into Chinese.

The automated systems consist of control, safety and alarm systems. Marine control systems are electric,hydraulic and pneumatic. During UMS period overnight, when the ship is at sea, the bridge will control the engines.Then when the remote control system breaks down, the engine will be controlled locally.And when entering and leaving port,we also control it from local position. There are so many instruments and buttons. They are all connected with the main engine and auxiliary machines. The main engine and auxiliary machines can be operated and turned on and off here.So that it's unnecessary for the engineer to keep watch on the engines.

**(三) Speaking Practice**

1. Group discussion

Work in groups. Look at the statements in the language bank task. Which of them are important aspects for marine automation system? Why?

2. Short talk

Now it is your chance to practice what you have learned from this task. Put your textbook away and give a short talk on the following topics. You should talk at least one minute. Don't be discouraged if you cannot make it. Review the task and try again. You are sure to do it better next time.

• marine automation system.

3. Role play

Work in groups or pairs and discuss the following topics. Then, you are advised to talk at least three minutes for each topic.

• Prompts: introducing marine automation system.

• The automation remote control system.

## 【 Unit Evaluation 】

The teacher evaluates the students on their performance and mutual evaluation results, the results in Table 6-4.

Table 6-4　Task Evaluation

| EVALUATION CONTENT | | | DISTRIBUTION SCORE | SCORE |
|---|---|---|---|---|
| Unit 5 Marine Signal System<br>Task1 Marine Alarm System (50%)<br>Task2 Marine Automation System (50%) | | | | |
| KNOWLEDGE EVALUATION | | | | |
| Ⅰ. Choice | | | 20 | |
| Ⅱ.Translation | 1.Translate new words and expressions into Chinese. | | 20 | |
| | 2.Translate the following sentences into English. | | 20 | |
| TIME: 30' | STUDENT SIGN: | TEACHER SIGN: | TOTAL: | |
| SKILL EVALUATION | | | | |
| Ⅲ. Speaking Practice<br>　　Role playing | | | 20<br>20 | |
| TIME: 30' | STUDENT SIGN: | TEACHER SIGN: | TOTAL: | |

# Unit 7

# Marine Communication and Navigation System

【Unit Goals】

1. Get to know ship's important cabin: bridge control room. Familiar with the basic marine communication and navigation equipment: GMDSS, INMARSAT-C mobile earth station, Sound powered telephone, VHF radio, GPS display unit and radar, etc.

2. Students can introduce the basic communication and navigation equipment in bridge control room to others in English. Moreover, they can talk to each other about the purpose of these equipment.

## Task 1   GMDSS

【Task goals】

1. Be familiar with GMDSS and get to know the definition of the Sea Areas for GMDSS.
2. Students can introduce the functions of the GMDSS in English and talk to each other about the definition of the Sea Areas for GMDSS.

【Knowledge linking】

What does the functions of the GMDSS in your mind?
Please look at the following pictures carefully and try to learn the terms:
(1) GMDSS (Fig. 7-1)
(2) INMARSAT-C mobile earth station (Fig.7-2)

### GMDSS

GMDSS stands for Global Maritime Distress and Safety System which is an internationally agreed-upon set of safety procedures, types of equipment, and communication protocols used to increase safety and make it easier to rescue distressed ships, boats and aircraft. [1]

GMDSS consists of several systems. The system is intended to perform the following functions: alerting (including position determination of the unit in distress),search and rescue coordination, locating, maritime safety information broadcasts, general communications, and bridge-to-bridge communications.(2) The goal of GMDSS is to virtually guarantee that complying vessels will be able to communicate with an onshore station at any time, from any location, in case of distress or to exchange safety-related information.

GMDSS defines four sea areas based upon the location and capability of onshore-based communication facilities.(3) The definition of the Sea Areas for GMDSS is outlined below.

Fig.7-1　GMDSS　　　　　　　　　　Fig.7-2　INMARSAT-C mobile earth station

**1. Sea Area A1**

It is an area within the radiotelephone coverage of at least one VHF coast station in which continuous Digital Selective Calling (DSC) alerting and radiotelephony services are available. Such an area could extend typically 30 nautical miles (56 km) to 40 nautical miles (74 km) from the Coast Station.

**2. Sea Area A2**

An area, excluding Sea Area A1, within the radiotelephone coverage of at least one MF coast station in which continuous DSC alerting and radiotelephony services are available. For planning purposes, this area typically extends to up to 180 nautical miles (330 km) offshore during daylight hours, but would exclude any A1 designated areas. In practice, satisfactory coverage may often be achieved out to around 400 nautical miles (740 km) offshore during night time.

**3. Sea Area A3**

It is an area, excluding sea areas A1 and A2, within the coverage of an Inmarsat geostationary satellite. This area lies between about latitude 76 Degree NORTH and SOUTH, but excludes A1 and/or A2 designated areas. Inmarsat guarantees their system will work between 70 South and 70 North though it will often work to 76 degrees South or North.

**4. Sea Area A4**

An area outside Sea Areas A1, A2 and A3 is called Sea Area A4. This is essentially the polar regions, north and south of about 76 degrees of latitude, excluding any A1 or A2 areas.

GMDSS sea areas serve two purposes: to describe areas where GMDSS services are available, and to define what radio equipment GMDSS ships must carry. Prior to the GMDSS, the number and type of radio safety equipment ships had to carry depended upon its tonnage. With GMDSS, the number and type of radio safety equipment ships have to carry depends upon the GMDSS areas in which they travel. To meet the requirement of the functional areas, the list of the minimum communications equipment needed for ships are(Fig.7-3):

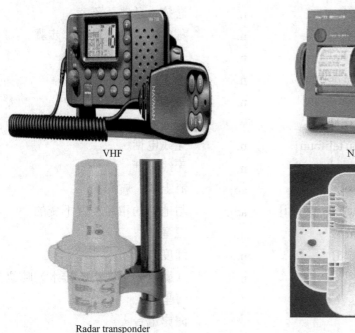
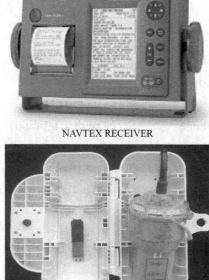

Fig. 7-3 Communications equipment

- Two-way VHF radiotelephone apparatus.
- Radar transponder operating in the 9 GHz band (SART).
- VHF radiotelephone with DSC and DSC Watch Receiver.
- International NAVTEX Receiver.
- 406 MHz EPIRB.
- Inmarsat EGC Receiver.

General functional requirements for GMDSS:

- Transmission of ship-to-shore distress alerts by at least two separate and independent means, using different radiocommunication service.
- Reception of shore-to-ship distress alerts.
- Transmission/reception of ship-to-ship distress alerts.
- Transmission/reception of search and rescue co-ordinating communications.
- Transmission/reception of on –scene communications.
- Transmission/reception of SART signals for locating.
- Transmission/reception of maritime safety information.
- Transmission/reception of general radiocommunication to/and from shore-based radio systems or networks.
- Transmission/reception of bridge-to-bridge communications.

## 【 New Words and Expressions 】

maritime　　　　　　　　　['mærɪtaɪm]　　　　　　　adj.　　　　海事的，海运上的

Marine Communication and Navigation System

| distress | [dis'tres] | n. | 悲痛；危难，不幸 |
| procedure | [prə'siːdʒə] | n. | 程序，手续；过程，步骤 |
| protocol | ['prəutə&#716;kɔːl] | n. | （数据传递的）协议 |
| determination | [di&#716;təːmi'neiʃən] | n. | 确定；测定， |
| coordination | [kəuˌɔːdn'eiʃən] | n. | 协调；和谐 |
| guarantee | [ˌɡærən'tiː] | v. | 保证，担保 |
| radiotelephone | ['reidiəu'telifəun] | n. | 无线电话 |
| radiotelephony | ['reidiəu'telefəni] | n. | 无线电话 |
| nautical | ['nɔːtikəl] | adj. | 海上的，航海的； |
| geostationary | [ˌdʒi(ː)əu'steiʃənəri] | adj. | 与地球的相对位置不变的 |
| satellite | ['sætəlait] | n. | 卫星 |
| latitude | ['lætitjuːd] | n. | 纬度 |
| tonnage | ['tʌnidʒ] | n. | （衡量船舶大小的排水）吨位 |

| nautical miles(n mile) | | | 海里 |
| Coast Station | | | 海岸电台 |
| Inmarsat(International Maritime Satellite Telephone Service) | | | 国际海事卫星 |
| geostationary satellite | | | 地球同步卫星 |
| polar region | | | 极地，近极区域 |
| Two-way VHF radiotelephone apparatus | | | 双向甚高频无线电话设备 |
| Radar transponder | | | 雷达应答器 |
| EPIRB (Emergency Position-Indicating Radio Beacon) | | | 应急无线电示位标 |
| EGC (Enhanced Group Call) | | | 增强群呼系统 |

【Notes】

(1) GMDSS stands for Global Maritime Distress and Safety System which is an internationally agreed-upon set of safety procedures, types of equipment, and communication protocols used to increase safety and make it easier to rescue distressed ships, boats and aircraft.

GMDSS 代表全球海上遇险和安全系统，它是用于提高航行安全性和便于海上遇难舰船、飞机搜救的一套国际认可的安全程序，设备和通信协议。

(2) The system is intended to perform the following functions: alerting (including position determination of the unit in distress), search and rescue coordination, locating, maritime safety information broadcasts, general communications, and bridge-to-bridge communications.

该系统具有以下功能：遇险报警（包括遇险单元的位置确定），搜救协调，定位，海上安全信息的播发，常规的公众业务通信和驾驶台对驾驶台的通信。

(3) GMDSS defines four sea areas based upon the location and capability of onshore-based communication facilities.

基于陆上通信设施的位置和能力，全球海上遇险和安全系统定义了 4 个海区。

## 【Task Implement】

### PART A  Reading Practice

#### INMARSAT

The international Maritime Satellite Organization (INMARSAT), a key player within GMDSS, is an international consortium comprising over 75 international partners who provide maritime safety communications for ships at sea.[1] In accordance with its convention, INMARSAT provides the space segment necessary for improving distress communications, efficiency and management of ships, as well as maritime correspondence services.

The basic components of the INMARSAT system include the INMARSAT space segment, Land Earth Stations (LES), also referred to as Coast Earth Stations (CES), and mobile Ship Earth Stations (SES).

The INMARSAT space segment consists of 11 geostationary satellites. Four operational INMARSAT satellites provide primary coverage, four additional satellites including satellites leased from the European Space Agency (ESA) and the International Telecommunications Satellite Organization (INTELSAT) serve as spares and three remaining satellites (leased from COMSAT Corporation, the U. S. signatory to INMARSAT) serve as back-ups.

The polar regions are not visible to the operational satellites and coverage is available from 70°N to 70°S.

The LES provide the link between the Space Segment and the land-based National/International fixed communications networks. These communications networks are funded and operated by the authorized communications authorities of a participating nation. This network links registered information providers to the LES. The data then travels from the LES to the INMARSAT Network Coordination Station (NCS) and then down to the SES's on ships at sea. The SES's provide two-way communications between ship and shore. INMARSAT A, the original INMARSAT system, operates at a transfer rate of up to 9600 bits per second and is telephone, telex and facsimile (fax) capable. It is being replaced by a similarly sized INMATSAT B system that uses digital technology to give better quality fax and higher data transmission rates.

INMARSAT C provides a store and forward data messaging capability (but no voice) at 600 bits per second and was designed specifically to meet the GMDSS requirements for receiving MSI data on board ship. These units are small, lightweight and use an omni-directional antenna.

### 【New Words and Expressions】

| | | | |
|---|---|---|---|
| consortium | [kənˈsɔːtiːəm] | n. | 组合，共同体 |
| comprise | [kəmˈpraiz] | v. | 由……组成；由……构成 |
| segment | [ˈsegmənt] | n. | 部分，环节 |
| lease | [liːs] | v. | 出租；租借 |
| LES (Land Earth Stations) | | | 地面站 |

CES (Coast Earth Stations)　　　　　　　　　岸站
SES (mobile Ship Earth Stations)　　　　　　船站
ESA (European Space Agency)　　　　　　　欧洲航天局
INTELSAT (International Telecommunications Satellite Organization)　　国际通信卫星组织
NCS (Network Coordination Station)　　　　网络协调站
omni-directional antenna　　　　　　　　　全向天线

【Notes】

1. The international Maritime Satellite Organization (INMARSAT), a key player within GMDSS, is an international consortium comprising over 75 international partners who provide maritime safety communications for ships at sea.

国际海事卫星组织是一个由超过 75 个国际成员组成的国际组织，它是 GNDSS 的主要组成部分，为海上航行的船舶提供海上安全通信。

## PART B　Role Playing

(A: worker in motor-vessel Noble Prince; B: worker at station)

A: Mayday Mayday Mayday.

This is motor-vessel Noble Prince.

B: Noble Prince, What happened?

A: I have struck a submerged object, taking in water fast, engine damaged.

B: What is the position?

A: In position forty-twofourteen degrees' north, sixteen seventeen degrees east.

B: How long can the vessel keep afloat?

A: I can not keep afloat more than three hours.

B: How many persons were seriously injured?

A: Chief engineer and two sailors seriously injured.

B: On what frequency is you keeping continuous watch?

A: I am keeping continuous watch on two one eight two kHz.

【Task Evaluation】

(一) Choice

1. With the help of GMDSS _____ can be alerted to a distress incident as soon as possible .

　A. all ships in a large sea area　　　　B. only the sea authorities ashore

　C. the SAR units ashore and at sea　　D. the port radios and the coast stations

2. The GMDSS defines four sea area based on the _____ .

　A. location and capacity of the facilities located on board ships

　B. Position and type of a sincere situation

　C. capacity and location of shore based communication facilities

D. position and capacity of mobile communication stations

3. An area within the coverage of at least one VHF shore station in which continuous DSC distress alerting is available is _____ .

A. sea area A1    B. sea area A2    C. distress area    D. GMDSS areas

4. Every ship, while at sea, _____ shall be capable.

A. of receiving shore-to-ship distress alerts
B. of transmitting and receiving MSI
C. of transmitting and receiving ship-to-ship distress alerts
D. A, B, C are all right

(二) Translate

1. Translate new words and expressions into Chinese.

Table 7-1    Translation

| | |
|---|---|
| 1. radiotelephone | |
| 2. NAVTEX | |
| 3. geostationary satellite | |
| 4. Radar transponder | |
| 5. Coast Station | |
| 6. EPIRB | |
| 7. nautical miles | |
| 8. latitude | |
| 9. Inmarsat | |
| 10. Two-way VHF radiotelephone apparatus | |
| 11. EGC | |
| 12. tonnage | |

A. 无线电话；B. 海岸电台；C. 地球同步卫星；D. 国际海事卫星；E. 雷达应答器；F. 海上安全信息播发系统；G. 双向甚高频无线电话设备；H. 应急无线电示位标；I. 增强群呼系统；J. 海里；K. 纬度；L. 吨位。

2. Translate the following sentences into Chinese.

GMDSS consists of several systems. The system is intended to perform the following functions: alerting (including position determination of the unit in distress), search and rescue coordination, locating, maritime safety information broadcasts, general communications, and bridge-to-bridge communications. The goal of GMDSS is to virtually guarantee that complying vessels will be able to communicate with an onshore station at any time, from any location, in case of distress or to exchange safety-related information.

GMDSS sea areas serve two purposes: to describe areas where GMDSS services are available, and to define what radio equipment GMDSS ships must carry. Prior to the GMDSS, the number and type of radio safety equipment ships had to carry depended upon its tonnage. With GMDSS, the

Marine Communication and Navigation System

number and type of radio safety equipment ships have to carry depends upon the GMDSS areas in which they travel.

**(三) Speaking Practice**

1. Group discussion

Work in groups. Look at the statements in the language bank task. What are the general functional requirements for GMDSS?

2. Short talk

Now it is your chance to practice what you have learned from this unit. Put your textbook away and give a short talk on the following topics. You should talk at least one minute. Don't be discouraged if you cannot make it. Review the task and try again. You are sure to do it better next time.

- The goal of GMDSS.
- The list of the minimum communications equipment needed for all ships.

3. Role play

Work in groups or pairs and discuss the following topics. Then, you are advised to talk at least three minutes for each topic.

- Prompts: Introducing general function requirements for GMDSS.
- Shipping Electric Installation.

# Task 2    Marine Communication System and Navigation Equipment

【Task Goals】

1. Get to know ship's communication system and navigation equipments. Familiar with the basic equipment: Automatic Telephone System, Sound powered telephone, Public Address System, radar, Compass and GPS.

2. Students can introduce the basic communication and navigation equipments in bridge control room to others in English and talk to each other about the purpose of these equipments.

【Knowledge linking】

What do ship's Communication System and Navigation Equipment include in your mind?

Please look at the following pictures carefully and try to learn the terms:

(1) Sound powered telephone (Fig. 7-4).

(2) VHF radio and telephone (Fig. 7-5).

(3) GPS display unit and radar (Fig.7-6).

## Task 2  Marine Communication System and Navigation Equipment

Fig. 7-4  Sound powered telephone

Fig. 7-5  VHF radio and telephone

 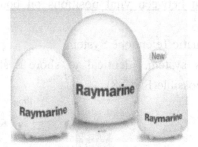

Fig. 7-6  GPS display unit and radar

### Marine Communication System and Navigation Equipment

Communication system and navigation equipment, indeed, are the ears and eyes of a ship. In this text, we will have a brief introduction of them.

### 1. Communication System

Communication system in a ship consists of internal communication system and external communication system. There is no a separated communication room on board, the communication equipment shall be installed in wheelhouse (Fig.7-7).

Internal communication system

(1) Talk-back system

This is network of microphone and loudspeakers, offers communication between the master station and a number of sub stations located in different parts of the vessel where communication is needed. The main station is located in the wheelhouse. Substations can communicate with the main station, but not with each-other. The network normally consists of wheelhouse, engine room, steering gear room and the mooring stations.

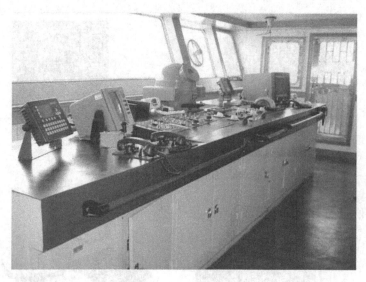

Fig. 7-7　Wheelhouse

(2) Sound Powered Telephone System

This system is independent from the ships power supply and meets the demands for emergency communication between vital positions on board, such as wheelhouse, central control room and engine room.[1]

(3) Automatic Telephone System

With this system, identical to shore system, two-way or duplex communication between telephones is possible(Fig.7-8).

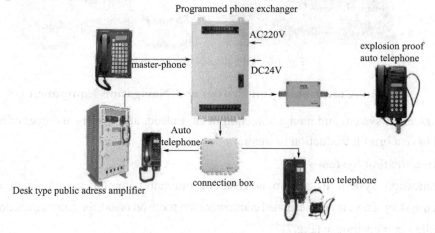

Fig.7-8　Automatic telephone system

(4) Public Address System

This is a one-way system, to address large quantities of people and paging, also is used to give general alarm signals.

## 2. Navigation Equipment

For navigation equipment normally including:

① One radar with ARPA ( Automatic Radar Plotting Aid) automatic warning system with rotating transmitting/receiving aerial, usually X-band (frequency 8-12GHz, wavelength 3cm).

② For ships larger than 500 GT a second radar, usually S-band (frequency 3-4 GHz, wavelength 10 cm ).

③ Two independent automatic position fixing systems: GPS, or more accurate DGPS with omni-directional satellite aerial and for DGPS also a parabolic differential aerial.

④ One Echo Sounder measuring waterdepth under the keel of the vessel.

⑤ One Log with speed and distance indicator.

⑥ One Magnetic Standard Compass.

⑦ One Gyro-compass

⑧ One Automatic Pilot controlling the course of the vessel.

⑨ AIS (Automatic Identification System), a transmitter that send information about the ship to adjacent ships and shore stations (Fig.7-9).

(1) Marine Radar

The word radar stands for radio detecting and ranging. It is a system by means of which it is possible to detect the presence of objects and to determine their velocity, direction and range (distance).[2] In addition, it can confirm some types of the detected objects. The radar can see in the dark or through heavy clouds. In foggy weather, radar on ships at sea helps prevent collisions. So it is really the eyes of a ship(Fig.7-10).

Fig.7-9   AIS                                    Fig.7-10   Radar

(2) Compass

Compasses are chief instruments on board to indicate the course of a ship, which may be subdivided into magnetic compass (Fig.7-11) and electrical compass in the light of their different working principles.

In spite of fact that a lot more navigation equipment of high accuracy has been invented ,the magnetic compass could not be spared yet by reason of its simplicity of construction, reliability of performance, convenience of application and independence of power supply.[3] But the magnetic compass has some weak points of its own, that is, the accuracy of magnetic compass is not as ideal as people might expect, since its pointing of direction will be affected both by the external magnetic field which has been slowly varying with time and by the magnetic objects around it.

Gyrocompass is also known as electrical compass, the working principle of which is quite another story. It applies the characteristics of a gyro to navigation, and what is more, its pointing of direction will be affected neither by the earth magnetic field nor by the magnetic objects around. Therefore, it obtains a high accuracy in direction pointing and a fine steadiness as well.

Fig.7-11　Magnetic compasses

(3) GPS

Today, GPS is the heart of virtually every electronic navigation system and is perhaps one of the most interfaced devices on board. It is the primary "talker" aboard most modern boats, sending its data to many other devices — the "listeners." It's quite common to have a single GPS receiver linked to one or more repeater displays, an autopilot, a VHF radio, radar, and a computer. Proper GPS installation and performance is key to both the functionality of many devices on board and the safety of the boat and crew.

【 New Words and Expressions 】

| | | | |
|---|---|---|---|
| microphone | [ˈmaikrəfəun] | n. | 扩音器，话筒 |
| loudspeaker | [ˈlaudˌspiːkə] | n. | 扬声器；喇叭 |
| duplex | [ˈdjuːpleks] | a. | 有两部分的 |
| radar | [ˈreidə] | n. | 雷达 |
| aerial/antenna | [ˈɛəriəl]/[ænˈtɛnə] | n. | 天线 |
| infrastructure | [ˈinfrəˌstrʌktʃə] | n. | 基础设施 |
| communication system | | | 通信系统 |
| navigation equipment | | | 航行设备 |
| internal communication system | | | 内部通信系统 |
| talk-back system | | | 对讲电话系统 |
| steering gear room | | | 舵机舱 |
| automatic telephone system | | | 自动电话系统 |
| sound powered telephone | | | 声力电话 |
| UPS (Uninterruptible Power System) | | | 不间断电源 |
| public adress system | | | 广播系统 |
| ARPA(Automatic Radar Plotting Aid) | | | 自动雷达标绘仪 |
| DGPS(Difference Global Positioning System) | | | 差分全球定位系统 |
| echo sounder | | | 回声测深仪 |

Task 2　Marine Communication System and Navigation Equipment

| | |
|---|---|
| log | 计程仪 |
| magnetic standard compass | 标准磁罗经 |
| automatic pilot | 自动驾驶仪 |
| international shore telephone | 国际通岸电话 |
| rescue coordination centers | 救援协调中心 |
| SSB (Single Side Band) | 单边带 |

【Notes】

(1) This system is independent from the ships power supply and meets the demands for emergency communication between vital positions on board, such as wheelhouse, central control room and engine room.

声力电话系统不需要船上电源供电，它可以满足船上像驾驶室、集控室和机舱等重要场所的紧急通信要求。

(2) It is a system by means of which it is possible to detect the presence of objects and to determine their velocity, direction and range (distance).

它是一个通过探测物体来确定物体的速度，方向和范围（距离）的系统。

(3) In spite of fact that a lot more navigation equipment of high accuracy has been invented ,the magnetic compass could not be spared yet by reason of its simplicity of construction, reliability of performance ,convenience of application and independence of power supply.

尽管已经发明了许多高精度的航海设备，但由于磁罗经结构简单，性能可靠，使用方便，不需要用电，所以磁罗经仍然在被使用。

【Task Implement】

### PART A　Reading Practice

#### Radio Communication system

Although communication technology is improving quickly, people at sea do not have access to the same communications infrastructure people ashore have. Like people ashore, Mariners need to access international shore telephone and data public switched networks. Additionally they need to access many maritime specific communications listed below:

Mariners need to be able to communicate with other ships of any size or nationality.

Mariners need to be able to receive and send urgent maritime safety information.

Mariners need to be able to send or receive distress alerts in an emergency to or from rescue coordination centers ashore and nearby ships anywhere in the world.

Radio Communication system on boats used to entail perhaps just a VHF radio telephone. But nowadays most boaters consider SSB, cell phones, satellite TV and/or Internet access basic requirements.

VHF radio is the most common of all marine electronic equipment used for boat-to-boat and boat-to-land communication. It operates in the frequency range of 156 MHz to174 MHz. In recent years, features such as digital selective calling (DSC), global positioning system (GPS), and the Global Maritime Distress and Safety System (GMDSS) have expanded the use and functionality of VHF radios by incorporating the ability to transmit time, position, and ownership information in the event of an emergency.

Single-sideband (SSB) radio is the long-range counterpart to VHF radio. Where marine VHF is limited to line-of-sight communications and a maximum of about 25 miles, SSB radio has the potential to transmit and receive over hundreds or even thousands of miles. An SSB radio bounces radio signals off the lower layers of the earth's atmosphere, which in turn reflect the signals back to earth. (You can think of SSB transmissions as giant triangles spanning many miles.)

【 New Words and Expressions 】

| | | | |
|---|---|---|---|
| mariner | ['mærɪnə] | n. | 船员，水手 |
| Radio communication system | | | 无线电系统 |
| VHF(Very High Frequency) | | | 甚高频 |
| DSC(digital selective calling) | | | 数字选择呼叫 |

## PART B    Role Playing

(A: chief officer; B: captain)

A: The new installed ARPA can not be used, Mr. Captain.

B: What's the matter?

A: The scanning line is dark red, and the background is black. Sometimes it is difficult to distinguish the scanning line on the display.

B: It must be designedly defective. I will send a cable to the manufacturer to ask for replacing the software.

A: Sir，The VHF transmitting/receiving convertion button is not working.

B: Let me check. Oh, the button is out of order. It can not be pushed down, inform radio officer to come with necessary tools.

A: OK.

B: Chief officer，Pleases switch on fine tunning button of compass.

A: OK，but the sensitivity is not enough. The gyro compass does not respond when the course changed within 1.5 degrees.

B: Well, I think we should do something.

【 Task Evaluation 】

(一) Choice

1._____ are the ears and eyes of a ship. In this text, we will have a brief introduction of them.
   A. communication system         B. navigation equipment         C. both A and B

2. Internal communication system in a ship including the following except_____.
   A. talk-back system              B. sound powered telephone system
   C. automatic telephone system    D. GMDSS

Task 2  Marine Communication System and Navigation Equipment

3. Frequency of X-band radar is _____.
A. 3~4 GHz    B. 5~6GHz    C. 1~2GHz    D. 8~9GHz
4. _____ are chief instruments on board to indicate the course of a ship.
A. adar    B. AIS    C. DSC    D. Compass
5. What equipment is used to measure waterdepth under the keel of the vessel?
A. echo sounder                 B. magnetic standard compass
C. talk-back system             D. automatic radar plotting aid

(二) Translation

1. Translate new words and expressions into Chinese (Table 7-2).

Table 7-2  Translation

| | |
|---|---|
| 1. gyro compass | |
| 2. magnetic compass | |
| 3. echo sounder | |
| 4. automatic telephone system | |
| 5. ARPA | |
| 6. UPS | |
| 7. sound powered telephone | |
| 8. automatic pilot | |
| 9. loudspeaker | |
| 10. microphone | |
| 11. navigation equipment | |
| 12. radar | |
| 13. Public Address System | |
| 14. VHF | |
| 15. talk-back system | |

A. 自动电话系统；B. 回声测深仪；C. 自动雷达标绘仪；D. 声力电话；E. 磁罗经；F. 自动驾驶仪；G. 不间断电源；H. 航行设备；I. 麦克风；J. 公共广播系统；K. 甚高频；L. 对讲系统；M. 陀螺罗经；N. 雷达；O. 扬声器。

2. Translate the following sentences into Chinese.

Compasses are chief instruments on board to indicate the course of a ship, which may be subdivided into magnetic compass and electrical compass in the light of their different working principles.

In spite of fact that a lot more navigation equipment of high accuracy has been invented, the magnetic compass could not be spared yet by reason of its simplicity of construction, reliability of performance, convenience of application and independence of power supply. But the magnetic compass has some weak points of its own, that is, the accuracy of magnetic compass is not as ideal as people might expect, since its pointing of direction will be affected both by the external magnetic field which has been slowly varying with time and by the magnetic objects around it.

Gyrocompass is also known as electrical compass, the working principle of which is quite another story. It applies the characteristics of a gyro to navigation, and what is more, its pointing of

Marine Communication and Navigation System

direction will be affected neither by the earth magnetic field nor by the magnetic objects around. Therefore, it obtains a high accuracy in direction pointing and a fine steadiness as well.

(三) **Speaking Practice**

1. Group discussion

Work in groups. Look at the statements in the language bank task. What equipment are included in the marine communication system and navigation equipment?

2. Short talk

Now it is your chance to practice what you have learned from this unit. Put your textbook away and give a short talk on the following topics. You should talk at least one minute. Don't be discouraged if you cannot make it. Review the task and try again. You are sure to do it better next time.

- communication system.
- navigation equipment.

3. Role play

Work in groups or pairs and discuss the following topics. Then, you are advised to talk at least three minutes for each topic.

- dialogue: A: chief officer; B: captain.
- Prompts: Introducing the equipment of marine communication system.
- Introducing navigation equipment.

## 【 Unit Evaluation 】

The teacher evaluates the students on their performance and mutual evaluation results, the results in Table 7-3.

Table 7-3    Task Evaluation

| EVALUATION CONTENT | | | DISTRIBUTION SCORE | SCORE |
|---|---|---|---|---|
| Unit 6 Marine Communication and Navigation System<br>Task1 GMDSS (50%)<br>Task2 Marine Communication System and Navigation Equipment (50%) | | | | |
| KNOWLEDGE EVALUATION | | | | |
| Ⅰ. Choice | | | 20 | |
| Ⅱ.Translation | 1.Translate new words and expressions into Chinese. | | 20 | |
| | 2.Translate the following sentences into English. | | 20 | |
| TIME: 30' | STUDENT SIGN: | TEACHER SIGN: | TOTAL: | |
| SKILL EVALUATION | | | | |
| Ⅲ. Speaking Practice<br>Role playing | | | 20<br>20 | |
| TIME: 30' | STUDENT SIGN: | TEACHER SIGN: | TOTAL: | |

# Unit 8

# Marine Electrical Maintenance and Trouble Shooting

【Unit Goals】

1. Familiar with the knowledge about marine electrical maintenance and trouble shooting.
2. Students can introduce marine electrical maintenance and trouble shooting to others in English and talk to each other about it fluently.

## Task 1  Marine Electrical Maintenance

【Task goals】

1. Get to know the knowledge about marine electrical maintenance.
2. Students can introduce the knowledge about marine electrical system maintenance to others in English and talk to each other about it fluently.

【Knowledge linking】

What do you think about marine electrical maintenance?
Please look at the following pictures carefully and grasp the knowledge:

(1) This service outlet was replaced by some one who didn't understand high voltage wiring and this is the result. The breaker was very old and the contacts fused closed and would no longer trip. This photo was taken during a survey while the wood behind the panel was burning. The owner showed no concern about it, thought it wasn't serious (Fig.8-1).

(2) Here's a good reason why this ribbed plastic conduit should not be used on boats. Not only is it highly flammable, but it spreads the fire (Fig.8-2).

(3) If you have electrical problems and your system looks something like this, then you needn't look much farther for the source of the problem ( Fig.8-3).

(4) Not every electrical system is going to be this neat, but this is the way it should be (Fig.8-4).

## Unit 8  Marine Electrical Maintenance and Trouble Shooting

Fig.8-1  Burned wood

Fig.8-2  Ribbed plastic

Fig.8-3  Electrical problem

Fig.8-4  Neat electrical system

(5) Corrosion takes its toll even on the interior of the boat due to leaks, salt air and high humidity. When tested, most of these connections had high resistance. This is the proper method to splice wires(Fig.8-5).

Fig.8-5  Splice wires

Fig.8-6  Wire bundle

(6) Close up of wire bundle above. These supposedly water proof wire connectors, on closer examination, are found to be full of water(Fig.8-6).

### Marine Electrical Maintenance

Let's begin with the fact that a boat is not a house or a car, simply because the later two don't float in water, which is what makes a boat inherently different. Especially a boat that floats in sea water because sea water is a fair conductor of electricity. Therefore, there are lots of additional rules about the materials and methods of installation that you won't find on land based vehicles or structures.[1] Because water (both inside and outside the boat) provides a very convenient ground path for electricity, we have to be a lot more careful how we do things.

## 1. Principles of Wiring

I would venture to say that half the electrical problems on boats result from improperly installed wiring. After the boat is built, there's no convenient way to route new wiring. But we need to understand that systems on boats are subject to high G-forces due to pounding, rolling and vibration.[2] Connections get stressed and wires rub and chafe against abrasive or sharp objects. It doesn't take much damage to wire insulation before you have a condition where stray current may develop. And the chance of finding a little bit of damage on one wire is about nil.

Must be routed in a suitable, dry area and be well secured. Should not be laying in bilge or in areas that get wet.

Must not be routed with pipes or hoses of any kind, and not be in contact with fuel tanks or fuel lines.

Splicing circuits should be avoided. If splicing is necessary, it should employ a proper terminal block, and not butt connectors (see above photo). Every splice in a circuit creates additional resistance, and the potential for the connection to come apart. Taped connections and wire nuts should not be used.

Wiring must be firmly secured and in locations where it won't get damaged. Should not be dangling or strung across open spaces. Use only plastic, not metal, clips to secure the wiring.

Must have chafing protection or conduit at vibration points around machinery.

Must not be in contact with, or proximity to machinery exhaust systems.

Wiring should be neat. A boat full of tangled wiring demonstrates unprofessionalism and the inability to fix something that goes wrong. An electrician can't trace a plate of spaghetti, and when something does go wrong, the cost of fixing it goes way up.

## 2. Grounds and Grounding

One of the least understood aspects of a boats electrical system, and the most troublesome, is the proper method of grounding. That we often get questions of whether AC or DC electrical equipment should be grounded to the boat's bonding system is illustrative of this point. AC and DC grounding systems are two separate systems, for distinctly different reasons. If you don't understand these systems, you run the distinct risk of creating a disaster. Actually, there are four separate ground systems: DC ground, AC ground, AC grounding (or bond), and the vessel's bonding system. You can add to this lightning and HF radio grounds as well. Do you know the principles of each? Are you sufficiently confused to discourage you from doing your own wiring? I hope so. For unless you understand each thoroughly, you're headed for trouble.

The AC ground and grounding systems are "free floating," meaning that they do not ground on the vessel, but only to shore.[3] The ground, or neutral, is a current carrying conductor, and is the source of many troubles because people do not regard it as such. The grounding, bond or green wire is the "safety" intended to channel current safely to ground in the event of a short circuit. Both of these circuits are capable of conducting current and can be the source of electrolysis when there are system faults with the dock or marina wiring. This is very easy to test for.

There is only one point where the DC side is grounded, and that is at the battery. It, too, is a "free floating" system in which nothing is ever grounded to any metallic part of the vessel, most especially not the bonding system. Just like a car sitting on rubber tires, completely insulated from earth potential, the battery itself provides the negative potential.

The bonding system, also green wire, has nothing to do with electrical systems. Underwater metals are simply wired together to equalize differences in potential of different kinds of metal. Nothing should ever be grounded to the bonding system. Unfortunately, some people don't understand this and use it to ground electrical equipment, occasionally with disastrous results.

## 【New Words and Expressions】

| maintenance | [ˈmeɪntənəns] | n. | 保养；维护；维修 |
| jury-rigged | [ˈdʒʊərɪˌrɪgd] | adj. | 临时或应急配备的 |
| electrolysis | [ɪˌlekˈtrɒləsɪs] | n. | 电解，电蚀；电蚀除瘤[毛发等] |
| vibration | [vaɪˈbreɪʃn] | n. | 摆动；震动； |
| abrasive | [əˈbreɪsɪv] | adj. | 有磨蚀作用的；摩擦的； |
| hose | [həʊz] | n. | 软管，胶皮管； |
| splicing | [ˈsplaɪsɪŋ] | v. | 绞接( splice 的现在分词 ) |
| tangle | [ˈtæŋgl] | vt.&vi. | （使）缠结，（使）乱作一团； |
| trace | [treɪs] | vt. | 跟踪，追踪；追溯，探索 |
| spaghetti | [spəˈgeti] | n. | 意大利面条；[电]漆布绝缘管 |
| bonding | [ˈbɒndɪŋ] | n. | 黏接；连（搭，焊，胶，粘）接 |
| illustrative | [ˈɪləstrətɪv] | adj.adv. | 解说性的;解说性地 |
| earth potential | | | 地电势 |
| negative potential | | | 负电势，负电位 |

## 【Notes】

(1) Therefore, there are lots of additional rules about the materials and methods of installation that you won't find on land based vehicles or structures.

因此，有许多关于安装的材料和方法的附加规则，这些你不会在陆上的车辆或建筑物上发现。

(2) But we need to understand that systems on boats are subject to high G-forces due to pounding, rolling and vibration.

但我们需要了解船上系统易遭受由于撞击、滚动和振动所产生的高重力。

(3) The AC ground and grounding systems are "free floating," meaning that they do not ground on the vessel, but only to shore.

交流接地和接地系统是"自由浮动",意味着它们不在船上做接地,但只到岸上做接地。

## 【Task Implement】

### PART A  Reading Practice

#### Main Circuit Protection and Circuit Breakers

Many people think that the circuit breakers on the dock protect their boat. They do not; they only protect the dock wiring. Your main circuit breaker protects your boat's systems. But what about that section of wiring and connectors between your main panel and the dock breaker? Well, the fact is that it is unprotected which is why so many fires occur. Check out all the top end boats and you will find that they have circuit protection located directly at the shore connectors. Which is why we recommend that you should too. Having slow blow cartridge fuses installed directly at the connectors can go a long way toward preventing fires and burned up shore cords, particularly if you are a traveler and frequently rely on uncertain power supplies. Circuit breakers should NEVER be installed on the exterior of the boat. Only gasketed, water proof cartridge holders should be used.(1)

Circuit breakers wear out, and when they do they work less well, or not at all. If you are using circuit breakers as ON/OFF switches, you are helping them wear out that much faster. It also damages breakers when you shut off equipment via the breaker. This causes arcing at the contact points which damages the points. When connecting and disconnecting shore power, you should always turn OFF equipment at the appropriate switch on the equipment. Then shut the main breaker off. Do not ever simply throw the main breaker off to shut down equipment that is operating. The circuit breaker arcs and damages it.

Also be aware that any equipment run by a motor, such as air conditioning and refrigeration equipment, start up with an initially much higher amperage than the normal running amperage. An air conditioner that runs at 14 amps may have a start up amperage of 20 amps, so that if you just go and turn all the equipment on at once, it overloads the system. Then the circuit breaker gets hot and won't stay engaged until it cools down. Ergo, start up heavy equipment one item at a time, allowing it time to cycle into its normal operating voltage before turning something else on. For example, don't turn the AC, refrigerator and icemaker all on at once and not expect the breaker to pop.(2)

## 【New Words and Expressions】

| dock | [dɒk] | n. | 码头 |
| circuit breaker | [ˈsəːkit ˈbreikə] | n. | 断路开关,断路器 |
| panel | [ˈpænl] | n. | 控制板 |
| exterior | [ɪkˈstɪərɪə(r)] | n. | 外部,外面,表面 |
| gasketed | [ˈgæskɪtɪd] | adj. | 填密的,用衬垫装配的 |
| icemaker | [aisˈmeɪkə] | n. | 制冰机 |
| cartridge fuses | [ˈkɑːtrɪdʒ fjuːz] | | 熔丝管,管形熔热 |

113

Marine Electrical Maintenance and Trouble Shooting

## 【Notes】

(1) Circuit breakers should NEVER be installed on the exterior of the boat. Only gasketed, water proof cartridge holders should be used.

断路器不应安装在船外。只应使用衬垫装配的，防水的盒夹。

(2) For example, don't turn the AC, refrigerator and icemaker all on at once and not expect the breaker to pop.

例如，不要期望把空调，冰箱，制冰机同时打开而断路器不跳闸。

## PART B  Role Playing

(A:cadet who comes on board for the first time; B: captain)

A: How do you arrange overhaul? Who makes the decision of the overhaul? When do you arrange overhaul?

B: The arrangement of the overhaul is based on the reasons for the machinery problem or the running time of the machine. In general, I will check the symptoms of the machinery during the operation of the machine. All problems are to be recorded for reference in the repair. When the main engine or other engine has run excessively, which means the time is more than the rated period, the engine must be repaired. In general, the chief engineer makes the repair decision in consultation with the shipmaster. The time shall be arranged appropriately. For example, when the ship is in port, the main engine is not used, So the main engine may be arranged for overhaul.

A: Will you show US your knowledge on different kinds of paint?

B: Yes, 1 will. The paints are divided into the following in accordance with the locations:deck paints, anchor and anchor chain paints, hull paints, waterline paints, bottom paints, steam gas tube paints ( used in the engine room and for coating hot pipes and so on). According to layers, the paints are divided into the following: primer and surface paints. According to the function, the paints are divided into the following: anti-corrosive paint, antifouling paint, anti-galvanic paint, boottopping green paint, light grey paint, surface paint, bituminous solution, red lead paint, and so on.

A: What is the safety procedure of overhauling the cylinder?

B: A safety meeting is necessary and all necessary procedures must be listed. Such as who decides the signals, the knocking signals for lifting up, slowing down, emergency stop, lifting down, etc. All persons must know the duties. One person should manage the tools on the spot. When lifting, no person is permitted to stand under the lifting load of the engine room crane or chain blocks to prevent any injury or casualty. After drawing out the piston, clearances shall be checked. The deformation or scar must be checked as well.

A: What types of maintenance and repair are there in general?

B: In general, the types of maintenance and repair are divided into voyage repair or ASM (at sea maintenance) and docking repair. If we evaluate according to the financial standards in the shipyard, we divide into the major repair and the minor repair and so on. In addition, the routine annual repair is called annual repair.

A: What are reasons for declination of precision, Performance, or efficiency of machinery?

B: Many reasons, such as wearing and tearing, corrosion, failure to maintain, failure to operate,

Marine Electrical Maintenance

faulty design reasons.

A: Why must we check the facilities periodically?

B: The reliability of the facilities and wearability of all components can be checked via a periodical check. The wear and tear condition of components and technical conditions of machinery, electrical parts, and lubricating systems can be examined for preventing potential danger and accidents as well.

A: How many approaches are there for dismantling?

B: Strike dismantling, pull dismantling, push dismantling, extreme temperature change dismantling and destroy dismantling.

A: What precautions do you take when machinery is overhauled for maintenance? What can be done to stop this occuring?

B: (1)Continual purification of the oil is essential, combined with frequent analysis. (2)All filters must be inspected and cleaned at regular intervals. (3)Keep oil and temperatures in good order.

A: After the overhaul of moving parts. what should be done in relation to the crankcase?

B: We shall check thoroughly to prove there are no rags or tools left behind inside the crankcase prior to boxing up. We shall check that all bolts inside the crankcase are suitably locked. We shall start L. O. pumps and check the flow from the bearings. We shall turn the engines by the turning gear. We shall check sounds and electric motor current. Then we shall make an inspection, 15-30 minutes after starting, one hour later and again when a full load is obtained.

## 【Task Evaluation】

### (一) Choice

1. Electric insulation is made of organic substances and so gradually _____ with age.
  A. deteriorates    B. increases    C. are fouled    D. becomes better
2. Time delayed or delayed action-type fuses are designed to _____.
  A. prevent grounds in branch circuits    B. prevent opens in motor circuits
  C. permit momentary overloads without melting    D. guard lighting and electronic circuits
3. The routine annual repair is called _____.
  A.annual repair    B. minor repair    C.major repair    D.voyage repair
4. The _____ is a software system to manage routine maintenance and repair work on board.
  A.WPS    B. PMS    C.IMO    D.UPS
5. How often will a vessel be repaired? In general, every _____ years.
  A.two    B.three    C.four    D.five

### (二) Translation.

1. Translate new words and expressions into Chinese (Table 8-1).

Table 8-1  Translation

| | |
|---|---|
| 1. maintenance | |
| 2. jury-rigged | |
| 3. electrolysis | |
| 4. vibration | |

续表

| 5. abrasive | |
| --- | --- |
| 6. hose | |
| 7. splicing | |
| 8. trace | |
| 9. spaghetti | |
| 10. bonding | |
| 11. earth potential | |
| 12. negative potential | |
| 13. circuit breaker | |
| 14. gasketed | |
| 15. cartridge fuses | |

A. 绞接；B. 断路开关，断路器；C. 负电势，负电位；D. 有磨蚀作用的，摩擦的；E. 摆动，震动；F. 电解，电蚀；G. 地电势；H. 软管，胶皮管；I. 填密的，用衬垫装配的；J. 熔丝管，管形熔热；K. 临时或应急配备的；L. 粘接；连（搭，焊，胶）接；M. [电]漆布绝缘管；N. 跟踪，追踪；O. 保养，维护，维修。

2. Translate the following sentences into Chinese.

The PMS stands for planned maintenance system. The PMS is a software system to manage routine maintenance and repair work on board. The ship can manage the maintenance and repair work easily using the PMS and the shipowner can conveniently access the PMS for monitoring. I had used the system when 1 worked on OSG. I listed the daily maintenance, weekly maintenance, and quarterly maintenance plans. I put them in the PMS system. All my senior staff could read them via the system. I printed them out and gave them to the second engineer and guided his routine work. I also told my staff that 1 would check their work daily. The company responsible persons might read my plan via the PMS. In short, PMS is helpful for maintenance and repair work.

(三) Speaking Practice

1. Group discussion

Work in groups. Which are important aspects for marine electrical maintenance? Why?

2. Short talk

Now it is your chance to practice what you have learned from this task. Put your textbook away and give a short talk on the following topics. You should talk at least one minute. Don't be discouraged if you cannot make it. Review the task and try again. You are sure to do it better next time.

• Marine electrical maintenance.

3. Role play

Work in groups or pairs and discuss the following topics. Then, you are advised to talk at least three minutes for each topic.

• A is a cadet visiting the ship. B is an electrician.
• Prompts: Introducing marine electrical maintenance.
• Marine electrical maintenance.

# Task 2  Electrical Trouble Shooting

## 【Task Goals】

1. Get to know different steps of the marine electrical troubleshooting. Familiar with the basic steps and tools: verify the problem, gather information, determine probable causes, narrow the list of causes, test all subsystems, digital multimeter, etc.

2. Students can introduce the knowledge about marine electrical trouble shooting to others in English and talk to each other about it fluently.

## 【Knowledge linking】

Could you illustrate what kinds of marine electrical troubles include onboard?
What is the difference between multimeter and ohmmeter?
Are you familiar with the electrician's tools? What are they?
Please look at the following pictures carefully and try to learn the terms.
(1) Voltage meter(Fig.8-7).
(2) Voltage measuring of the battery(Fig.8-8).
(3) Marine pilers(Fig.8-9).
(4) Tool kit(Fig.8-10).

Fig.8-7    Voltage meter

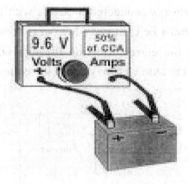

Fig.8-8    Voltage measuring of the battery

Fig.8-9    Marine pilers

Fig.8-10    Tool kit

## Electrical Trouble Shooting

The marine environment can be especially harsh on the components of your boat's electrical system. When trouble occurs you will want the capability to make accurate and reliable judges quickly, so troubleshooting is very important onboard for electricians.

Electrical personnel use many different types of measuring instruments. Some jobs require very accurate measurements while other jobs need only rough estimates. Some instruments are used solely to determine whether or not a circuit is complete. The most common measuring and testing instruments are voltmeters, ammeters, ohmmeters, multimeter, wattmeters, and watt-hour meters.

### 1. Voltmeters

The voltmeter is a much more accurate measurement than the voltage tester. Because voltmeters are connected in parallel with the circuit or the component being considered, it is necessary that they have relatively high resistance. The internal resistance keeps the current through the meter to a minimum. The lower the value of current through the meter, the less effect it has on the electrical characteristics of the circuit.

The sensitivity (therefore the accuracy) of the meter is stated in ohms per volt ($\Omega/V$). The higher the ohms per volt are, the better the quality of the meter. High values of ohms per volt minimize any change in circuit characteristics.

CAUTION: Do not leave a meter connected with the polarity reversed.

### 2. Ammeters

Ammeters are designed to measure the amount of current flowing in a circuit or part of a circuit. They are always connected in series with the circuit component being considered. The resistance of the meter must be extremely low so it does not restrict the flow of current through the circuit. When measuring the current flowing through very sensitive equipment, even a slight change in current caused by the ammeter may cause the equipment to malfunction (Fig. 8-11).

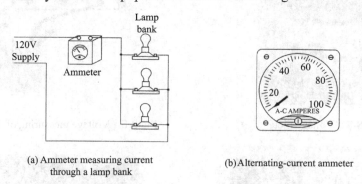

(a) Ammeter measuring current through a lamp bank

(b) Alternating-current ammeter

Fig.8-11  Ammeters

### 3. Megohmmeter (Megger)

A megohmmeter, commonly known by the trade name Megger, is an instrument used to measure very high values of resistance. For example, it is used to measure the resistance of the insulation on circuit conductors and motor windings. A megohmmeter is designed to measure the resistance in megohms; one megohm ($M\Omega$) is equal to one million ohms.

### 4. Multimeters

Multimeters are designed to measure more than one unit. For example, the volt-ohm-milliammeter, measures D. C. and A. C. voltages, D. C. current, and resistance. The advantage of this type of meter is that measurements can be taken with or without deenergizing the circuit (Fig. 8-12).

The multimeter has two kinds: the analog multimeter uses a standard meter movement with a needle. The digital multimeter uses an electronic numerical display. These two kinds of multimeters have some common grounds:

Fig.8-12  Multimeter

(1) Both have a positive jack and a common jack for the test leads.

(2) Both have a function switch to select D. C. voltage, A. C. voltage, D. C. current or resistance.

(3) Both have a range switch for accurate readings.

### 5. Basic troubleshooting steps

While solving more complicated problems has become more sophisticated, the basic processes haven't changed. Problem solving is not always easy, and to be done properly and efficiently, several steps must be taken in logical order:[1]

- Verify the problem.
- Gather information.
- Determine probable causes.
- Narrow the list of causes.
- Test all subsystems.

Following these logical steps to troubleshooting may seem like the medical history a doctor gathers when trying to figure out what ails you, and for good reason: the method works.[2] Used in combination with the best, most capable equipment, this method will definitely increase your odds for success.

### 6. Troubleshooting example

As the article space constraints, we only take battery troubleshooting for example.

Often the first sign of a battery problem will occur when the starter won't turn the engine over. Use your multimeter to get a rough idea of the battery's state of charge. To perform a no-load test, set the digital multimeter switch function to Volts DC and measure across the terminals. Compare your readings to the graph in Fig.8-13.

The voltage test tells only the state of charge, not the battery condition. To gain additional information about the battery's condition, test the specific gravity of the electrolyte in each cell using a hydrometer.[3] If the specific gravity is low but relatively the same across all cells, recharging may be able to bring the battery back to good health, unless the plates are sulfated. If one cell shows a specific gravity much lower than the rest, the cell is probably dead and recharging will not help.

In a lead-acid battery, each cell produces about 2.1 volts at full charge. Therefore, a 12V battery has 6 cells in series. If the no-load test reads 10V instead of 12V, a dead cell is likely and the battery should be replaced.

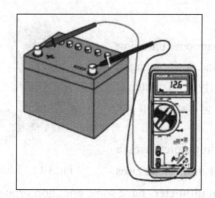 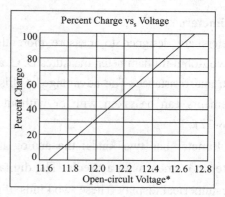

Fig. 8-13　Measuring System Voltage

Sulfated plates can be detected by measuring the output voltage under load (after the battery has been charged). Typical results for a good battery are given in Fig.8-14 below[4].

```
Load test @ 1/2 CCA Rating
8.5V @ 0 °F (-18 °C)
8.8V @ 30 °F (-1 °C)
9.4V @ 50 °F (10 °C)
9.6V @ 70 °F (21 °C)
```

Fig. 8-14

## 【New Words and Expressions】

| | | | |
|---|---|---|---|
| personnel | [ˌpəːsəˈnel] | n. | (总称)人员 |
| voltmeter | [ˈvəultˌmiːtə] | n. | 电压表 |
| ammeter | [ˈæmitə] | n. | 电流表，安培计 |
| ohmmeter | [ˈəumˌmiːtə] | n. | 电阻表，欧姆计 |
| multimeter | [mʌlˈtimitə] | n. | 万用表 |
| wattmeter | [ˈwɔtmiːtə] | n. | 功率表，瓦特计 |
| troubleshooting | [ˈtrʌblʃuːtiŋ] | n. | 故障查找 |
| logical order | | | 逻辑顺序 |
| verify | [ˈverifai] | vt. | 核实 证明 判定 |
| lead-acid | | | 铅酸的 |
| in series | | | 连续地，串联 |
| tool kit | | | 工具包 |

## 【Notes】

(1) Problem solving is not always easy, and to be done properly and efficiently, several steps must be taken in logical order:

解决问题并不容易，为了正确有效的解决问题，必须依逻辑顺序按下述几个步骤进行：

(2) Following these logical steps to troubleshooting may seem like the medical history a doctor gathers when trying to figure out what ails you, and for good reason: the method works.

遵循故障查询的逻辑步骤，看起来像医生试图找出你怎么啦时,收集病史,这样做有充分的理由：因为这个方法行之有效。

(3) To gain additional information about the battery's condition, test the specific gravity of the electrolyte in each cell using a hydrometer

为了获得关于电池状况的其他信息，用比重计测试每节电池中电解液的比重。

(4) Sulfated plates can be detected by measuring the output voltage under load (after the battery has been charged). Typical results for a good battery are given in Figure 8-14 below.

硫酸板块可以通过测量负载情况下的输出电压来检测（电池充电后）。在下面的图 8-14 中给出好电池的典型的测试结果。

## 【 Task Implement 】

### PART A  Reading Practice

Alternator Decisions and Recommendations(Table 8-2).

**Table 8-2  Alternator Decisions and Recommendations**

| Decision | Action |
| --- | --- |
| No Problems | The system is showing normal output from the alternator. No problem detected. |
| No Output | The alternator is not providing charging current to the battery.<br>• Check the belts to ensure the alternator is rotating with the engine running. Replace broken or slipping belts and retest.<br>• <u>Check all connections to and from the alternator, especially the connection to the battery. If the connection is loose or heavily corroded, clean or replace the cable and retest.</u>[1]<br>• If the belts and connections are in good working condition, replace the alternator. (Older vehicles and modern boats with high-output alternators often use external voltage regulators, which may require only replacement of the voltage regulator.) |
| Low Output | The alternator is not providing enough current to power the system's electrical loads and charge the battery.<br>• Check the belts to ensure the alternator is rotating with the engine running. Replace broken or slipping belts and retest.<br>• Check the connections from the alternator to the battery. <u>If the connection is loose or heavily corroded, clean or replace the cable and retest.</u>[2] |
| High Output | The voltage output from the alternator to the battery exceeds the normal limits of a functioning regulator.<br>• Check to ensure there are no loose connections and that the ground connection is normal. If there are no connection problems, replace the regulator. (Most alternators have a built-in regulator requiring you to replace the alternator. In older vehicles and some modern boats with high-output alternators that use external regulators, you may need to replace only the voltage regulator. )<br>The regulator controls voltage output based on the battery voltage, underhood (or engine room) temperature, and vehicle loads used. <u>In other words, it controls the maximum voltage the system can produce based on the current needs and amount of current that can be produced by the spinning of the rotor in the alternator.</u>[3] The normal high limit of a typical automotive regulator is 14.5 volts ±0.5. Refer to the manufacturer specifications for the current limit, which may vary by vehicle type.<br>A high charging rate will overcharge the battery and may decrease its life and cause it to fail. If the battery test decision is REPLACE and the charging system test shows a HIGH OUTPUT, check the battery's electrolyte levels. A symptom of overcharging is battery fluid spewing through the vent caps, which causes low electrolyte levels and will harm the battery. |

Unit 8  Marine Electrical Maintenance and Trouble Shooting

续表

| Decision | Action |
|---|---|
| Excessive Ripple | One or more diodes in the alternator are not functioning or there's stator damage, which is shown by an excessive amount of AC ripple current supplied to the battery.<br>• Make sure the alternator mounting is sturdy and that the belts are in good shape, and functioning properly.(4) If the mounting and belts are good, replace the alternator. |
| Open Phase | The EXP has detected an open phase within the alternator. Replace the alternator. |
| Open Diode | The EXP has detected an open diode within the alternator. Replace the alternator. |
| Shorted Diode | The EXP has detected a shorted diode within the alternator. Replace the alternator. |

## 【New Words and Expressions】

| | | | |
|---|---|---|---|
| alternator | [ˈɔːltəneɪtə(r)] | n. | 交流发电机 |
| belt | [belt] | n. | 传送带 |
| retest | [ˌriːˈtest] | n.& v. | 再测验，再考验 |
| corrode | [kəˈrəʊd] | vt.& vi. | 使腐蚀，侵蚀 |
| spew | [spjuː] | vt.& vi. | 涌出，射出；渗出 |
| built-in | [bɪlt ɪn] | adj. | 嵌入的；内置的；固有的 |
| underhood | [ˈʌndəhʊd] | n. | 发动机舱 |
| shorted | [ʃɔːtid] | adj. | 短路的 |
| diode | [ˈdaɪəʊd] | n. | 二极管 |
| voltage regulator | | | 稳压器，电压调节器，调压器 |
| excessive ripple | | | 过度波动 |
| battery fluid | | | 蓄电池液 |

## 【Notes】

(1) Check all connections to and from the alternator, especially the connection to the battery. If the connection is loose or heavily corroded, clean or replace the cable and retest.

检查所有进出发电机的连接，特别是至电池的连接。如果连接松动或严重腐蚀，清洗或更换电缆并重新测试。

(2) Check the connections from the alternator to the battery. If the connection is loose or heavily corroded, clean or replace the cable and retest.

检查所有进出发电机的连接，特别是至电池的连接。如果连接松动或严重腐蚀，清洗或更换电缆并重新测试。

(3) In other words, it controls the maximum voltage the system can produce based on the current needs and amount of current that can be produced by the spinning of the rotor in the alternator.

换句话说，它控制系统基于电流需要产生的最大电压和旋转发电机转子产生的电流量。

(4) Make sure the alternator mounting is sturdy and that the belts are in good shape, and functioning properly.

确保发电机的安装坚固，且带况良好，且功能正常。

## PART B  Role Playing

(A: cadet who comes on board for the first time; B: captain)

A: Could you tell me the main reason for seeing blue smoke exhausted from the diesel engine?

B: It is possibly due to leak of lubricant which being burnt in the diesel engine.

A: Could you tell me the main reason for seeing yellow smoke exhausted from the diesel engine?

B: The sulphur content in the oil is higher than normal.

A: Could you tell me the main reason for seeing white smoke exhausted from the diesel engine?

B: The water content is much higher than normal.

A: Could you tell me the main reason for seeing black smoke exhausted from the diesel engine?

B: The possible reasons are as follows: discharge valve damage or overload operation of diesel engine, or leakage of nozzle, or the incomplete combustion in the cylinder because not enough fresh air was pumped.

A: What signs indicate a scavenge fire has started?

B: The following signs are symptoms that a scavenge fire may occur: (1)Turbo—charger surging; (2)High scavenge space temperatures; (3)High exhaust temperatures; (4)High cooling water outlet temperatures; (5)Blistering paint on scavenge space doors.

A: What can cause a well-maintained bearing to suffer overheating?

B: Overheating takes place if L.O. becomes corrosive or contaminated. Perhaps, the L.O. supply fails. The cooler problems may be caused if the L.O. temperature is higher. If the bearing adjustment is wrong. such as the clearances are inappropriate, the bearing may suffer overheating.

A: What are the causes of scavenge fires?

B: (1)Wearing of mechanical components. (2)Faulty fuel injection. (3)Inefficient exhaust system. (4)Incorrect cylinder lubrication-oil leaks into scavenge space. (5)Insufficient drainage of scavenge drains. (6)Piston rings are broken.

A: What can be done to prevent scavenge fires?

B: (1)Prevent the build-up of oil and sludge in the scavenge space. (2) Ensure that the internal surfaces of the space are kept reasonably clean. (3) Carry out routine piston ring inspections. (4)Ensure scavenge air temperature is not above 55℃. (5)Ensure drains are blown and drains are proved clear. (6)Check the cylinder oil injection timings.

A: What action will you take when you a report has been given to you that the running of the main engine is abnormal?

B: I will immediately give the order to slow the main engine to the lowest safe rpm and contact the Bridge to request permission to stop. I will give the order to increase cylinder lubrication.

## 【Task Evaluation】

### (一) Choice

1. When there is a fire in a large electric motor, normally the very FIRST step is to _____.
   A. secure the electric supply    B. ventilate area to remove smoke
   C. start the fire pump and lead out hose    D. apply foam

2. _____ are designed to measure more than one unit.

A. Megohmmeters　　　B. Voltmeters　　　C. Multimeters　　　D. Ammeters

3. A _____ is an instrument used to measure very high values of resistance.

A. Megohmmeter　　　B. Voltmeters　　　C. Multimeter　　　D. Ammeters

4. _____ are designed to measure the amount of current flowing in a circuit or part of a circuit.

A. Megohmmeters　　　B. Voltmeters　　　C. Multimeters　　　D. Ammeters

5. _____ are connected in parallel with the circuit or the component being considered, it is necessary that they have relatively high resistance.

A. Megohmmeters　　　B. Voltmeters　　　C. Multimeters　　　D. Ammeters

**(二) Translation.**

1. Translate new words and expressions into Chinese (Table 8-3).

**Table 8-3　Translation**

| | |
|---|---|
| 1. verify the problem | |
| 2. gather information | |
| 3. determine | |
| 4. probable causes | |
| 5. narrow the list of causes | |
| 6. tool kit | |
| 7. lead-acid battery | |
| 8. ammeter | |
| 9. excessive ripple | |
| 10. voltage regulator | |
| 11. troubleshooting | |
| 12. ohmmeter | |
| 13. logical order | |
| 14. Test all subsystems | |
| 15. battery fluid | |
| 16. multimeter | |
| 17. voltmeter | |

A. 工具包；B. 万用表；C. 验证问题；D.电压表；E.缩小原因列表；F.电流表，安培计；G. 触电死亡；H. 收集信息；I.功率表，瓦特计；J.故障查找；K.铅酸电池；L. 逻辑顺序；M. 稳压器，电压调节器，调压器；N.电阻表，欧姆计；O. 过度波动；P.蓄电池液；Q.检测子系统。

2. Translate the following sentences into Chinese.

Electrical personnel use many different types of measuring tools. Some jobs require very accurate measurements while other jobs need only rough estimate. Some tools are used solely to determine whether or not a circuit is complete. The most common measuring and testing tools are digital multimeter and etc. The digital multimeter is used to test some basic electrical components commonly found on inboard marine engines including batteries, starters, alternators, and ignition systems. But the applications don't end here. Once you own a digital multimeter, you will be able to check the wiring on your boat trailer, perform corrosion potential testing on your zinc/bonding system, and even check the wiring in your house and car. When you think of the various electrical items that you want to add to your boat, you quickly realize that a good quality digital multimeter is an essential part of your boat's tool kit.

(三) Speaking Practice

1. Group discussion

Work in groups. Look at the statements in the language bank task. Work in groups. Which are important aspects for marine troubleshooting? Why?

2. Short talk

Now it is your chance to practice what you have learned from this task. Put your textbook away and give a short talk on the following topics. You should talk at least one minute. Don't be discouraged if you cannot make it. Review the task and try again. You are sure to do it better next time.

• Marine electrical troubleshooting.

3. Role playing

Work in groups or pairs and discuss the following topics. Then, you are advised to talk at least three minutes for each topic.

• A is a cadet visiting the ship. B is an electrician.
• Prompts: Introducing marine electrical troubleshooting.
• Marine electrical troubleshooting.

## 【 Unit Evaluation 】

The teacher evaluates the students on their performance and mutual evaluation results, the results in Table 8-4.

**Table 8-4　Task Evaluation**

| EVALUATION CONTENT | | | DISTRIBUTION SCORE | SCORE |
|---|---|---|---|---|
| Unit8 Marine Electrical Maintenance and Trouble Shooting<br>Task1　Marine Electrical Maintenance　(50%)<br>Task2 Electrical Trouble Shooting(50%) | | | | |
| KNOWLEDGE EVALUATION | | | | |
| Ⅰ. Choice | | | 20 | |
| Ⅱ.Translation | 1.Translate new words and expressions into Chinese. | | 20 | |
| | 2.Translate the following sentences into English. | | 20 | |
| TIME: 30' | STUDENT SIGN: | TEACHER SIGN: | TOTAL: | |
| SKILL EVALUATION | | | | |
| Ⅲ. Speaking Practice<br>　　Role playing | | | 20<br>20 | |
| TIME: 30' | STUDENT SIGN: | TEACHER SIGN: | TOTAL: | |

# Unit 9

# Marine Electrical Test

## 【Unit Goals】

1. Get to know different items of the marine electrical test. Familiar with the basic words and expressions: mooring test, sea trial, parallel test, calibrate, meg-ohmmeter etc.
2. Students can introduce marine electrical test in English. They can talk to each other about it fluently.

## Task  Marine Electrical Test

### 【Knowledge linking】

What does marine electrical test include in your mind?
Please look at the following pictures carefully and try to learn the terms:

(1) Multimeter (Fig.9-1)

Fig.9-1  Multimeter

(2) Megger/meg-ohmmeter (Fig.9-2)
(3) Circuit analyzer(Fig.9-3)

Fig.9-2  Megger/meg-ohmmeter         Fig.9-3  Circuit analyzer

## Marine Electrical Test

Marine electrical test consists of mooring test and sea trial. On the ship, after the end of all electrical equipment installation, power tests should be carried out. The purpose is to test the integrity of its performance after the demolition, transportation, installation onto the ship. Time and procedures of test can be determined according to the extent of completion of the equipment testing. <u>Some equipment, which is not directly related to protection with the ship's navigation, in principle, should have completed the inspection of mooring test; some equipment after the mooring test still need to make effective use of sea trial.</u>[1]

All tests and inspections listed in these documents are to be witnessed by the owner's supervisors and class surveyor as applicable. However, in case that the supervisor dose not attend these tests or inspections on any reasons of his own convenient, these tests and inspections are to be entrusted to the classification surveyors or inspectors of the ××× quality control Department.

1. Tools and measuring equipment for test (Table 9-1).

**Table 9-1 Tools and measuring equipment for test**

| Measuring equipment | Tool |
|---|---|
| DC 500V portable megger (100 meg-ohm. transistor type)<br>Portable AC voltmeter/ammeter of clamp-on type（卡箍式）<br>Portable circuit tester<br>Voltage detectors<br>Portable DC voltmeter<br>Standard hydrometers（湿度表）<br>Thermometers（温度表）（－20℃ ～ +100℃）<br>Beaker（烧杯）[1 liter（升）] | Electric soldering iron（电烙铁）(100W AC 220V) with two spare heating elements<br>Soldering iron (40W AC 220V) with two spare heating elements |

2. Mooring Test Items are as follow
   ➢ <u>Main Generator & Main Switchboard</u>[2] (Table 9-2).

**Table 9-2 Mooring test items**

| No. | Mooring Test Items |
|---|---|
| 1 | Test procedure for D/G<br>    Insulation resistance measurement test<br>    Generator engine safety device test<br>    D/G load test and generator operation load test<br>    Load characteristic test<br>    Transient voltage regulation test<br>    Governor test<br>    G/E Starting interlock test<br>    G/E Starting test |
| 2 | Test procedure for parallel running test<br>    Generator control system<br>    The relevant alarms are to be confirmed during test<br>    Parallel running by manual operation<br>    The auto/manual generator control shall be confirmed by main switchboard |
| 3 | Test procedure for main switchboard<br>    Main switchboard protection device test |

Fig.9-4 is Load and performance test for generator.
   ➢ Em'cy Generator and Em'cy Switchboard.
   ➢ Motor and Motor Controllers.

Fig.9-4  Load and performance test for generator

Operation of motors shall be confirmed during sea trial or in port according to the schedule of machinery part.
- ➢ Pump Auto Stand-By Start and Auto Change-Over.
- ➢ Insulation Resistance Measurement.
- ➢ Automation System.

Automation and control equipment shall be tested or calibrated on sea trial or in port.Individual trials of auxiliary engines, deck machinery, steering gear, life boat with davits, accommodation ladder, safety system, controls, communication and signal equipment, light installation, domestic machinery arrangement for water and oil and other equipment important for the operation of the vessel, excepts M/E Dock trial, should be carried out to demonstrate satisfactory workmanship and proper working order.
- ➢ Navigation, Communication and Radio System.

Navigation and radio equipment shall be tested or calibrated on sea trial or in port.
- ➢ Lighting System.

This category includes all lighting circuits, both AC and DC, with their different power supply considerations:cabin lights, navigation lights, convenience lights.Distribution circuit of power lighting shall be thoroughly measured their insulation resistance by DC 500V ohmmeter. AC power sources consist of shore-power isolation transformers and AC generators, both of which are AC current producers. The transformer is a point of distribution on board the boat; it is supplied by the shore-power feed but electrically isolated from it.

<u>Light circuits are simple. All we need is power supplied from a source and a good return path to ground. The primary concerns are of course electrical continuity and sufficient voltage throughout the circuit, especially in the case of navigation lights.</u>[3]
- ➢ Other Tests.

Operation of other electrical equipment shall be confirmed before delivery.

Electrical systems are to be tested under working condition to the satisfaction of the attending surveyor, and surveyor may require additional testing on the rule base, if deemed necessary.

## Marine Electrical Test

### 【New Words and Expressions】

| | | | |
|---|---|---|---|
| megger | ['megə] | n. | 兆欧表，摇表 |
| meg-ohmmeter | | n. | 兆欧表，摇表 |
| mooring | ['mɔːrɪŋ] | n. | 停泊处；系泊用具，系船具；下锚 |
| mooring test | | | 系泊试验 |
| trial | ['traɪəl] | n. | 测试，试验 |
| sea trial | | | 试航 |
| soldering iron | | | 烙铁 |
| performance | [pəˈfɔːməns] | n. | 履行；性能；表现；演出 |
| impedance | [ɪmˈpiːdns] | n. | 阻抗，全电阻；电阻抗 |
| calibrate | [ˈkælɪbreɪt] | vt. | 校准 |
| davit | [ˈdævɪt] | n. | 吊艇架 |
| ladder | [ˈlædə] | n. | 梯子 |
| ohmmeter | [ˈəʊmiːtə(r)] | n. | 欧姆表 |
| accommodation ladder | | | （船的）舷梯 |
| workmanship | [ˈwɜːkmənʃɪp] | n. | 技艺，工艺 |
| insulation resistance | | | 绝缘电阻 |
| shore-power | | | 岸电 |
| lighting circuits | | | 照明电路 |

### 【Notes】

(1) Some equipment, which is not directly related to protection with the ship's navigation, in principle, should have completed the inspection of mooring tests; some equipment after the mooring test still need to make effective use of sea trial.

有些与船舶的航行保障没有直接关系的设备，原则上应已完成系泊试验的检验，有些设备还需要利用海试测试有效性。

(2) Main Generator & Main Switchboard(Table 9-2).
主柴油发电机和主配电板（Table 9-2 参考译文见 Table 9-3）

**Table 9-3　主柴油发电机和主配电板**

| 序号 | 系泊试验项目 |
|---|---|
| 1 | 柴油发动机试验程序<br>　　绝缘电阻测量<br>　　柴油发电机安全装置试验<br>　　柴发负荷试验和发电机运行试验<br>　　负荷特性试验<br>　　瞬态电压调节试验<br>　　调速器试验<br>　　柴发启动连锁试验<br>　　柴发启动试验 |

# Unit 9  Marine Electrical Test

续表

| 序号 | 系泊试验项目 |
|---|---|
| 2 | 并车试验程序<br>　发电机控制系统<br>　在试验期间相关报警应交验<br>　手动并车<br>　在主配电板试验期间交验发电机手动/自动控制 |
| 3 | 主配电板试验程序<br>　主配电板保护装置试验 |

(3) Light circuits are simple. All we need is power supplied from a source and a good return path to ground. The primary concerns are of course electrical continuity and sufficient voltage throughout the circuit, especially in the case of navigation lights.

照明电路很简单。从电源到地有一个良好的回路就可以保证照明电路能正常工作了。我们主要关注电路的导通和有足够的电压供给电路，尤其是对于导航灯。

## 【Task Implement】

### PART A    Reading Practice

Mooring test scheme for electrical part refer to Table 9-4.

**Table 9-4    Mooring test scheme for electrical part**

| NO. | CONTENT |
|---|---|
|  | GENERAL<br>总则 |
| 1 | MAIN GENERATOR & MAIN SWITCHBOARD<br>主柴油发电机和主配电板 |
| 2 | EM'CY GENERATOR AND EM' CY SWITCHBOARD<br>应急发电机和应急配电板 |
| 3 | MOTOR AND MOTOR CONTROLLERS<br>电机及其控制器 |
| 4 | PUMP AUTO STAND-BY START AND AUTO CHANGE-OVER<br>泵的自动起停与自动切换 |
| 5 | INSULATION RESISTANCE MEASUREMENT<br>绝缘电阻测量 |
| 6 | OTHER TESTS<br>其他系统 |
| 7 | AUTOMATION SYSTEM<br>自动化系统 |
| 8 | NAVIGATION,COMMUNICATION AND RADIO SYSTEM<br>航行、通信和无线电系统 |
| 9 | LIGHTING SYSTEM<br>照明系统 |

以主柴油发电机和主配电板系泊试验为例：

MAIN GENERATOR & MAIN SWITCHBOARD（主柴油发电机和主配电板试验）

1. General 通用要求

(1) The generators are to be loaded with load bank(PF=0.8).

发电机应带负荷试验（功率因数为 0.8）。

(2) The instrument on the main switchboard is to be used for the measurement in principle.

原则上可以使用主配电板上的仪表做测量。

2. Equipment particulars 设备详细信息

  2.1 Diesel generator     柴油发电机

    2.2.1 Diesel engine     柴油机

- Maker：×××　　制造厂：×××
- Model: 6DK-20e　　机型：6DK-20e
- Number of Set : 3 Sets　　台数：3 台
- Rated output/Revolution : 910kW / 900RPM/Min

  额定输出功率/转数：910kW/ 900 转/min

    2.2.2 Generator     发电机

- Maker：×××　　制造厂：×××
- Type : 1FC5564　　型号：1FC5564
- Number of Set : 3 Sets　　台数：3 台
- Rated output : 1137.5 kVa / 900rpm/Min　　额定输出：11137.5 kVa / 900 转/min
- Power Factor : 0.8　　功率因数：0.8
- Rated voltage : 450V　　额定电压：450V
- Rated current : 1460A　　额定电流：1460A
- Insulation class : F　　绝缘等级：F 级
- Phase : 3PH　　相数：3 相
- IP Grade : IP44　　防护等级：IP44

  2.2 Switchboard   主配电板

- Maker：×××　　制造厂：×××

3. Test procedure for D/G　　主柴发试验程序

  3.1 Insulation resistance measurement: Refer to Table 9-5 （绝缘电阻测量见表 9-5）。

Table 9-5　Insulation resistance measurement

| TABLE 9-5<br>表 9-5 | | HULL No.：<br>船号： | | OWNER：<br>船东： | | CLASS：<br>船级社： | | |
|---|---|---|---|---|---|---|---|---|
| ITEM：DIESEL GENERATOR<br>项目：柴油发电机 | | | | LOCATION：E/R<br>位置：机舱 | | | | |
| KIND OF INSP.: INSULATION RESISTANCE MEASUREMENT<br>检查内容：绝缘电阻测量 | | | | DATE：<br>日期： | | | | |
| No.<br>序号 | DESCRIPTION<br>内容 | No.1 D/G<br>1 号柴油发电机 | | No.2 D/G<br>2 号柴油发电机 | | No.3 D/G<br>3 号柴油发电机 | | REMARK<br>附　注 |
| | | HOT COND.<br>热态 | COLD COND.<br>冷态 | HOT COND.<br>热态 | COLD COND.<br>冷态 | HOT COND.<br>热态 | CLOD COND.<br>冷态 | |
| 1 | STATOR WINDING<br>定子绕组 | | | | | | | |
| 2 | SPACE HEATER<br>空间加热器 | | | | | | | |

3.2 Generator engine safety device test: Refer to Table 9-6（柴油发电机安全装置试验见表9-6）.

**Table 9-6　Generator engine safety device**

| TABLE 9-6 表9-6 | HULL No.: 船号： | | OWNER: 船东： | | CLASS: 船级社： |
|---|---|---|---|---|---|
| ITEM: DIESEL GENERATOR 项目：柴油发电机 | | | LOCATION：E/R 位置：机舱 | | |
| KIND OF INSP.: SAFETY DEVICE TEST 检查内容：柴发安全装置试验 | | | DATE: 日期： | | |

| NO. 序号 | DESCRIPTION 项目内容 | DESIGN VALUE 设定值 | RESULT 试验结果 | | | REMARK 附注 |
|---|---|---|---|---|---|---|
| | | | NO.1 D/G 1号柴油发电机 | NO.2 D/G 2号柴油发电机 | NO.3 D/G 3号柴油发电机 | |
| 1 | SAFETY TRIP 安全停车 | | | | | |
| | OVERSPEED TRIP 超速停车 | 1035rpm | | | | A,D |
| | L.O. PRESSURE LOW TRIP 滑油压力低停车 | 0.2Mpa | | | | A,D |
| | JACKET WATER HIGH TEMP. TRIP 缸套冷却水温度高停车 | 90℃ | | | | A,D |
| 2 | READY TO START 准备启动 | | | | | |
| | TURNING BAR 盘车杆 | | | | | |
| | PRIMING L.O.LOW INLET 预供滑油入口压力低 | | | | | |

Note: 1.　A: Alarm,　　D: Display
　　 1.　A:报警　　　D:显示

　　　　Q.C.　　　　　　　　OWNER　　　　　　　　NK

　　3.2.1 Over speed trip　　超速停车
　　3.2.2 High cooling water temperature alarm and /or trip
　　　　冷却水温度高报警和/或停车
　　3.2.3 L.O low pressure alarm and/or trip　　滑油压力低报警和/或停车
　　3.3 D/G load test and generator operation load test: Refer to Table 9-7（柴发负荷试验和发电机运行试验见表9-7）

**Table 9-7  D/G load test and generator operation load test**

| TABLE9-7 表 9-7 | | HULL No.: 船号: | | OWNER: 船东: | | | CLASS: 船级社: | | |
|---|---|---|---|---|---|---|---|---|---|
| ITEM: NO.1 GENERATOR 项目：1号发电机 | | | | | | LOCATION: E/R 位置：机舱 | | | |
| KIND OF INSP.: LOAD TEST 检查内容：负荷试验 | | | | | | DATE 日期： | | | |
| TIME (MIN) 时间 | | | | 20 | 20 | 20 | 60 | 5 | REMARK 备注 |
| ITEM 项目 | | | | | | | | | |
| LOAD (%)负荷 | | | | 25 | 50 | 75 | 100 | 110 | |
| OUTPUT(kW)功率 | | | | | | | | | |
| VOLTAGE (V)电压 | | | | | | | | | |
| CURRENT( A)电流 | | | | | | | | | |
| FREQUENCY (Hz)频率 | | | | | | | | | |
| WINDING TEMP（℃） 绕组温度 | | | R | | | | | | |
| | | | S | | | | | | |
| | | | T | | | | | | |
| BEARING TEMP（℃） 轴承温度 | | | | | | | | | |

ENGINE ROOM TEMP.:

机舱环境温度：

Note：Measure and record main bearing temperature of engine after 100% load test with the spot thermometer.

注：满负荷后用点温计测量和记录主轴承温度.

The generator load tests are to use water resistance load band and to be done with power factor = 0.8, increase generator load gradually from zero to overload, measure the following relevant data during the test and record them.

用水电阻做发电机负荷试验，功率因数=0.8，从空载到过载逐渐增加发电机负荷，在试验期间测量并记录如下相关数据。

    Alternator：Output (kW), Voltage (V)  发电机负荷：输出功率（kW），电压（V）
    Current (A), Frequency (Hz)  电流（A），频率（Hz）
    Winding temp. per phase (℃)  每相绕组温度(℃)
    Engine: Revolution (R.P.M),  柴油发电机负荷：转数（rpm）
    L.O pressure  滑油压力
    L.O temperature  滑油温度
    Cooling F.W pressure  冷却淡水压力
    Cooling F.W temperature  冷却淡水温度
    Exhaust gas temperature  排气温度
    Other necessary data  其他需要数据

3.4 Load characteristic test: Refer to Table 9-8（负荷特性试验见表 9-8）.

Table 9-8  Load characteristic test

| TABLE9-8 表9-8 | | HULL No.: 船号: | | OWNER: 船东: | | | | CLASS: 船级社: | | | |
|---|---|---|---|---|---|---|---|---|---|---|---|
| ITEM: DIESEL GENERATOR 项目：柴油发电机 | | | | | | LOCATION: E/R 位　置：机舱 | | | | | |
| KIND OF INSP.: LOAD CHARACTERISTIC TEST 检查内容：负荷特性试验 | | | | | | DATE: 日　期： | | | | | |
| | | LOAD(%) 负荷 | 100 | 75 | 50 | 25 | 0 | 25 | 50 | 75 | 100 | REMARK 备注 |
| | | TOTAL/kW 总功率 | 910 | 683 | 455 | 228 | 0 | 228 | 455 | 683 | 910 | |
| | | TIME/MIN 时间 | 10 | 5 | 5 | 5 | 5 | 5 | 5 | 5 | 10 | |
| | | ITEM 项目 | | | | | | | | | | |
| NO.1 D/G 1号柴油发电机 | OUTPUT/kW （输出功率） | | | | | | | | | | | |
| | CURRENT（电流）/A | | | | | | | | | | | |
| | VOLTAGE（电压）/V | | | | | | | | | | | |
| | FREQUENCY（频率）/Hz | | | | | | | | | | | |
| NO.2 D/G 2 | …… | | | | | | | | | | | |
| NO.3 D/G 3 | …… | | | | | | | | | | | |

3.5 Transient voltage regulation test 瞬态电压调节试验

3.6 Governor test 调速器试验

3.7 G/E Starting interlock test　　柴油发电机启动连锁试验

3.8 G/E Starting test 启动试验

4. Test procedure for parallel running test:并车试验程序

4.1 Generator control system 发电机控制系统

4.2 The relevant alarms are to be confirmed during test. Refer to: onboard test list for AMS
在试验期间相关报警应交验。见：监测报警系统船上试验列表。

4.3 Parallel running by manual operation　手动并车

4.4 The auto/manual generator control shall be confirmed by Main switchboard.
在主配电板试验期间交验发电机手动/自动控制。

5. Test procedure for main switchboard 主配电板试验程序

   5.1 Main switchboard protection device test　　主配电板保护装置试验

   　5.1.1 ACB over current trip test (L.T.D 、S.T.D) at ACB test position
   　　　发电机主开关 ACB 过流脱扣试验（长延时、短延时）

   　5.1.2 Preferential trip test at ACB test position　　优先脱扣试验

   　5.1.3 Reverse power trip at ACB actual position　　逆功率脱扣试验

   　5.1.4 Under voltage trip at ACB test position　　电压低脱扣试验

   　5.1.5 Interlocking confirmation　　　　　　　　联锁功能确认

   5.2 Test method:试验方法

Each over current relay of ACB is to be tested with simulate current of secondary circuit of current transformer at the following setting value. In case of preference trip, confirm that the consumers listed in the record page ×××are to be automatically tripped.

每台发电机主开关 ACB 的过流继电器按下述设定值用电流互感器次级电路的模拟电流试验。当优先脱扣时，确认列在第×××页的负载自动脱扣。

1) Under voltage trip    失压脱扣
2) Reverse power trip    逆功率脱扣

5.3 Heavy consumer starter request test    重载询问试验

When the heavy consumer equipment sends starting request to MSB, if the running generator's capacity is not big enough, the stand-by generator will automatically start and automatically synchronizing and in parallel running, automatically load sharing, and then sends out starting available signal; if the running generator's capacity is big enough to start heavy consumer, then MSB sends out starting available signal.

当发出大功率用户启动指令后，运行发电机剩余容量不足以启动大功率用户时，将自动启动备用发电机，备用发电机自动同步、自动并车，自动负荷分配，然后发出大功率用户启动信号，允许启动；若运行发电机剩余容量足够启动大功率用户时，则直接发出大功率用户启动信号，启动大功率电机。

## 【 New Words and Expressions 】

| | | | |
|---|---|---|---|
| rated output | | | 额定输出 |
| power factor | | | 功率因数 |
| insulation class | | | 绝缘等级 |
| insulation resistance | | | 绝缘电阻 |
| IP grade | | | 防护等级 |
| trip | [trɪp] | n.&v. | 跳闸 |
| governor | [ˈgʌvənə(r)] | | 调速器 |
| stator | [ˈsteɪtə] | | 定子 |
| winding | | | 定子绕组 |
| safety trip | | | 安全停车 |
| turning bar | | | 盘车杆 |
| bearing | | | 轴承 |
| L.O PRESSURE | | | 滑油压力 |
| interlock | | | 联锁 |
| exhaust gas temperature | | | 排气温度 |

## PART B    Role Playing

(S-Surveyor, E-Electrician)

S: A dynamic balance test should be carried out to the rotor of the generator. Please carry out the protection tests on board. You should include no-voltage, over-load and reverse power test. Please apply a load trial after the generator is refitted. I shall attend these tests. Please tell me in advance when you are going to carry out the tests.

E:OK.

S:After the over current test, please hand over three copies of the record to the electrical engineer.

E:OK

S:After trial, you must give me five copies of the record.

E:Let's me check up the records.

## 【Task Evaluation】

### (一) Choice

1. _____ should have completed the inspection of mooring test; _____ after the mooring test still need to make effective use of sea trial.

   A. Some equipment, all equipment      B. Some equipment, Some equipment
   C. all equipment, Some equipment      D. all equipment, all equipment

2. What does test procedure for D/G include?

   A. Insulation resistance measurement test
   B. Generator engine safety device test
   C. D/G load test and generator operation load test
   D. A+B+C

3. _____ shall be tested or calibrated on sea trial or in port.

   A. charging and Discharging Boards      B. Navigation and radio equipment
   C. Automation and control equipment      D. B and C

4. AC power sources consist of _____, both of which are AC current producers.

   A. DC generators
   B. motor
   C. shore-power isolation transformers and AC generators
   D. charging & discharging panel

5. What does mooring test item include?

   A. main generator & main switchboard, motor and motor controllers, inavigation, communication and radio system
   B. emergency switchboard
   C. insulation resistance measurement, lighting system,
   D. A+B+C

### (二) Translation

1. Translate new words and expressions into Chinese (Table 9-9).

Table 9-9    Translation

| | |
|---|---|
| 1. insulation resistance measurement | |
| 2. mooring test | |
| 3. sea trial | |
| 4. governor test | |

续表

| | |
|---|---|
| 5.light circuits | |
| 6. parallel running test | |
| 7.megger/meg-ohmmeter | |
| 8.electrical test | |
| 9. Parallel running by manual operation | |
| 10.power factor | |
| 11.Under voltage trip | |
| 12.Reverse power trip | |
| 13.L.O pressure | |
| 14.stator winding | |
| 15.rated voltage | |

A. 功率因数；B. 系泊试验；C. 照明电路；D. 绝缘电阻；E. 额定电压；F. 航行试验；G. 手动并车；H. 兆欧表；I. 失压脱扣；J. 调速器试验；K. 并车试验；L. 逆功率脱扣；M. 滑油压力；N. 电气试验；O. 定子绕组。

2. Translate the following sentences into Chinese.

(1) Maker's shop test

Electric equipment shall be inspected and tested in accordance with the Rule, Regulations, and the Maker's usual practice.

Owner's representative can attend the shop test of main equipment and necessary test records shall be submitted to the Owner as follows:

- Main switchboard
- Emergency switchboard
- Motor starters

(2) On board test

At the completion of installation, the electric equipment shall be inspected and/or tested in accordance with the Rules, Regulations, and under supervision of the Owner's representative.

The inspection and/or tests shall be carried out as follows:

(1) Generator and generator panel

The electric load for generator on board tests shall be of water rheostat (power factor: 1) on the shore.

- Load test;
- Parallel running test (except emergency generator) under actual ship's operation.

The test for shifting the load from one (1) diesel generator to another set shall be carried out and vice versa.

- Protective test;
- Over-current trip;
- Under Voltage trip;

## Unit 9 Marine Electrical Test

- Reverse power trip (except emergency generator) ;
- Preferential trip (except emergency generator) ;
- Insulation resistance test;
- Automatic starting, synchronizing and load sharing;
- Test for main D/G generators;
- Automatic starting test for emergency generator.

(2) Motor

Motor together with their associated control gears and transformers shall be run under normal operating condition to make sure of the performance.

(3) Lighting equipment

On/off test and installation inspection shall be carried out for all lighting equipment, including navigation and signaling lights etc.

(4) Interior communication and nautical equipment

Interior communication test shall be carried out by present operating on board.

Magnetic standard compass shall be compensated at sea trial, and the adjustment certificate issued by the Builder shall be submitted to the vessel.

(5) Radio equipment

To obtain the safety Radio telegraphy certificate, the test and inspection shall be given by the inspection authority in accordance with the requirements of SOLAS.

(6) Insulation resistance

Insulation resistance for feeder circuits shall be measured.

### (三)Speaking Practice

1. Group discussion

Work in groups. Look at the statements in the language bank task. Which of them are important aspects for mooring test? Why?

2. Short talk

Now it is your chance to practice what you have learned from this unit. Put your textbook away and give a short talk on the following topics. You should talk at least one minute. Don't be discouraged if you cannot make it. Review the task and try again. You are sure to do it better next time.
- Alternator Set and Associated Switchboard.
- Lighting System.

3. Role play

Work in groups or pairs and discuss the following topics. Then, you are advised to talk at least three minutes for each topic.
- Prompts: introducing the mooring test.
- Automation System(its function and related equipment).
- Lighting System

### 【 Unit Evaluation 】

The teacher evaluates the students on their performance and mutual evaluation results, the results in Table 9-10.

Marine Electrical Test

Table 9-10  Task Evaluation

| EVALUATION CONTENT | | | DISTRIBUTION SCORE | SCORE |
|---|---|---|---|---|
| Unit 9 Marine Electrical Test | | | | |
| KNOWLEDGE EVALUATION | | | | |
| Ⅰ. Choice | | | 20 | |
| Ⅱ. Translation | 1. Translate new words and expressions into Chinese. | | 20 | |
| | 2. Translate the following sentences into English. | | 20 | |
| TIME: 30' | STUDENT SIGN: | TEACHER SIGN: | TOTAL: | |
| SKILL EVALUATION | | | | |
| Ⅲ. Speaking Practice Role playing | | | 20 20 | |
| TIME: 30' | STUDENT SIGN: | TEACHER SIGN: | TOTAL: | |

# Unit 10

# Lists and Documents for Electrical Engineer's Profession

【Unit Goals】

1. Get to know what the lists and documents for electrical engineer's profession contained. Familiar with the format and the relevant requirements of the lists and documents for electrical engineer's profession.

2. Basic knowledge of the lists and documents for electrical engineer's profession introduction.

## Task 1　Documents for Repairs

【Task goals】

1. Get to know what documents for repairs contained.
2. Familiar with the format and the relevant requirements of documents for repairs.
3. Students can talk about the knowledge about documents for repairs in English to each other fluently.

【Knowledge linking】

What does documents for repairs contain in your mind?
(一) Ship Principal Specifications
SHIP'S NAME:M/V Leizhouhai
L.O.A　　　　　　　213.7m
BREADTH　　　　　32.4m
DEPTH　　　　　　18m
G.R.T　　　　　　　33539.01t
DISPLACEMENT　　26896.31t
DRAFT( FULL): 13.8m
BUILDER: Denmark
DATE OF BUILDING: 1982

Electric Department
1) No.1 Alternator
A. C. 440 V, 60 Hz, 1360 kVA 3 phase
Type:GFV 4632B-8
Serial No. : 80018160 GS1
Manufacturer: FUJI ELECTRIC CO. LTD.
Date of manufacture: 1980. 2

The alternator to be dismounted and transported to workshop and then to be disassembled. <u>The rotor and stator to be cleaned by special cleaner, dried and painted with one coat of insulating paint.</u>[(1)] The slip ring to be machined. All carbon brushes to be renewed. Bearings to be examined and re-newed if any damage to be found (spares to be supplied by ship). The rust on the cooling fan of driving end to be removed and painted with one coat of paint. The alternator to be shifted on board, remounted and recoupled in order. Insulation test to be carried out together with owner and recorder.

<u>At last, running test without load to be carried out for 30 minutes, then 25%, 50%, 75% load running test each for one hour respectively, various records to be handed over to ship in triplicate.</u>[(2)]

2) Switchboard

The following tests to be carried out on the ACB ( main switch) of main switchboard:
① Over load test;
② Low voltage test;
③ Reverse power test.

The above mentioned ACB to be adjusted, if its acting time can't meet the current regulation. The results of the action to be recorded and handed over to ship in triplicate.

The automatic voltage regulator to be examined and repaired as follows:
SCR self-excited constant unit, type: TUR.
Emergency generator, AC 440V, 60 Hz, 75 kW.
The voltage oscillate regularly under any loads.

It produces little effect when adjusting the voltage setting potentiometer. All SCR parameters are normal when tested by owner. To be examined and eliminate the trouble.

Electrical power station automation device (frequency and load regulator, automatic closing device) to be examined and repaired.

(1) When No.1 and No.2 generators running in parallel and the load is stable, the distribution difference of the active power is large ±20% of the generator's rated power. Automatic regulating is invalid. To be examined, and adjusted within ±15% of rated power.

(2) Harbour generator

When it runs at 60% load, the stand-by generator started up automatically. It has been adjusted by ship, but invalid. To be examined and to set the stand-by generator to start up at 80% load of the harbour generator.

(3) Instruments

Following instruments to be examined and adjusted, the records to be handed over to ship in triplicate.
① 4 pcs of voltmeters    AC 440V;
② 3 pcs of ammeters    150 A;

③ 2 pcs of power meters    150 kW;
④ 2 pcs of frequency meters    40~70 Hz;
⑤ 2 pcs of factor meters;
⑥ 2 pcs of synchro indicators.

(4) Electrical Motor and Converter

Motors ( squirrel cage type)

Following electrical motors to be dismounted and transported to workshop, all windings to be cleaned thoroughly, dried and painted with a coat of insulation paint. All bearings to be cleaned, greased, and to be renewed with Yard's spares, if any damage to be found. The motors to be reassembled and shifted on board and remounted in order. <u>The insulation to be tested together with ship's engineer, running test to be carried out, and the records to be handed over to ship in triplicate.</u>[3]

① No. 1 motor of main engine lub, oil pump.

AC 440 V, 60 Hz, 40 kW, 1750 r/min

② No.2 motor of main engine sea water pump.

AC 440 V, 60 Hz, 42 kW, 1755 r/ruin

③ No. 1 motor of M. E. injector cooling pump.

AC 440 V, 60 Hz, 2 kW,1740 r/min

④ No. 2 motor of Aux, engine sea water pump.

AC 440 V, 60 Hz, 4 kW, 1750 r/min

⑤ 1 pc of steering gear hydraulic pump (No.2).

AC 440 V, 60 Hz, 15 kW, 1760 r/min

⑥ No. 1 windlass motor.

AC 440 V, 60 Hz, 40 kW, 1740 r/min

(5) Lighting System

One pc of water-tight lamp above the water-tight door on the boat deck side has been damaged, to be renewed with ship spare.

10 pcs of fluorescent lamps of line No. 4 in accommodation, their insulation resistance have been lower than 0.04 megerohm for a long time. Both the insulation of the lightening equipments and the connection boxes are normal when checked by ship, 15 m of cable to be renewed.

(6) Navigation Light and Mast Light

The following renewed lighting equipment must possess with the certificate confirmed by the register of shipping.

One piece of aft mast navigation lamp to be renewed with Yard's spare.

The mast strong light equipment (220V/400W) on port side of hold No.4 is damaged by corrosion to be renewed. 5 m of cable from power socket to mast house to be renewed. The cable to be laid through iron pipe (Lighting equipment to be supplied by Yard).

If same type of lighting equipment can't be found other types with same power can be replaced.

(7) Control Boxes and Distribution Boxes

The electrical work for a new installation of lub oil purifier is as follows:

① One piece of starter box supplied by ship to be installed. The cable to be connected.

② The cable from power distribution box No.3 to starter box to be laid on original cable guide plate.

The length of cable is about 12m. All the cable and its accessories to be supplied by Yard.

(8) Emergency Power Source

4 groups of batteries of emergency lighting 24V, the solution of battery to be refilled and charged then shifted on board and remounted in order.

(9) Automation and Remote Controls

The blade angle of controllable pitch propeller to be examined and adjusted.

The controllable pitch propeller (C. P. P.) is operated with "follow up" made on the bridge and in the control room.

There is 0.60°~1° of difference between the actual angle and the electro indicating angle.

① To coordinate with repair works, the mechanical drive to be examined and adjusted.

② Relevant feed back potentiometer to be examined and adjusted and to be renewed if any damage to be found (the spare to be supplied by ship).

③ After the whole system has been examined and adjusted the error between the operating order angle and actual angle should be less than 0.3 degree.

Main engine remote control system ( type: DMS990) to be examined and repaired.

① When main engine operates with "remote operation" mode it is not obvious when the engine is beyond critical speed to be examined and adjusted.

② When the operating handle is in "full" position after main engine started the engine is still running at slow speed. We have checked that the regulating air pressure is normal and the servomotor and the regulating system of main engine are normal. To be examined and readjusted by shipyard and eliminate the trouble.

(10) Electrical Heater

Main engine fuel oil heater.

Two groups of heating coil have been burnt to be removed and renewed with Yard's spare.

(11) Alarm System

The alarm of oil mist detector of main engine some times misalarmed. To be examined and the trouble to be eliminated.

10 pcs of cargo hold smoke detectors. The sensor have been damaged to be renewed with Yard's spare.

* An "A" ladder or movable stagings are needed for this work.

(12) Kitchen Electric Utensils

The heater of bread baking oven is damaged to be renewed with ship's spare. The temperature switch is damaged, to be renewed with Yard's spare. Another 2 pcs of temperature switches to be handed over to ship as spare parts.

(13) Other Works

General Notice

① Unless otherwise specified, the shipyard is to furnish the necessary labours, materials and/or equipments to complete every item of repair work.

② All workmanship and material to be of the first class quality and to the satisfaction of the Owner and Classification Society concerned.

③ The tender must cover and include the work herein specified as well as necessary removing transportation: staging and accessory works connected therewith.

## (二) Agreements

### 1. Agreement

This is to confirm that following agreement has been made by and between Shanghai Ocean Shipping Company (hereinafter referred to as the Owner) and Mitsui Engineering & Shipbuilding Co., Ltd. (hereinafter referred to as Mitsui), in respect of Owner's Repair Account to M/V "YUHE" completed on 25th November, 1988 at our Yura Dockyard, as follows.

(1) The Owner's Repair Account have been settled and agreed as follows:

| | |
|---|---|
| Drydocking & Repairs Account | ¥ 13 101 600 |
| Total | ¥ 13 101 600 |
| Special Discount Including | |
| Friend Ship Reduction | ¥ 13 131 600 |
| Balanced Owner's Account | ¥ 9 970 000 |

(2) The above agreed amount shall be paid by the owner to Mitsui within three (3) months after completion of repairs.

Date: 22nd February, 1989

China Ocean Shipping Company          Mitsui Engineering & Shipbuilding
Head Office                                               Co., Ltd. Yura Dockyard

### 2. Agreement of voyage repair works

This agreement is made on between x x x x Shipping. Co. (hereinafter called party A) & ××××Ocean Shipping Voyage Repair Dockyard (hereinafter called party B) in connection with party A's consigning of ship voyage repair engineering, on the basis of friendship and mutual benefits.

(1) <u>Party B should fulfill the voyage repair works which party A consigned and party B received, with high quality and being on schedule.</u>[4] Party B undertakes a guarantee period of 3 months counted from the date on execution of repaired works consigned by party A, party B are bound as soon as possible to repair or replace with new material at their own expense if there is any defects happened on works done, which is due to improper material or careless workmanship or design.

<u>Party A reserve the right to remove the defects by his own means at another shipyard, if party B has no ability to remove defects in due time or in the event of danger to the ship or her cargo or when necessary because of service reason.</u>[5]

(2) Through consultation with and agreed by the two parties, the voyage repair settlement charge should based on the "Price List for Ship Repair" applied from 1 st July 1985 by China National Machinery Import and Export Co. Shanghai Branch, and multiplied by coefficient $K = 0.7$.

(3) After being in receipt of the party B's repair bill, the settlement charge should paid to party B within 15 days.

(4) Each voyage repair settlement charge consists of two parts means first 90% of the above charge being repair charge and second 10% of the above charge being rapid repair reward.

(5) Party B will carry out its job on board during normal working hour unless otherwise agreed by both parties, party B is obliged to reduce transportation and all other accessory costs such as tug boat, floating crane etc. as much as possible.

(6) This agreement comes into force on 1 st Jan. 1986 and is to be extended automatically for the next coming year if no objection is raised by any of the parties concerned.

Each Party has a right to terminate this agreement by notifying to other party in written three months beforehand.

(7) This agreement is made out in English and Chinese each in two originals, one of each for the undersigned parties.

Party A                    Party B
× × × ×                   × × × ×  Ocean
Shipping Co.              Shipping Voyage Repair Dockyard

## (三) Quotation

( No.   )                              Data: 20th November, 1989

Messrs, China Ocean Shipping Co.
    Dalian Branch

Dear Sirs:

In compliance with your kind inquiry for drydocking repair for M. V. …we have pleasure in quoting you as follow:

    Price :                    _____
    Working Period:           _____
    Place of Delivery:        _____
    Terms of Payment:         _____
    Terms of Validity:        _____
    Remarks: For itemized prices see below

Ishikawajima-Harima Heavy Industries Co. Ltd.

Looking forward to receiving your favorable reply, we are

Your very truly

Chief of Ships Repairing Business Section, Nagoya Shipyard

                                                          Signature_____

The sample of Quotation (Table 10-1).

**Table 10-1    Quotation**

| ITEM | QUANTITY | DESCRIPTION | UNIT PRICE | AMOUNT |
|------|----------|-------------|------------|--------|
|      |          |             |            |        |

## (四) Bill

    × × × × × ×  Company

Ship's Name: MV  × × ×

Kind of Works:

Owner's general repairs

Period :

From 15th t0 20th June, 1989

    Furnished all necessary labor, materials and equipment to accomplish all works on the subject vessel in our shipyard, as shown in the attached sheets.

    Total Amount:    Yen 13 500 000—

    Description         Amount

Bill File No. 2424-624-30 ￥ 13 500 000—

(Owner's General Repairs)
The sample of Bill (Table 10-2).

×××× Co, Ltd

Table 10-2  Bill

| ITEM | DESCRIPTION | AMOUNT |
|---|---|---|
| 402 | Electric Department<br>Following motors dismounted from deck, landed and opposite side bearing renewed with ship's supply.<br>1) Air condition motor: 32 kW ×1 set<br>2) Deck vent fan motor: 11 kW 5 sets<br>Bearing No. 6311zz ×8pcs.<br>Bearing No. 6313zz ×2pcs.<br>For the above, fan casings, steel nets and packing dismounted and reinstalled with following materials supplied by ×××.<br>M20×70×100 PCS<br>M8×10×50 PCS | ¥629 300— |
| 403 | Signal light removed, existing foundation modified, new signal light furnished and installed and cables connected, then tested. | ¥124 000— |

### (五) Vouchers

Ship's name _____                Orderer _____
Working _____                    Working period
Working place _____              From _____
Details Works _____              to _____
                                    Service engineering section

I certify that the above mentioned works have been finished.
Date_____    Signature_____

### (六) Claims on guarantee repairs

In the period of our second and third voyages, dating from 5th March t0 2th July, the following defects were found. We claim for guarantee repair.

(1) One coil of main contactor in the control box of the shaft generator was found short-circuit.

(2) On the date of 20th, March we found overheat on the bearing of No. 1 compressor motor and it was stopped at once.

The above-mentioned damage (defects) has ( have) been caused from improper fitting and/or inferior materials used, so that we hold you responsible for making compensation of the same for our Losses (Table 10-3).[6]

Table 10-3  Guarantee repair list

| Ship's Name<br>"YIN HE" | Guarantee Rep. No.<br>101 | Date |
|---|---|---|
| Hull No.<br>204 | Dept.<br>ELECTRIC | |
| Unit    Maker<br>M/E Lub. oil Back pressure<br>Flush Filter | HDW | |
| Defect Report<br>The coil of differential pressure indicator $Ap_1$ was bum out | | |
| Action | | |

1) Stop operation
2) Renew (Table 10-4)

**Table 10-4　Renew**

| Pieces | Spare Parts | Part No. |
|---|---|---|
| 1 | Please supply one new for spare part | |
| Chief Engineer | | Master |
| | Comment HDW | |

### (七) Order list

To:_____Co.                                                    Date:_____

Dear Sirs:

　　Please supply my vessel M. V._____with the following ship's stores ( engine parts) :
1) ××××
2) ××××

　　　　　　　　　　　　　　　　　　　　　　　　Chief Engineer_____
　　　　　　　　　　　　　　　　　　　　　　　　Chief Electrician_____

OR: Please supply my vessel M. V._____with the undermentioned engine parts (electrical appliances) and stores at your earliest convenience.

OR: You are kindly requested to arrange delivery of the undermentioned items, if possible before the 10th inst.

OR: You are kindly requested to arrange for the supply of the following stores prior to our departure at_____( date ) .

OR: Please kindly supply the following engine parts ( electrical appliances) to our vessel M. V_____at_____anchorage.

### (八) Invoice

Original (Table 10-5).

**Table 10-5　Invoice**

　　　　　　　　　　　　　　　　　　　　　　　　　　　　　　　　No.:_____
　　　　　　　　　　　　　　　　　　　　　　　　　　　　　　　　Part :_____
　　　　　　　　　　　　　　　　　　　　　　　　　　　　　　　　Date :_____
　　　　　　　　　　　　　　　　　　　　　　　　　　　　　　　　To_____

| Description & Particulars | Unit | Quantity Supplied | Unit | Amount |
|---|---|---|---|---|
| | | | | |

Total:

　　　　　　　　　　　　　　　　　　　　　　　　　　　　　Received Correct
Note:_____　　　　　　　　　　　　　　　　　　　　　　　Master's
Signature_____

　　　　　　　　　　　　　　　　　　　　　　　Ch/Engineer Signature_____

# Unit 10  Lists and Documents for Electrical Engineer's Profession

## 【New Words And Expressions In Text】

| | | | |
|---|---|---|---|
| breadth | [bredθ] | n. | 船宽 |
| depth | [depθ] | n. | 型深 |
| displacement | [dɪsˈpleɪsmənt] | n. | 排水量 |
| draft | [drɑːft] | n. | 吃水 |
| Denmark | [ˈdenmɑːk] | n. | 丹麦 |
| alternator | [ˈɔːltəneɪtə(r)] | n. | 交流发电机 |
| manufacturer | [ˌmænjuˈfæktʃərə(r)] | n. | 制造厂 |
| dismount | [dɪsˈmaʊnt] | v. | 拆卸 |
| workshop | [ˈwɜːkʃɒp] | n. | 车间 |
| disassemble | [ˌdɪsəˈsembl] | v. | 解体，分解 |
| cleaner | [ˈkliːnə(r)] | n. | 清洁剂 |
| dried | [draɪd] | v. | 烘干 |
| machine | [məˈʃiːn] | v. | 光车 |
| rust | [rʌst] | n. | 铁锈 |
| potentiometer | [pəˌtenʃiˈɒmɪtə(r)] | n. | 电位器 |
| eliminate | [ɪˈlɪmɪneɪt] | v. | 排除 |
| invalid | [ɪnˈvælɪd] | adj. | 无效的 |
| grease | [griːs] | n. | 润滑脂 |
| lub = lubricating | [ˈluːbrɪkeɪtɪŋ] | n. | 润滑 |
| injector | [ɪnˈdʒektə] | n. | 喷油器 |
| aux. = auxiliary | [ɔːgˈzɪliəri] | adj. | 辅助的 |
| corrosion | [kəˈrəʊʒn] | n. | 锈蚀 |
| purifier | [ˈpjʊərɪfaɪə(r)] | n. | 分油机 |
| accessory | [əkˈsesəri] | n. | 属具 |
| relevant | [ˈreləvənt] | adj. | 相应的 |
| critical | [ˈkrɪtɪkl] | adj. | 临界的 |
| servomotor | [ˈsɜːvəʊˈməʊtə] | n. | 伺服电动机 |
| mist | [mɪst] | n. | 雾 |
| sensor | [ˈsensə(r)] | n. | 传感器 |
| ladder | [ˈlædə(r)] | n. | 梯子 |
| staging | [ˈsteɪdʒɪŋ] | n. | 脚手架 |
| labour | [ˈleɪbə(r)] | n. | 劳动力 |
| tender | [ˈtendə(r)] | n. | 报价（投标价） |
| workmanship | [ˈwɜːkmənʃɪp] | n. | 工艺 |
| owner | [ˈəʊnə(r)] | n. | 船东 |
| therewith | [ðeəˈwɪð] | adv. | 与此；随即 |
| principal specification | | | 要素 |
| Leizhouhai | | | "雷州海" |
| L. O. A. = length overall | | | 总长 |

## Task 1 Documents for Repairs

| | |
|---|---|
| G. R. T. = gross weight | 总重 |
| one coat of | 一层，一度 |
| slip ring | 滑环 |
| driving end | 拖动端，原动机侧 |
| on board | 船上 |
| in order | 就绪 |
| running test without load | 空载试验 |
| hand over to ship | 交船 |
| in triplicate | 一式三份 |
| ACB = air circuit breaker | 空气断路器 |
| reverse power test | 逆功率试验 |
| SCR = silicon controlled rectifier | 可控硅 |
| active power | 有功功率 |
| factor meters | 功率因数表 |
| synchro indicator | 同步指示器，同步表 |
| stand-by | 备用 |
| yard's spares | 船厂提供的备件 |
| M. E. = main engine | 主机 |
| aux. Engine | 辅机，发电机，原动机 |
| steering gear | 舵机 |
| register of shipping | 船舶登记局 |
| windlass motor | 卧式锚机 |
| follow up | 随动 |
| mast house | 桅楼 |
| feed back | 反馈 |
| baking oven | 烘箱 |
| classification society | 船级社 |

【Notes】

(1) The rotor and stator to be cleaned by special cleaner, dried and painted with one coat of insulating paint.

转子和定子是用专用清洁剂清洗，烘干，涂上一层绝缘漆。

(2) At last, running test without load to be carried out for 30 minutes, then 25%, 50%, 75% load running test each for one hour respectively, various records to be handed over to ship in triplicate.

最后，无负载运行测试需要 30min，随后分别进行 25%，50%，75%负载运行测试每一个一小时，交付船东各种记录一式三份。

(3) The insulation to be tested together with ship's engineer, running test to be carried out, and the records to be handed over to ship in triplicate.

绝缘与船上的工程师一起进行测试，进行运行试验，并将记录交付船东一式三份。

(4) Party B should fulfill the voyage repair works which party A consigned and party B received, with high quality and being on schedule.

Unit 10　Lists and Documents for Electrical Engineer's Profession

乙方应履行甲方委托乙方接收的船修工程，高质量和按时完成。

(5) Party A reserve the right to remove the defects by his own means at another shipyard, if party B has no ability to remove defects in due time or in the event of danger to the ship or her cargo or when necessary because of service reason.

如果在预定的时间或在对船舶或船上货物有危险情况下或由于服务的必要，乙方没有能力排除故障，甲方有权按照自己的方式在其他船厂排除故障。

(6) The above-mentioned damage (defects) has ( have) been caused from improper fitting and/or inferior materials used, so that we hold you responsible for making compensation of the same for our losses.

上述损坏（故障）是由于装修不当和/或劣质材料的使用造成的，所以我们认为你们应该负责对我们的损失作出同样的补偿。

## 【Task Evaluation】

### （一）Choice

1. The following tests to be carried out on the ACB ( main switch) of main switchboard:①Over load test;②_____;③Reverse power test.

　　A. High voltage test　　　　　　　　B. Under voltage test
　　C. Over voltage test　　　　　　　　D. Low voltage test

2. All windings to be cleaned thoroughly, dried and painted with a coat of _____.

　　A. insulation paint　　B. colorful paint　　C. scarlet paint　　D. black paint

3. After being examined and adjusted, the error of the blade angle of controllable pitch propeller between the operating order angle and actual angle should be less than_____degree.

　　A. 0.1　　　　B. 0.2　　　　C. 0.3　　　　D. 0.4

4. Party A reserve the right to remove the defects by his own means at another shipyard, if party B has no ability to remove defects in due time or in the event of danger to the ship or her cargo or when necessary because of _____.

　　A. materials reason　　　　　　　　B. service reason
　　C. high quality　　　　　　　　　　D. mechanical damage

5. At last, running test _____ to be carried out for 30 minutes, then 25%, 50%, 75% load running test each for one hour respectively, various records to be handed over to ship in triplicate.

　　A. 10% load　　B. full load　　C. half load　　D. without load

### （二）Translation

1. Translate new words and expressions into Chinese (Table 10-6).

Table 10-6　Translation

| | |
|---|---|
| 1.breadth | |
| 2.depth | |
| 3.displacement | |
| 4.draft | |
| 5.manufacturer | |

| | 续表 |
|---|---|
| 6.dismount | |
| 7.disassemble | |
| 8.machine | |
| 9.rust | |
| 10.potentiometer | |
| 11.grease | |
| 12.lub = lubricating | |
| 13.injector | |
| 14.accessory | |
| 15.workmanship | |
| 16.principal specification | |
| 17.L. O. A. =length overall | |
| 18.G. R. T. = gross weight | |
| 19.slip ring | |
| 20.driving end | |
| 21.stand-by | |
| 22.yard's spares | |
| 23.register of shipping | |
| 24.mast house | |
| 25.baking oven | |

A. 桅楼; B. 船舶登记局; C. 船厂提供的备件; D. 总长; E. 要素; F. 工艺; G. 属具; H. 喷油器; I. 润滑; J. 光车; K. 解体，分解; L. 拆卸; M. 吃水; N. 烘箱; O. 制造厂; P. 排水量; Q. 润滑脂; R. 备用; S. 型深; T. 拖动端，原动机侧; U. 滑环; V. 总重; W. 铁锈; X. 船宽; Y. 电位器

2. Translate the following sentences into Chinese.

Following electrical motors to be dismounted and transported to workshop, all windings to be cleaned thoroughly, dried and painted with a coat of insulation paint. All bearings to be cleaned, greased, and to be renewed with Yard's spares, if any damage to be found. The motors to be reassembled and shifted on board and remounted in order. The insulation to be tested together with ship's engineer, running test to be carried out, and the records to be handed over to ship in triplicate.

(三) Speaking Practice

1. Group discussion

Work in groups. Look at the statements in the language bank task. Which of them are important aspects for the lists and documents for electrical engineer's profession? Why?

2. Short talk

Now it is your chance to practice what you have learned from this unit. Put your textbook away and give a short talk on the following topics. You should talk at least one minute. Don't be discouraged if you cannot make it. Review the text and try again. You are sure to do it better next time.

- the ship principle specification
- agreement
- quotation

3. Role play

Work in groups or pairs and discuss the following topics. Then, you are advised to talk at least three minutes for each topic.

- A is a cadet who doesn't know the principles about the lists and documents for electrical engineer's profession. B is an electrician.
- Prompts: Introducing the knowledge about the lists and documents for electrical engineer's profession.
- the lists and documents for electrical engineer's profession (the ship principle specification, agreement, quotation, bill and etc.) .

## Task 2   Certificates, Letters, Telegram & Telex

【 Task goals 】

1. Get to know the knowledge about certificates,letters, telegram & telex.
2. Familiar with the format and the relevant requirements of certificates,letters, telegram & telex.
3. Students can talk about the knowledge about certificates,letters, telegram & telex in English to each other fluently.

【 Knowledge linking 】

How to write certificates,letters, telegram & telex in your mind?

(一) Certificates

**Classification Certificate for Generating Plant**

No._____

Kind of ship_____                    Name of ship_____
Registered number_____
Port of Registry_____              Water in which trading is engaged_____
Ship's Owner_____                   Gross tonnage_____
Capacity of the generating rated voltage_____   Plant_____
                                                                   Rated Current_____

Rated Speed_____
  Number, Type and Capacity of Generator
  Main_____
  Reserve_____

This is to **certify** that the generating plant of the vessel has been surveyed at Shanghai by the Register of CCS on the 1st of Oct. 1988 and found in a good condition satisfying with the requirement of the Rule, the particulars being indicated as above. In consequence of the above stated the generating plant of this vessel is classed "_____".

Task 2 Certificates, Letters, Telegram & Telex

Signature of director of<br>
Register of Shipping of_____<br>
Date_____

## Test Certificate for AC-Motor

We hereby certify that the AC-Motor described in the following was tested by our surveyor.

Date of test <u>June 29th, 1989</u>      Supplier <u>ASEA Brown Boveri Ltd</u>

Quantity <u>1</u>      Serial - No. <u>HM 1004 206</u>

Type <u>AQVY 450/06-183</u>      Type of construction <u>VI</u>

Rated output <u>1300 kW</u>      Operation <u>S2 - 30 min</u>

Rated current <u>286A</u>      Protection <u>IP 23</u>

Rated voltage <u>3300 V</u>      Insulation class <u>F</u>

Speed <u>1183 rpm</u>      Power factor <u>0. 83</u>

Rated frequency <u>60 C/s</u>      Ambient temperature <u>45℃</u>

Connection <u>Star</u>

**Table 10-7　Performance Test and Load Characteristic**

| Item | Current /A | speed /rpm |
|---|---|---|
| Momentary excess torque | 515 | 1160 |
| Rated output | 286 | 1183 |
| 50% load | 149 | 1192 |
| 25% load | 93 | 1196 |
| No-load | 64 | 1200 |

\* Motors for windlasses and steering gears see rules for Electrical Plants

Temperature rises (Table 10-8) after heating test run until the final temperatures are reached.

**Table 10-8　Temperature rises**

| Stator 500℃ | Rotor- |
|---|---|
| Slip rings- | Bearing 32℃/46℃ |

A heating test run was carried out with

    Machine No. <u>HM 1004 206</u> Certificate No.<u>45 321 AB</u>

    Induced over voltage test t0 1.5 times rated voltage

    Test voltage <u>4950 V</u> Duration <u>180s</u>

    Overspeed test t0 1.2 times the max. speed

    Not required for motors with squirrel cage rotors

    High voltage test

    Test voltage <u>7600 V</u> Frequency <u>50 Hz</u> Duration <u>60s</u>

    Insulation resistance <u>>4000 M Ω</u>

Remarks: The heat run test has been carried out by the Two-frequency Method.

Supplier order No. <u>1-266 989-750-29000</u>

Customer's order No._____ Shipyard_____ Perspective use <u>Bow thruster</u> Hull No. <u>COSCO</u>

As a sign of testing the motor was marked as follow

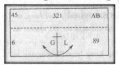

                     Place and Date_____
               Surveyor to Germanische Lloyd_____

## (二) Letter

Dear Sirs,

  MV " x x x "

  We enclosed herewith one copy of our repair account covering the work carried out on the captioned vessel during the period 23rd to 27th November, 1988 as follows:

| Bill No. | Description | Amount |
|---|---|---|
| 0049/12-88 | No. 2 Generator repair | HK & 73 432. 00 |

  We also enclose one photostat signed worklist for your information.

  In accordance with the terms already advised, please arrange settlement of this account within to days from date hereof.

  Any queries concerning this account must be reported to us by letter and/or telex within 30 days of receipt.

  Please arrange payment in Hong Kong Dollars, Our Bankers are ×××××××  Our Account number is ××××.

  We reserve the right to charge interest on overdue amounts in accordance with our standard conditions.

  Thanking you in anticipation.

                           yours faithfully
                           × × × × ×  Ltd.

## (三) Telegram & Telex

### Telegram

TO AB AGENCY HAMBURG

  ETA HAMBURG SRD AUTOPILOT FOUND OUT OF OPERATION TYPE AEG PLS ARRANGE SURVEYOR SHIPYARD ENGINEER ABOARD HAVE IT REPAIRED URGENTLY

### TELEX

| | |
|---|---|
| TO: HANYUAN Technical Service Center | TELEFAX: |
| ATTN: Mr. × × × | 040/310753 |
| FM: CONFM, COSCO SHANGHAI | Our REF. No. |
| | 54389884 |

Dear Sirs,

                       Ref.: MV "Xing Hai He" SG system

  The Fax writer by Mr. Mersmann, Siemens, and transfered from your company had been received. We fully understand the point of view on rehabilitation of the operation of the SG system on captioned vessel.

Task 2  Certificates, Letters, Telegram & Telex

Firstly, we should mention that the vessel was taken from "Hong Kong Island" company in March 1989, the SG system can be operation but not so satisfactory until September 1989 caused by short circuit due to pollution of inside busbars by suction of oily air.

Of course, first of all, we should order spare parts and the Maker, Siemens, have the responsibility to supply the spare parts that owner needed. <u>Our philosophy is that we try to do our best to find what is the real reason to disturb the system and get a correct way or direction to solve the existing problem.</u>[(1)] Therefore we have organized our engineer to take installation, measuring and commissioning the whole system at the beginning of February, 1990 in order to sweep off some unimportant point and make our own experience on operation, finally may leave some difficulty point to asking Siemens engineer to come on board to save money and time.

<u>Would you please understand our situation and we believe the good relationship between Siemens and COSCO, they will give us full support.</u>[(2)] The firm order we have given for three months please urge Siemens and we are eagerly waiting for the reply.

Best Regards.

Jan 8, 1990

Signature _____

## (四) Telegram & Telex Abbreviations in Common Use (Table 10-9)

**Table 10-9  Telegram & Telex Abbreviations**

| | | |
|---|---|---|
| ABSOLLAT | ABSOLUTE LATEST | 最迟 |
| ABT | ABOUT | 大约 |
| A/C | ACCOUNT | 账 |
| ACDG | ACCORDING | 按照 |
| ACDGLY | ACCORDINGLY | 照着办，相应地 |
| ACK | ACKNOWLEDGE | 已告和收到 |
| ACPT | ACCEPT | 接受，认可 |
| ACPTBL | ACCEPTABLE | 可接受的 |
| ADDTL | ADDITIONAL | 附加的，另外的 |
| ADIF | ADVICE IF | 如果……请即告知 |
| ADV | ADVICE | 通知 |
| AFT | AFTER | 以后 |
| AGN | AGAIN | 再，又 |
| AGR | AGREE | 同意，赞同 |
| AGRT | AGREEMENT | 同意，协议 |
| AIRG | AIRING | 航寄 |
| ALDY | ALREADY | 已经 |
| AMND | AMEND | 修改 |
| APPLIC | APPLICATION | 申请书，申报单 |
| APPREC | APPRECIATE | 欣赏，意识到 |
| ARRNG | ARRANGE | 安排 |
| APPROX | APPROXIMATELY | 大约，接近于 |
| ARRV | ARRIVE | 到达 |
| ASAP | AS SOON AS POSSIBLE | 尽快 |
| ATTN | ATTENTION | 注意 |

## Unit 10  Lists and Documents for Electrical Engineer's Profession

续表

| | | |
|---|---|---|
| AVGE | AVERAGE | 平均 |
| BCAUS | BECAUSE | 因为 |
| BEF | BEFORE | 以前 |
| BEGG | BEGINNING | 开始 |
| BTWN | BETWEEN | 在……中间 |
| BYRETLX | BY RETURN TLX | 电传答复 |
| CERT | CERTIFICATE | 证书 |
| CFM | CONFIRM | 确认 |
| CNCL | CANCEL | 取消 |
| CONC | CONCERNNING | 关于 |
| COOP | COOPERATION | 合作 |
| CUD | COULD | 能够 |
| DD | DATED | 注有日期的 |
| DECI | DECISION | 决定 |
| DELY | DELIVERY | 交货 |
| DEPT | DEPARTMENT | 部门 |
| DESP | DESPATCH | 发送，派遣 |
| DIRTLY | DIRECTLY | 直接地 |
| DISC | DISCUSS | 商议 |
| DPT | DEPATURE | 开航 |
| DTL | DETAIL | 细节 |
| ENQRY | ENQUIRY | 询问，询价 |
| ERLY | EARLY | 早的 |
| ETA | ESTIMATED TIME OF ARRIVAL | 估计到达时间 |
| ETD | ESTIMATED TIME OF DEPARTURE | 估计开航时间 |
| EXCLDG | EXCLUDING | 把……除外 |
| EXPLN | EXPLAIN | 解释 |
| FLT | FLIGHT | 航班 |
| FLW | FOLLOW | 跟随 |
| FM | FROM | 从 |
| FURTHM | FURTHERMORE | 此外 |
| FYI | FOR YOUR INFORMATION | 供你方参考 |
| GUAR | GUARANTEE | 担保 |
| HV | HAVE | 有 |
| HWEVR | HOWEVER | 无论如何 |
| IMMDLY | IMMEDIATELY | 立即 |
| IMPS | IMPOSSIBLE | 不可能 |
| INCL | INCLUDING | 包括 |
| INF | INFORM | 通知 |
| INSPTN | INSPECTION | 检验 |
| LAT | LATEST | 最迟 |
| MAX | MAXIMUM | 最大的 |
| MFR | MANUFACTURE | 制造 |
| MID | MIDDLE | 中间 |
| MIN | MINIMUM | 最小的 |

续表

| | | | |
|---|---|---|---|
| MKR | MAKER | | 制造者 |
| MSG | MESSAGE | | 信息 |
| N | AND | | 和 |
| NCRY | NECESSARY | | 必要的 |
| NEGO | NEGOTIATE | | 谈判 |
| NIG | NOTHING | | 没有东西 |
| N.O.S | NOT OTHERWISE SPECIFIED | | 未另列明的 |
| NTD | NOTED | | 已注意到 |
| O/A | OUR ACCOUNT | | 由我方支付 |
| OBT | OBTAIN | | 获得 |
| O.K. | ALL RIGHT | | 行，好 |
| OL | OUR LETTER | | 我方信件 |
| OPT | OPTION | | 选择 |
| ORIG | ORIGINAL | | 正本 |
| OT | OUR TELEGRAM | | 我方电报 |
| OTHWS | OTHERWISE | | 否则 |
| PAYMT | PAYMENT | | 付款 |
| PKG | PACKAGE | | 件 |
| PLS | PLEASE | | 请 |
| POSS | POSSIBLE | | 可能的 |
| PREP | PREPARE | | 准备 |
| PREV | PREVIOUS | | 以前的 |
| PROB | PROBABLE | | 大概的 |
| QLTY | QUALITY | | 质量 |
| QNTY | QUANTITY | | 数量 |
| QSTN | QUESTION | | 问题 |
| RCV | RECEIVE | | 收到 |
| RDY | READY | | 准备好 |
| REF | REFERENCE | | 参考 |
| REP | REPLY | | 回答 |
| REPR | REPRESENTATIVE | | 代表 |
| REQR | REQUIRE | | 需要 |
| RESPLY | RESPECTIVELY | | 各自的 |
| RESV | RESERVE | | 保留 |
| RGDS | REGARDS | | 关于，敬意 |
| RVT | REVERT | | 再洽 |
| RYL | REFER TO YOUR LETTER | | 请参阅你方的信件 |
| RYTLX | REFER TO YOUR TELEX | | 请参阅你方的电传 |
| SCHED | SCHEDULED | | 排定的 |
| SEAFRT | SEA FREIGHT | | 海运运费 |
| SEP | SEPARATE | | 个别的，分离的 |
| SHPD | SHIPPED | | 已装运 |
| SHUD | SHOULD | | 就，万一，必须 |
| SMPL | SAMPLE | | 样品 |
| SORI | SORRY | | 对不起 |

*157*

续表

| STP | STOP | 停 |
|---|---|---|
| SUGG | SUGGEST | 建议 |
| SUPP | SUPPLY | 提供 |
| TEL | TELEGRAPH | 电报发送 |
| TEMP | TEMPORARY | 暂时的 |
| TGM | TELEGRAM | 电报 |
| THFOR | THEREFORE | 因此 |
| THRU | THROUGH | 通过 |
| TKS | THANKS | 感谢 |
| TLX | TELEX | 电传 |
| TOC | TOGETHER | 共同 |
| TTL | TOTAL | 总额，总的 |
| U | YOU | 你 |
| UNACPTBL | UNACCEPTABLE | 不能接受的 |
| UNRCVD | UNRECEIVED | 未收到 |
| UOS | UNLESS OTHERWISE | 除非另有说明 |
| UR | YOUR | 你的 |
| URGT | URGENT | 紧急的 |
| VSL | VESSEL | 船 |
| VVVVV | NO OUTGOING CIRCUIT | 无外线 |
| W | WITH | 和……一起 |
| WL | WILL | 将，就会 |
| W/O | WITHOUT | 没有 |
| WT | WEIGHT | 重量 |
| WDU | WOULD | 将 |
| YC | YOUR CABLE | 你方电报 |
| YL | YOUR LETER | 你方来信 |
| YTLX | YOUR TELEX | 你方电传 |
| ZSWK | THIS WEEK | 本周 |

## 【New Words And Expressions】

| | | | |
|---|---|---|---|
| certificate | [səˈtɪfɪkət] | n. | 证明书；文凭 |
| classification | [ˌklæsɪfɪˈkeɪʃn] | n. | 分类；分级；类别 |
| connection | [kəˈnekʃn] | n. | 连接；联系，关系；连接点 |
| torque | [tɔːk] | n. | （尤指机器的）扭转力；转（力） |
| overdue | [ˌəʊvəˈdjuː] | adj. | 过期的；延误的，迟到的；未兑的； |
| amount | [əˈmaunts] | n. | 总额；金额 |
| rated voltage | | | 额定电压 |
| insulation class | | | 绝缘种类[等级] |
| power factor | | | 功率因数 |
| rated frequency | | | 额定频率 |
| ambient temperature | | | 环境温度；背景温度；周围温度 |

## 【Notes】

(1) Our philosophy is that we try to do our best to find what is the real reason to disturb the system and get a correct way or direction to solve the existing problem.

我们的理念是，我们尽力找到妨碍系统的真正原因并得到一个解决现有问题正确的方法或方向。

(2) Would you please understand our situation and we believe the good relationship between Siemens and COSCO, they will give us full support.

你能理解我们的处境，并且我们相信西门子和中远关系很好，他们会给我们充分的支持。

## 【Task Evaluation】

### (一) Choice

1. We should order spare parts and the Maker, Siemens, have the responsibility to supply the spare parts that _____ needed.
   A. company      B. maker      C. owner      D. manufacturer
2. The abbreviation of "NO OUTGOING CIRCUIT" is _____.
   A. VVVVV       B. VSL         C. URGT       D. UR
3. The abbreviation of "REFER TO YOUR LETTER" is _____.
   A. RGDS        B. RVT         C. RYL        D. RYTLX
4. The abbreviation of "PREPARE" is _____.
   A. POSS        B. PREP        C. PREV       D. PROB
5. The abbreviation of "ACCORDING" is _____.
   A. ACDG        B. ACDGLY      C. ACK        D. ACPT

### (二) Translation

1. Translate new words and expressions into Chinese (Table 10-10).

**Table 10-10   Translation**

| | |
|---|---|
| 1. certificate | |
| 2. classification | |
| 3. connection | |
| 4. torque | |
| 5. overdue | |
| 6. amount | |
| 7. rated voltage | |
| 8. insulation class | |
| 9. power factor | |
| 10. rated frequency | |
| 11. ambient temperature | |

A. 功率因数；B. 额定频率；C. 额定电压；D. 绝缘种类[等级]；E. 总额,金额；F. 过期的,延误的,迟到的,未兑的；G. 分类,分级,类别；H. 连接,联系,关系,连接点；I. 证明书,文凭；J.（尤指机器的）扭转力；K. 环境温度,背景温度,周围温度。

2. Translate the following sentences into Chinese.

Lists and Documents for Electrical Engineer's Profession

Of course, first of all, we should order spare parts and the Maker, Siemens, have the responsibility to supply the spare parts that owner needed. Our philosophy is that we try to do our best to find what is the real reason to disturb the system and get a correct way or direction to solve the existing problem. Therefore we have organized our engineer to take installation, measuring and commissioning the whole system at the beginning of February, 1990 in order to sweep off some unimportant point and make our own experience on operation, finally may leave some difficulty point to asking Siemens engineer to come on board to save money and time.

### (三) Speaking Practice

1. Group discussion

Work in groups. Look at the statements in the language bank task. Which of them are important aspects for certificates, letters, telegram & telex? Why?

2. Short talk

Now it is your chance to practice what you have learned from this unit. Put your textbook away and give a short talk on the following topics. You should talk at least one minute. Don't be discouraged if you cannot make it. Review the text and try again. You are sure to do it better next time.

- certificates.
- letters.
- telegram.
- telex.

3. Role play

Work in groups or pairs and discuss the following topics. Then, you are advised to talk at least three minutes for each topic.

- A is a cadet who doesn't know the principles about certificates, letters, telegram & telex.

  B is an electrician.
- Prompts: Introducing the knowledge about certificates, letters, telegram & telex.
- the lists and documents for electrical engineer's profession (certificates, letters, telegram & telex).

## Task 3   Business Writing Relating to Electro-technical Officer

### 【Task Goals】

1. Get to know the knowledge about business writing relating to electro-technical officer.

2. Familiar with the format and the relevant requirements of business writing relating to electro-technical officer.

3. Students can talk about the knowledge about business writing relating to electro-technical officer in English to each other fluently.

## Task 3  Business Writing Relating to Electro-technical Officer

【 Knowledge linking 】

How to write business writing relating to electro-technical officer in your mind?

### (一) Requests for repair

Attention: Technique Department
Carbon copy: (shipowner)
Subject: Application for Technician
July 10 , 2010

Dear Sir,

　　Please be advised that my weather facsimile machine broke down and needs repair. I would be much appreciated if you could arrange for a technician to come on board for repair as soon as we arrive Singapore. My latest ETA is 1500hrs 12th July.
　　Thanks for your attention.

Truly yours,

_____
Master of M. V. "××"


ATTN: TECH DEPT
CC: (shipowner)
SUBJ: APLCTN FOR. TECH
JUL 10, 2010

DEAR SIR,
　　PLS BE ADVD THAT MY WX FAX BROKE N NEEDS REPAIR. I'D BE MUCH APPRECIATED IF U CLD ARRG A TECH ON BOARD FOR REPAIR AS WE ARR SIN. MY ETA 121500HRS JUL.
　　TKS FOR ATTN.

TRULY YOURS,

_____
MASTER/M. V. "×××"


### (二) Order for spare parts

Attention: Sales Department
Carbon copy: (shipowner/charterer)
Subject: Spare Parts
July 11, 2010
Dear Sir,

161

Lists and Documents for Electrical Engineer's Profession

  I have the honor to inform you that we would like to place an order for a certain number of spare parts from your shipyard.[1] Enclosing herewith is a copy of spare parts list. If possible, please deliver the order on board at SINGAPORE. Our ETA/ETD are 1500hrs 12th/2100hrs 14th July. If some parts are not available, could you kind to manage and send them to our next port of call PORT KELANG, Malaysia by air? All the expenses will be for charterer's account.

  Your immediate attention and early reply will be appreciated.

Truly yours,


———————————
Chief Engineer of M. V. ×××

ATTN: SALES DEPT
CC : ( shipowner/char)
SUBJ: SPARE PARTS
JULY 11, 2010

DEAR SIR,
  I V THE HONOR TO IFM U THAT WE D LIKE TO OD SPARE PTS FM UR SPYD. ENCL IS THE LIST. IF PSBL, PLS DEL THE OD ON BOARD AT SIN. OUR ETA/ETD 121500/142100. IF SOME PTS U/A, CLD U MNGE N SD THEM TO NXT PORT OF CALL PORT KELANG, MSIA BY AIR? ALL EXP WL BE FOR CHAR'S ACCT.
  UR IMD ATTN N ELY RE WL BE APPRECIATED.

TRULY YOURS,


———————————
C/E, M. V. ×××

  (三) **Reports on damages & repairs**
Attention: Technique Department
Carbon copy: (shipowner)
Subject: Gyrocompass Repeater Trouble
July 12, 2010

Dear Sir,
  My master gyrocompass is all right, but port and starboard side repeaters follow incorrectly. Would you please arrange for a specialist boarding to fix the problem before departure? My ETD is 2100hrs 14th, July.

Thanks for your kind cooperation.

Best regards

Truly yours,

_____
Master of M. V. "×××"

ATTN: TECH DEPT
CC: (shipowner)
SUBJ: GYRO RPTR TROUBLE
JUL 12, 2010

DEAR SIR,
　　MY GYRO OK, BUT P&S REPEATERS FLW INCORRECTLY. WD U PLS ARRG A SP BOARDG TO FIX PB B4 DEP? ETD 142100HRS.

TKS FOR UR KIND COOP

B RGDS,

TRULY YOURS,

_____
MASTER,　M. V. "×××"

**(四) Application for assistant**
Attention: Agent
Carbon copy: ( shipowner/charterer)
Subject: Application for Shore Assistant
July 13, 2010

Dear Sirs,
　　<u>Please kindly arrange for shore gang to move my engine room heavy supplies during stay at port as soon as possible. All expenses incurred will be for charterer's account.</u>[2]
　　Thank you in anticipation for your early attention.

Regards.

Truly yours,

_____

Lists and Documents for Electrical Engineer's Profession

Captain ×××

ATTN: AGT
CC : ( shipowner/chat)
SUBJ: APLCTN FOR SHORE ASST
JUL 13, 2010

DEAR SIRS,
 PLS ARRG SHR GANG TO MV MY ENG-RM HV SPLY DURG STAY AT PT ASAP. ALL EXP INCURD WL BE FOR CHAT'S ACCT.
 TKS FOR UR ELY ATTN.

RGDS,

TRULY YOURS,

_____
CAPT ×××

## 【New Words And Expressions In Text】

| | | | |
|---|---|---|---|
| shipowner | [ˈʃɪpəʊnə(r)] | n. | 船东 |
| technician | [tekˈnɪʃn] | n. | 修理技师 |
| charterer | [ˈtʃɑːtərə] | n. | 租船人 |
| port | [pɔːt] | n. | 左舷 |
| starboard | [ˈstɑːbəd] | n. | 右舷 |
| incur | [ɪnˈkɜː(r)] | v. | 招致，引起 |
| break down | | | 故障 |
| ETA ( Estimated Time of Arrival) | | | 预计到达时间 |
| M. V. (Motor Vessel) | | | 机动船 |
| spare part | | | 备件 |
| ETD ( Estimated Time of Departure) | | | 预计离港时间 |

## 【Notes】

(1) I have the honor to inform you that we would like to place an order for a certain number of spare parts from your shipyard.
我荣幸地通知您，我们想从你们的船厂订购一定数量的备件。

(2) Please kindly arrange for shore gang to move my engine room heavy supplies during stay at port as soon as possible. All expenses incurred will be for charterer's account.
船舶在港期间请尽快安排码头港转移我轮机舱的重负荷。一切费用由承租人承担。

## Task 3　Business Writing Relating to Electro-technical Officer

【Task Implement】

### PART A　　Reading Practice

#### The Procedure of Arranging for the Ship's Repair

The arrangement of ship's repair is a bottom up and top down procedure. Actually, the ship will arrange personnel to check for needed repairs themselves. All items to be repaired will be lodged in the repair list. The document will be sent to the shipping company. The shipping company will confirm the items.[(1)] They may add or cut down some items in accordance with the budget. Officers in charge of the ship's repair will offer and negotiate with the shipyard. They may discuss the prices of the repair, quality or standard of the repair, time or period of the repair, and other issues. As soon as they have made agreements, they will sign a contract. The contract will be returned to the shipping company. The company will arrange the cargo plan in order to guarantee that the ship being repaired will sail to the shipyard in a designated period of time.[(2)] Before the repair, engineers from the shipyard will come on board to check all things to be repaired. They may arrange gangs of workers to meet the repair items. All crew members must be responsible for monitoring working conditions, quality of repair, safety measures on the spot. If any unsafe measures or substandard repairs has been found, the message will be collected and the shipmaster will consult with the engineers from the shipyard immediately. The engineers from shipyard will correct their repair to meet the standard. Upon completion of the repair, staffs from the shipping company and crew members will check the repair work thoroughly. The ship is only maneuvered to depart from the shipyard with satisfactory repair. As a general rule, the crew members will continue to observe the working conditions of the ship until half a year has past.

【New Words and Expressions】

| | | | |
|---|---|---|---|
| procedure | [prəˈsiːdʒə(r)] | n. | 程序，手续；工序，过程，步骤 |
| budget | [ˈbʌdʒɪt] | n. | 预算；预算案 |
| negotiate | [nɪˈɡəʊʃɪeɪt] | vi. | 谈判，协商，交涉 |
| contract | [ˈkɒntrækt] | n. | 契约；婚约 |
| maneuver | [məˈnuːvə] | vt. | 操纵 |
| substandard | [ˌsʌbˈstændəd] | adj. | 不够标准的，低等级标准 |
| crew member | [kruː ˈmembə] | | 队员 |
| in accordance with | [in əˈkɔːdəns wið] | | 与……一致，依照 |

【Notes】

(1) The document will be sent to the shipping company. The shipping company will confirm the items.
该文件将被发送到船舶公司。船舶公司将确认项目。

(2) The company will arrange the cargo plan in order to guarantee that the ship being repaired will sail to the shipyard in a designated period of time.
为了保证在指定的时间内，船舶航行到船厂修理，公司将安排货物运输计划。

Unit 10  Lists and Documents for Electrical Engineer's Profession

## PART B  Role Playing

(A: cadet who comes on board for the first time; B: captain)

A: How often will a vessel be repaired?

B: It may match up to the ship's survey and it may be dependent upon the ship's condition. In general, every five years, the ship will be executed for renewal of it's certificates. The ship's surveyors from the classification society will board the ship. They may give the shipowner's recommendations. To combine with the running problems of the ship, the shipowner will consider the major repair arrangement for the ship. So, the ship may possibly perform a docking repair within 5 years. For two voyage repairs, it is within an 18 month interval.

A: What kinds of repair classes for machinery are there?

B: Many types, such as small scale, middle scale or large scale depending upon the size of the work. On the other hand, it may include standard work or periodical repair work.

A: What kinds of repair classes for machinery are there?

B: Many types, such as small scale, middle scale or large scale depending upon the size of the work. On the other hand, it may include standard work or periodical repair work.

A: Why must we check the facilities periodically?

B: The reliability of the facilities and wearability of all components can be checked via a periodical check. The wear and tear condition of components and technical conditions of machinery, electrical parts, and lubricating systems can be examined for preventing danger and accidents as well.

A: What is the repair list? What should be borne in mind when writing a repair list?

B: The repair list is a combination of repair items from the checklist. A standard item of repair includes: coded numbers for the item, names of the place, damage description, repair standard or requirement of repair, and so on. In general, all facilities and equipment belonging to the deck department management are in one group, whereas those belonging to the engine department managements are in another group. When writing a repair list, it is necessary to write symptoms and requirement of repairs in more detail. In addition, the repair items shall be checked again and again. This is to ensure that the important items are ensured to be included.

## 【Task Evaluation】

(一) Choice

1. The repair list is a combination of repair items from the ＿＿＿＿.
   A. repair columns          B. building list
   C. check items             D. repair items

2. What kinds of repair classes for machinery are there? Many types, such as small scale, middle scale or large scale depending upon the ＿＿＿＿of the work.
   A. big         B. depth         C. size         D. scale

3. How often will a vessel be repaired? It may match up to the ship's survey and it may be dependent upon the ship's condition. In general, every ＿＿＿＿ years.
   A. five        B. four          C. three        D. two

## Task 3  Business Writing Relating to Electro-technical Officer

4. As a general rule, the crew members will continue to observe the working conditions of the ship until _____ has past.

A. two years          B. one and half a year
C. half a year        D. a year

5. The document will be sent to the shipping company. The shipping company will confirm the items. They may add or cut down some items in accordance with the _____.

A. list      B. budget      C. price      D. usual

### (二) Translation

1. Translate new words and expressions into Chinese (Table 10-11).

**Table 10-11  Translation**

| | |
|---|---|
| 1. shipowner | |
| 2. technician | |
| 3. port | |
| 4. starboard | |
| 5. break down | |
| 6. ETA ( Estimated Time of Arrival) | |
| 7. M. V. (Motor Vessel) | |
| 8. spare part | |
| 9. ETD ( Estimated Time of Departure) | |
| 10. budget | |
| 11. negotiate | |
| 12. contract | |
| 13. maneuver | |
| 14. substandard | |
| 15. crew member | |
| 16. in accordance with | |

A. 谈判，协商，交涉；B. 契约；婚约；C. 操纵；D. 队员；E. 不够标准的，低等级标准；F. 右舷；G. 船东；H. 左舷；I. 修理技师；J. 预计到达时间；K. 预算；预算案；L. 预计离港时间；M. 备件；N. 机动船；O. 故障；P. 与……一致，依照。

2. Translate the following sentences into Chinese.

Before the repair, engineers from the shipyard will come on board to check all things to be repaired. They may arrange gangs of workers to meet the repair items. All crew members must be responsible for monitoring working conditions, quality of repair, safety measures on the spot. If any unsafe measures or substandard repairs has been found, the message will be collected and the shipmaster will consult with the engineers from the shipyard immediately. The engineers from shipyard will correct their repair to meet the standard. Upon completion of the repair, staffs from the shipping company and crew members will check the repair work thoroughly. The ship is only

Unit 10  Lists and Documents for Electrical Engineer's Profession

maneuvered to depart from the shipyard with satisfactory repair. As a general rule, the crew members will continue to observe the working conditions of the ship until half a year has past.

(三) Speaking Practice

1. Group discussion

Work in groups. Look at the statements in the language bank task. Which of them are important aspects for business writing relating to electro-technical officer? Why?

2. Short talk

Now it is your chance to practice what you have learned from this unit. Put your textbook away and give a short talk on the following topics. You should talk at least one minute. Don't be discouraged if you cannot make it. Review the text and try again. You are sure to do it better next time.

- requests for repair.
- order for spare parts.
- reports on damages & repairs.
- application for assistant.

3. Role play

Work in groups or pairs and discuss the following topics. Then, you are advised to talk at least three minutes for each topic.

- A is a cadet who doesn't know the principles about business writing relating to electro-technical officer.

B is an electrician.

- Prompts: Introducing the knowledge about business writing relating to electro-technical officer.
- business writing relating to electro-technical officer (requests for repair; order for spare parts; reports on damages & repairs; application for assistant).

【 Unit Evaluation 】

The teacher evaluates the students on their performance and mutual evaluation results, the results in Table 10-12.

Table 10-12  Unit Evaluation

| EVALUATION CONTENT | | | DISTRIBUTION SCORE | SCORE |
|---|---|---|---|---|
| Unit 10 Lists and Documents for Electrical Engineer's Profession<br>Task1 Documents for Repairs (30%)<br>Task2 Certificates,Letters,Telegram & Telex(30%)<br>Task3 Business Writing Relating to Electro-technical Officer(40%) | | | | |
| KNOWLEDGE EVALUATION | | | | |
| Ⅰ. Choice | | | 20 | |
| Ⅱ.Translation | 1.Translate new words and expressions into Chinese. | | 20 | |
| | 2.Translate the following sentences into English. | | 20 | |
| TIME: 30' | STUDENT SIGN: | TEACHER SIGN: | TOTAL: | |
| SKILL EVALUATION | | | | |
| Ⅲ. Speaking Practice<br>Role playing | | | 20<br>20 | |
| TIME: 30' | STUDENT SIGN: | TEACHER SIGN: | TOTAL: | |

# Practical Training 1

【Training Goals】

1. Practice some terms talking about marine power system, communication and navigation equipment etc.
2. Practice the expressions about main marine electrical equipment.

【Training Content】

## Marine Electrical Equipment

**1. 电力推进装置及配套设备和辅助电气设备**

电力推进装置为推进装置服务的配套设备和对船舶安全必不可少的辅助电气设备。

Electrical propelling machinery associated equipment together with auxiliary services essential for the safety of the ship

**(1) 电力推进装置及配套设备**

| | |
|---|---|
| 动力系统 Power system | 应急蓄电池组 Emergency accumulator battery |
| 电动机 Motor | 重要用途电气设备 Electrical equipment for essential services |
| 变压机 Transformer | 照明系统 Lighting system |
| 蓄电池 Battery | 主照明系统 Main lighting system |
| 电力设备 Electrical power equipment | 应急照明系统 Emergency lighting system |
| 电子设备 Electronic equipment | 临时应急照明系统 Temporary emergency lighting system |
| 馈电线 Feeder | 船内通信系统 Internal communication system |
| 区配电板 Section board | 广播系统 Command broadcasting system |
| 分配电板 Distribution board | 传令钟系统 Telegraph system |
| 电缆 Cable | 电话系统 Commanding telephone system |
| 断路器 Breaker | 轮机员呼叫系统 Engineer's alarm system |
| 熔断器 Fuse | 船内报警系统 Internal alarm system |
| 电力设备 Electrical power equipment | 探火和失火报警系统 Fire detection and fire alarm systems |
| 主发电机 Main generator | 灭火剂施放预告报警 Pre-warnings for the release of extinguishing media |
| 应急发电机 Emergency generator | 通用应急报警系统 General emergency alarm system |
| 主配电板 Main switchboard | 水密门关闭报警 Watertight doors closing alarm |
| 应急配电板 Emergency switchboard | |
| 应急蓄电池充放电板 Emergency accumulator battery charging and discharging board | |

## (2) 重要用途电气设备 Electrical equipment for essential services

| | |
|---|---|
| 空压机 Air compressor | 舱底泵 Bilge pump |
| 空气泵 Air pump | 冷藏机械 Refrigerating machinery |
| 循环和冷却水泵 Circulating and cooling water pump | 机炉舱通风机 Ventilating fans for engine and boiler rooms |
| 油头冷却泵 Fuel valve cooling pump | 锅炉强迫通风机 Fans for forced draught to boilers |
| 滑油泵 Lubricating oil pump | 自动喷水系统 Automatic water sprinkler system |
| 冷凝器循环泵 Condenser circulating pump | 压力水雾灭火系统 Water-spraying fire-extinguishing system |
| 抽吸泵 Extraction pump | 探火和失火报警系统 Fire detection and fire alarm system |
| 增压风机 Scavenge blower | |
| 分油机 Oil separator | 法定航行设备 Navigational aids (required by statutory regulations) |
| 燃油泵 Oil fuel pump | |
| 燃油燃烧装置 Oil fuel burning unit | 法定通信设备 Communication equipment (required by statutory regulations) |
| 给水泵 Feed water pump | |
| 舵机 Steering gear | 航行灯 Navigation light |
| 锚机 Windlass | 特殊用途灯 Special purpose lights |
| 消防泵 Fire pump | |

## 2. 无线电设备 Radio Equipment

| | |
|---|---|
| 无线电台 Radio station | 窄带印字电报 NBDP radiotelegraphy (narrow band direct printing radiotelegraphy) |
| 无线电台（救生艇手提式） Radio apparatus | 高频窄带印字电报 HF NBDP radiotelegraphy |
| **无线电通信设备 Equipment for radio communication** | 直接印字电报 Direct-printing radiotelegraphy |
| 无线电装置 Radio installation | 航行警告电传接收机 NAVTEX receiver |
| 甚高频无线电装置 VHF radio installation (very high frequency radio installation) | 加强群呼接收机 EGC receiver |
| 中频无线电装置 MF radio installation (medium frequency radio installation) | 高频直接印字无线电报接收机 HF direct-printing radiotelegraphy receiver |
| 中/高频无线电装置 MF/HF radio installation (medium/high frequency radio installation) | 船用雷达应答器 Ship's radar transponder |
| 国际海事卫星组织船舶地面站 INMARSAT SES (International Maritime Satellite Organization ship earth station) | **无线电导航设备 Radio navigational equipment** |
| | 雷达 Radar |
| | 环视雷达 All-round looking radar |
| 遇险报警辅助设施 Secondary means of distress alerting | (海上)避碰雷达 Anticollision radar |
| 接收海上安全信息的设备 Facilities for reception of maritime safety information | 自动跟踪雷达 Automatic-tracking radar |
| | 信标雷达 Beacon radar |
| | 探测雷达 Detection radar |
| 应急无线电示位标 EPIRB (emergency position-indicating radio beacon) | 搜索雷达 Search radar |
| | 警戒雷达 Warning radar |
| 极轨道卫星 COSPAS-SARSAT | 雷达反射器 radar reflector |
| 国际海事卫星 INMARSAT | 折叠式雷达反射器 collapsible radar reflector |
| 甚高频数字选择呼叫 VHF DSC | 罗经 Compass |
| 卫星应急无线电示位标 Satellite EPIRB | 主罗经 Master compass |
| 甚高频应急无线电示位标 VHF EPIRB | 磁罗经 Magnetic compass |
| 救生用无线电通信设备 Life-saving radio communication apparatus | 电罗经 Gyro compass |
| | 操舵罗经、驾驶罗经 Steering compass |
| 双向甚高频无线电话设备 Two-way VHF radiotelephone apparatus | **天线 Antenna** |
| | 仿真天线 Artificial antenna |
| 甚高频无线电话 VHF radio telephone | 定向天线 Directional antenna |
| 声力电话 Sound powered telephone | 环状天线 Loop antenna |
| 对讲电话 Walkie talkie | 鞭状天线 Whip antenna |
| 数字选择性呼叫编码器 DSC encoder (digital selective calling encoder) | 室外天线 Outdoor antenna |
| | 雷达天线 Radar antenna |
| 数字选择性呼叫值班接收机 DSC watch receiver (digital selective calling watch receiver) | 无线电天线 Radio antenna |
| | 接收天线 Receiving antenna |
| | 发射天线 Transmitting antenna |

### 3. 发电机和电动机 Generator and motor

发电机 Generator
原动机 Prime mover
发电机组 Generating set
主发电机 Main generator
辅助发电机 Auxiliary generator
应急发电机 Emergency generator
备用发电机 Reserve (stand-by) generator
直流发电机 D.C. (Direct current) generator
交流发电机 A.C. (Alternating current) generator
无刷发电机 Brushless generator
轴带发电机 Shaft-driven generator
柴油(机驱动)发电机 Diesel (-driven) generator
燃气轮机（驱动）发电机 Gas turbine (driven) generator
防滴式发电机 Drip-proof generator
电动发电机 Electric motor generator
三相发电机 Three-phase generator
多相发电机 Polyphase generator
单极发电机 Unipolar generator
串励发电机 Series generator
并励发电机 Shunt generator
复励发电机 Compound wound generator
自励发电机 Exciterless generator
恒流发电机 Constant current generator
恒速发电机 Constant speed generator
恒功率发电机 Constant power generator
恒压发电机 Constant voltage generator
自励恒压式交流发电机 Self-regulated type A.C. generator
并联运行直流发电机 D.C. generator running in parallel

发生器 Generator
泡沫发生器 Froth (foam) generator
惰性气体发生器 Inert gas generator
脉冲发生器 Pulse generator
信号发生器 Signal generator
涡流发生器 Vortex generator
造波机 Wave generator

电动机 Motor
Electric motor
交流电动机 A.C. (alternating-current) motor
直流电动机 D.C. (direct-current) motor
多相异步电动机 Polyphase asynchronous motor
多相凸极同步电动机 Polyphase salient synchronous motor
多相隐极同步电动机 Polyphase non-salient synchronous motor
多相异步结构同步电动机 Pylyphase asynchronous construction synchronous motor
自动同步电动机 Auto-synchronous motor
电容式电动机 Capacitor motor
笼型三相异步电动机 cage three-phase asynchronous motor
整流子电动机 Commutator motor
变极电动机 Change-pole motor
变速电动机 Change-speed motor
复励电动机 Compound motor
差励电动机 Differential motor
推斥电动机 Repulsion motor
可逆电动机 Reversible motor
感应电动机 Induction motor
伺服电动机 Servo motor
通用电动机 Universal motor
全封闭式电动机 Totally-enclosed motor
分相电动机 Split-phase motor
调速电动机 Varying-speed motor
驱动电动机 Drive (driving) motor
控制电动机 Control motor
电动机架 Motor frame
电动机壳 Motor casing(shell)
（电动机的）电气控制箱 control box
换向器 Commutator
整流子片 Commutator segment

### 4. 配电系统 Distributing system

直流双线绝缘系统  D.C. two wire insulated system
直流负极接地的双线系统  D.C. two wire system with negative pole earthed
直流利用船体作负极回路的单线系统  D.C. single wire system with negative to hull return
交流单相双线绝缘系统  A.C. single phase two wire insulated system
交流单相一线接地的双线系统  A.C. two wire system with one pole earthed
交流单相一线利用船体作回路的单线系统  A.C. single wire system with hull return
交流三相三线绝缘系统  Three phase A.C. three wire insulated system
交流三相中性点接地的四线系统  Three phase A.C. four wire system with neutral earthed
交流三相利用船体作中性线回路的三线系统  Three phase A.C. three wire system with neutral earthed and the hull serving as neutral wire
主电源  Main source of power
应急电源  Emergency source of power
蓄电池组  Accumulator battery
应急蓄电池组  Emergency accumulator battery
临时应急蓄电池组  Temporary accumulator battery
蓄电池  Accumulator, battery
充电/放电  Charge/discharge
电耦合  Electric coupling
电平  Level
电键  Key
电刷  Brush
矽钢片  Silicon steel sheet
电瓶车  Electromobile
电网  Electrical network
接线箱  connection box
岸电箱  shore (power) connection box
配电箱  distribution box
**汇流排  Busbar**
主汇流排  Main busbar
分区配电板汇流排  Sub-switchboard busbar
裸主汇流排  Bare main busbar
均压汇流排  Phase (pole) busbar
中性线汇流排  Equalizer busbar
相（极）汇流排  Neutral busbar
直流汇流排  D.C. busbar
交流汇流排  A.C. busbar
裸线  Bare conductor
接地线  Earth connection
中性线  Neutral wire

正极  Positive pole
负极  Negative pole  配电板  Switchboard
主配电板  Main switchboard
电力推进装置配电板  Switchboard for electric propulsion installation
应急配电板  Emergency switchboard
蓄电池充放电板  Battery charging and discharging board (panel)
分配电板  Distribution board
区配电板  Section board
控制屏  Control panel
绕组  Winding
定子绕组  Stator winding
转子绕组  Rotor winding
整流绕组  Commutating winding
励磁绕组  Exciting winding
补偿绕组  Compensating winding
复激绕组  Compound winding
同心绕组  Concentric winding
合成绕组  Concentrated winding
阻尼绕组  Damping winding
差动绕组  Differential winding
磁场绕组  Field winding
多层绕组  Multi-layer winding
低压绕组  Low-voltage winding
前进绕组  Progressive winding
后退绕组  Retroprogressive winding
串激绕组  Series winding
并激绕组  Shunt winding
并联绕组  Parallel winding
分级绕组  Step winding
电枢绕组  Armature winding
重叠绕组  Cumulative winding
**保护  Protection**
过载保护  Overload protection
逆功率保护  Reverse power protection
欠压保护  Under voltage protection
断路保护  Short circuit protection
过电流保护  Protection against excess current
阴极电流保护装置  Cathodic current protection
**振荡  Oscillation**
电振荡  Electric oscillation
电磁振荡  Electromagnetic oscillation
强迫振荡  Forced oscillation
自由振荡  Free oscillation
谐波振荡  Harmonic oscillation
弛张振荡  Relaxation oscillation
高频振荡  High frequency oscillation

## 5. 变流机、变压器、收发送机等以及开关

变流机 Converter
变流机组 Converter set
充电变流机 Charging converter
探照灯变流机 Searchlight converter
透平变流机 Turbo converter

变压器 Transformer
风冷式变压器 Air blast transformer
气冷式变压器 Air-cooled transformer
耦合变压器 Couple transformer
升压变压器 Booster transformer
级联变压器 Cascade transformer
恒流变压器 Constant-current transformer
配电变压器 Distribution transformer
三相变压器 Three-phase transformer
三（芯）柱变压器 Three-column transformer
三绕组变压器 Three-winding transformer
灯丝变压器 Filament transformer
仪量变压器 Potential transformer
照明变压器 lighting transformer
电力变压器 power transformer
调节变压器 Regulating transformer
串联变压器 Series transformer
静电变压器 Static transformer
抽头（多节）变压器 Tapped transformer
降压变压器 Step-down transformer
增压变压器 Step-up transformer

发射机、发送机 Transmitter
雷达发射机 Radar transmitter
无线电发送机 Radio transmitter
舵角发送机 Rudder angle transmitter
液压(功率)发送机 Hydraulic (power) transmitter
自差确定信号发送机 Calibration transmitter
方位发送机 Bearing transmitter
差动式同步发送机 Selsyn differential transmitter
距离及偏差发送机 Range and deflection transmitter
定向发送机 Directional transmitter
调频发送机 Frequency modulation transmitter
干扰发射机 Jamming transmitter
转数发送机 Revolution transmitter
激光发射机 Laser transmitter
声呐发射机 Sonar transmitter
主发射机 Main transmitter

备用发送机 Reserve transmitter
视频发射机 Video transmitter
发报机 Telegraph transmitter
中短波发信机 Medium-shirt wave transmitter

接收机 Receiver
交流接收机 A.C. (alternating current) receiver
自差式接收机 Autodyne receiver
声接收机 Acoustic receiver
全波接收机 All-wave receiver
无线电接收机 Radio receiver
无线电信标接收机 Radio beacon receiver
罗经接收机 Compass receiver
雷达接收机 Radar receiver
舵角接收机 Rudder angle receiver
跟踪接收机 Track receiver
自动同步接收机 Selsyn receiver
目标方位接收机 Target bearing receiver
超外差接收机 Superheterodyne receiver
单通道接收机 Single-channel receiver
单频收信机 Single-frequency receiver
单回路接收机 Single-circuit receiver
单边带接收机 Single-sideband receiver
警告接收机 warning receiver
脉冲压缩接收机 Pulse compressive receiver
气象传真接收机 Radio weather facilities

收发器 Transreceiver

调整器 Regulator
电压调整器 Voltage regulator
自励恒压装置 Self-excitation voltage regulator
自动调整器 Automatic regulator
供水调整器 Feed water regulator
电流调整器 Current regulator
励磁调整器 Field regulator
相位调整器 Phase regulator
电位调整器 Potential regulator
分级调整器 Step voltage regulator
温度调整器 Temperature regulator

整流器 Rectifier
铝整流器 Aluminum rectifier
固体整流器 Dry rectifier
全波整流器 Full-wave rectifier
半波整流器 Half-wave rectifier
汞(水银)整流器 Mercury rectifier

汞弧整流器 Mercury-arc rectifier
硒整流器 Selenium rectifier
可控硅整流器 Silicon-controlled rectifier
硅整流器 Silicon rectifier
硫化物整流器 Sulphide rectifier
振动整流器 Vibrating rectifier

继电器 Relay
辅助继电器 Auxiliary relay
闭(联)锁继电器 Block relay
离心继电器 Centrifugal relay
闭合(合闸)继电器 Closing relay
控制继电器 Control relay
电流继电器 Current relay
定时限继电器 Definite time relay
隔离继电器 Disconnecting relay
吸持继电器 Holding relay
阻抗继电器 Impedance relay
脉冲继电器 Impulse relay
感应式继电器 Induction relay
瞬动继电器 Instantaneous relay
联锁继电器 Interlocking relay
中和继电器 Neutral relay
失压继电器 No-volt relay
速动继电器 Quick-acting relay
速放继电器 Quick-releasing relay
逆电流继电器 Reverse current relay
逆功率继电器 Reverse power relay
反相继电器 Reverse-phase relay
短路继电器 Short-circuit relay
热继电器 Thermal relay
热电子继电器 Thermionic relay
限时(延时)继电器 Time-lag relay
定时继电器 Timing relay
脱扣（切断）继电器 Trip relay

开关 Switch
自动开关 Automatic switch
辅助开关 Auxiliary switch
转换开关 Change-over switch
万能转换开关 Universal change-over switch
整步开关 Synchronizing switch
接触开关 Contact switch
控制开关 Control switch

延迟开关 Delay switch
双联开关 Coupled twin switch
双极开关 Double-pole switch
双投开关 Double-throw switch
接地开关 Grounding switch
拍动开关 Flap switch
浮动开关 Float switch
平板开关 Flush switch
闸刀开关 Knife switch
闭合开关 Closing switch
隔离开关 Isolating switch
限位开关 Limit switch
舵角限位开关 Rudder limit switch
横向限位开关 Trolley limit switch
联锁开关 Interlocking switch
行程开关 Position switch
总开关 Main switch
主令开关 Master switch
常开(闭)按钮开关 Normally opened(closed) push switch
电源开关 Power switch
速断开关 Quick break switch
保险开关 Safety switch
串并联开关 Series-parallel switch
手捺开关 Snap switch
同步开关 Synchro switch
制动开关 Tappet switch
终点开关 Terminal switch
三向开关 Three-way switch
反向开关 Reversing switch
旋转开关 Rotary switch
遥控开关 Remote switch
音量控制开关 Volume control switch
多极联动开关 Multipole linked switch

断路器 Breaker
空气断路器,空气断路开关 Air circuit breaker(ACB)
断路器 Circuit breaker
主开关 Main circuit breaker
自动开关 Automatic circuit breaker
自动空气开关 Automatic air circuit breaker
油断路器、油开关 Oil circuit breaker
快断路器 Quick-break circuit breaker

熔断器 Fuse
封闭式熔断器 Enclosed-type fuse
插入式熔断器 Push-in fuse
螺旋式熔断器 Screw-plug fuse, screw-in type fuse
快速熔断器 Quick-acting fuse
管式熔断器 Cartridge fuse

制动器 Brake
圆盘制动器 Disk (disc) brake
涡流制动器 Eddy-current brake
电动制动器 Electric brake
电磁制动器 Electromagnetic brake
紧急制动器 Emergency brake
摩擦制动器 Friction brake
脚踏制动器(脚刹车) Foot brake
手制动器(手刹车) Hand brake
液位(水力)制动器 Hydraulic brake
磁铁制动器 Magnetic brake
气压制动器 Pneumatic brake
螺线管制动器 Solenoid brake

接触器 Contactor
主接触器 Main contactor
辅助接触器 Auxiliary contactor
时间接触器 Timing contactor
加速接触器 Accelerating contactor
线路接触器 Line contactor
制动接触器 Brake contactor, damping contactor
电磁接触器 Magnetic contactor
继电接触器 Relay contactor
启动接触器 Starting contactor
正反转(方向)接触器 Reversing contactor
触头 Contact

控制器 Controller
自动控制器 Automatic controller
鼓形控制器 Drum controller
电控气压控制器 Electro-pneumatic controller
手动控制器 Hand controller
磁控制器 Magnetic controller
速度控制器 Speed controller
主（总）控制器 Main controller
主令控制器 Master controller
通用控制器 Universal controller
凸轮控制器 Cam-operated controller

放大器 Amplifier
声频放大器 Audio-frequency amplifier
级联放大器 Cascade amplifier
扼流圈耦合放大器 Choke-coupled amplifier
(直)线性放大器 Linear amplifier
光电(流)放大器 Photoelectric cell amplifier
光电管放大器 Photo-electric tube amplifier
功率放大器 Power amplifier
推挽式放大器 Push-pull amplifier
射频、高频放大器 Radio-frequency amplifier
谐振放大器 Turned amplifier
半导体放大器 Semi-conductor amplifier
电子管放大器 Valve (electronic) amplifier

电容器 Capacitor (condenser)
电解电容器 Chemical capacitor
云母电容器 Mica capacitor
纸质电容器 Paper capacitor
蜡质电容器 Paraffined capacitor
瓷电容器 Porcelain capacitor
可变电容器 Variable capacitor

消音器 Silencer
电抗器 Reactance（并车电抗器 Paralleling reactance）
电位器 Potentiometer
调速器 Governor
变流器、倒换器 Inverter（倒相器 Phase inverter）
可控硅逆变器 Thyristor inverter
自动拍发器 Auto keying device
离子传感器 Ion fire detection
频率合成器 Frequency synthesizer
扬声器 Loudspeaker
对时喇叭 Timing loudspeaker
耳机 Headphones
分股耳机 Split headphones
播音机 broadcaster
无线电测向仪 Radio direction finder
测深仪 Echo sounder
计程仪 Log
相序表 Phase meter
万用表 Multimeter
电流表 Ampere meter
电压表 Voltmeter
兆欧表 Megohmmeter

## 6. 电缆、电路、电线以及照明装置

**电缆 Cable**
船用电缆 Marine cable
充电电缆 Charging cable
混合电缆 Compound (composite) cable
同轴电缆 Concentric cable
连接电缆 Connecting cable
配电电缆 Distribution cable
馈电电缆 Feeder cable
照明电缆 Lighting cable
主干电缆 Trunk cable
均压线电缆 Equalizer cable
石棉电缆 Asbestos cable
铠装电缆 Armoured cable
成束电缆 Bunched cable
薄膜电缆 Grout cable
铜质(护套)电缆 Copper-sheathed cable
铅包电缆 Lead-covered cable
塑料电缆 Plastic cable
橡胶电缆 Rubber cable
多芯电缆 Multiple core cable; Multiple conductor cable
三芯电缆 Triple-core (three core) cable
动力电缆 Power cable
海底电缆 Submarine cable
软花线 Plaited cable
导电线芯 Conductor
电缆槽 Cable trunk, cable channel
连接箱 Connection box
联接箱 Coupling
导板 Cable tray
管道 Cable conduit
管子 Cable pipe
护套 Sheath
铅合金护套 Lead-alloy sheath
铜质护套 Copper sheath
非金属护套 Non-metallic sheath
防护覆盖层 Protective covering
金属编织层铠装防护覆盖层 Metal-braid armour protective covering
纤维编织防护覆盖层 Fibrous braid protective covering
电缆敷设路线 Cable runs
绝缘带 Insulating tape
黄腊带 Yellow varnished cambric tape

**电路 Circuit**
交流电路 Alternating current circuit
直流电路 Direct current circuit
电路 Electric circuit
线路 Line circuit
主电路 Main circuit
分电路 Branch circuit, sub-circuit

次级(副边)电路 Secondary circuit
初级(原边)电路 Primary circuit
电源(动力)电路 Power circuit
推进电路 Propulsion circuit
操纵电路 Maneuvering circuit
控制电路 Control circuit
供电电路 Supply circuit
输入电路 Input circuit
输出电路 Outlet circuit
天线电路 Antenna circuit
接收电路 Receiving circuit
通信电路 Communication circuit
信号电路 Signal circuit
照明电路 Lighting circuit
集成电路 Integrated circuit
闭合电路 Close circuit
补偿电路 Compensating circuit
线路板 Circuit panel
印制电路板 Printed circuit board

**线路（/线） Line**
分支线 Branch line
馈电线路 Feeder line
高压线 High tension line
电源线 Power line
单线线路 Single-wire line
架空线路 Overhead line
实线 Solid line

**电线 Wire (Electric wire)**
铝线 Aluminum wire
铜皮皮线 Armoured wire
铅皮包线 Lead covered wire
胶皮线 Rubber-covered wire
引入线 Lead-in wire
裸线 Bare wire
裸铜线 Bare copper wire
电池接线 Battery wire
双芯塑料线 Double core plastic wire
地线 Earth wire; grounding wire
接地导线 Grounded transmitting wire
绝缘线 Insulated wire
耐燃线 Slow-burning wire
焊锡线 Soldering wire
镀锡线 Tinned wire
多股绞合线 Stranded wire (cable)
中性线 Neutral wire
馈电线 Feeder
保险丝 Fuse
电热丝 Heating resistance wire
电话线网 Telephone wire

线圈 Coil
工作线圈 Actuating coil
空心线圈 Air-core coil
合闸线圈 Closing coil
阻尼线圈 Damping coil
复合线圈 Compound coil
扁平线圈 Disc coil
励磁线圈 Exciting coil
环状线圈 Encirclement coil
屏蔽线圈 Shielding coil
灭弧线圈 Blow-out coil
空载扼流线圈 No-load choke coil
接触线圈 Contactor's coil
接线端 Terminal
入端 Input terminal
分路线头 Tapping (branch) terminal
引入端 Leading-in terminal
引出端 Leading-out terminal
接线盒 Terminal box
照明系统 Lighting system
照明装置 Light (lighting) installation
照明灯具 Lighting fittings, Lighting fixtures, Lamps and lanterns
照明 Lighting, illumination
装货甲板照明 Cargo lighting
电气照明 Electric lighting
应急照明 Emergency lighting
机舱照明 Engine room lighting
局部照明 Local lighting
固定照明 Fixed lighting
檐板照明 Cornice lighting
壁灯 Panel lighting
灯 Light
尾（航行）灯 After light, Stern light
船首灯、旗杆灯 Bow light, Stem light
航行灯 Navigation light
桅灯 Mast(head) light
锚灯 Anchor light
右舷灯 Green side light, Starboard (side) light
左舷灯 Red side light, Port (side) light
失控灯 Not under command light
拖带灯 Towing light
艇甲板灯 Boat deck light
航标灯 Beacon light
浮标灯 Buoy light
固定灯 Fixed light
装货灯 Cargo light
闪光灯 Flashing light
探照灯（用于货舱照明） Flood light
探照灯 Search light
信号灯 Signal light

防爆灯 Explosion proof light
遇险信号灯 Distress light
警告灯 Warning light
白炽灯 Incandescent light
荧光灯 Fluorescent light
可携照明灯 Portable luminaire
电标志 Electrical signs
灯 Lamp
弧光灯 Arc lamp
气体放电灯 Gas discharge lamp
蓄电池灯 Battery lamp
(小)艇甲板灯 Boat deck lamp
桥楼信号灯 Bridge lamp
篷顶灯 Ceiling lamp
白昼信号灯 Daylight signaling lamp
指示灯 Indicating lamp, pilot lamp
日光灯 Daylight lamp
荧光灯 Fluorescent lamp
白炽灯 Incandescent lamp
防爆灯 Explosion-proof lamp
火警指示灯 Fire lamp
聚光灯 Projector lamp
防水灯 Waterproof lamp
壁灯 Wall lamp
吊灯 Pendent lamp
台灯 Desk lamp
手提灯 Portable lamp
床头灯 Bed lamp
镇流器 Ballast coils (for daylight lamp)
手电筒 Electric torch, flashlight
(电子)管 Tube
放大管 Amplifier tube
绝缘套管 Insulating tube
检波管 Detector tube
电子管 Electronic tube
离子管 Ionic tube
功率管 Power tube
整流管 Rectifying [Rectifier] tube
弯瓷管 Angle porcelain tube
二极管 Two-electrode tube, diode
波导管 Wave guide tube
灯泡 Bulb
灯丝 Filament
灯杆 Post
灯头、灯座 Holder
灯罩 Shade
灯台 Stand
插头 Plug
插座 Socket

### 7. 报警系统与信号设备

报警系统 Alarm system
报警器 Alarm
报警装置 alarm device
声响报警器 Acoustic alarm
声光报警装置 Audible and visual alarm
自动报警器 Auto(automatic) alarm
火灾警报器 Fire alarm
施放 CO2 报警器 CO2 releasing alarm
烟气报警器 Smoke alarm
过载报警装置 Overload alarm
紧急警铃 Emergency-alarm
蜂鸣器 buzzer
警报器 alarm buzzer
信号设备 Signaling equipment
白昼信号灯 Daylight signaling lamp
号钟 Bell
号灯 Light
号笛 Whistle, siren
号角 Horn
号锣 Gong
号钟 Bell
号型 Shape
报警信号 alarm signal
声响报警信号 audible alarm signal
浮游烟气信号 buoyant smoke signal
遇难(求救)信号/遇险信号 distress signal
火警信号 fire (alarm) signal
灯光信号 Light signal
劳兰警告信号 Loran alarm signal
海上(通信)信号 nautical signal
全向信号 omnidirectional signal
降落伞信号 parachute signal

烟雾信号 smoke signal
音响信号 sound signal
视觉信号 visual signal
警告信号 Warning signal
引航信号 pilot signal
检疫信号 quarantine signal
通行(要求让路)信号 right-of-way signal
火箭信号 rocket signal
航行灯发生故障时能发出声响和视觉信号的自动指示器 Automatic indicator giving an audible and visual indication of failure of the navigation light
自动拍发器 Auto keying device
闪光信号、照明弹 Flare
手把火焰信号 Hand flare
红火号 Red hand flare
救生圈烟火信号 Life buoy flare
火箭照明弹 Rocket flare
火箭降落伞照明信号 Rocket parachute flare
火箭 Rocket
抛绳火箭 Line throwing rocket
抛绳器（装置） line throwing apparatus
警报 Warning
避碰警报 Collision-avoidance warning
强(烈)风警报 Gale warning
寒潮警报 Cold wave warning
冰情警报 Ice warning
无线电航行预告 Wireless navigational warning
欠电压报警 Under-voltage warning
CO2 预施放报警 Pre-warning device for releasing of CO2
CO2 施放预告信号 Preliminary warning of discharging of CO2
手动失火报警按钮 Manually operated call points
灯标 Light beacon

## 【Training Evaluation】

| 考核内容 | | 所占比例 | 分数 |
|---|---|---|---|
| 知识考核 | | 40% | |
| 准确掌握船舶电站、电力拖动系统设备的英文铭牌 | | 20 | |
| 准确掌握船舶信号、电工工艺系统设备的英文铭牌 | | 20 | |
| 技能考核 | | 60% | |
| 个人考核 | 说出船用电气设备英文名称20个以上 | 30 | |
| 小组考核 | 以小组为单位，任选船舶某电气系统设备，背写出设备的中英文名称30个以上，填写附表 | 30 | |
| 总分 | | | |

## Practical Training 1

附表

| NO. | CHINESE PLATE | ENGLISH PLATE |
|-----|---------------|---------------|
|     |               |               |

# Practical Training 2

## 【Training Goals】

(1) Practice some technical terms talking about equipment testing.
(2) Practice the expressions about testing and submission.
(3) Practice some useful sentences and patterns for monitoring & alarm points list.

## 【Training Content】

### Expressions for Testing and Submission

**(一) 谈论接线 Talking about wire connecting**

1. 芯线是按图纸接的（按规范、标准、X 船级社）。The core wire was connected according to the drawing (spec,standard,classification society rules).
2. 线没有接。The wire hasn't been connected.
3. 线接错了。The wire was connected in wrong way.
4. 现在就接。You must connect the wire at once.
5. 没有芯线套管吗？（你们现在就套）Is there the core wire sleeve? (You must put on the sleeve at once.)
6. 芯线太粗（细/长/短）。 The core wire is thick (thin / long / short).
7. 芯线没有拧紧（太松）。 The core wire hasn't been tightened enough. (It's too loose.)
8. 芯线没有压销桩铜接头（你们马上就压）。The core wire hasn't been fixed with a pin copper connection. (You must fix it at once.)
9. 铜接头没有压紧。 The copper connection hasn't been tightened.
10. 接线桩不牢。 The terminal isn't firm.
11. 芯线和接线柱接触不好。 The core wire doesn't connect the terminal well.
12. 你有没有铜接头（或销状铜接头）。 Do you have any pin copper connections?
13. 你要多少尺寸的接头？ What's the size of the connection?
14. 芯线断了（破损了）。 The core wire is broken(damaged).
15. 线接得（不美观）不规范，重接（返工）。The wire wasn't connected according to the rules. You must reconnect it.
16. 是否就这一根重接？I only need to reconnect this wire. Am I right?
17. 这一根电缆要换。This piece of cable should be replaced.
18. 是否可以不换? Is it necessary to replace it?
19. 这种接法我们不能接受（不符合规范）。We can't agree with this connection method (It's

not up to the rules).

    20. 如何接才是正确得？ What's the right connection method?

    21. 检验接线是否正确 Please check the wire connecting method!

    22. 接线柱上怎么没有弹簧垫圈（或锁紧螺母）？ Where's the spring ring (lock nut) on the terminal?

    23. 接线号码不对（号码没错）. The number of the connection wire is wrong. (The number is right.)

    24. 你看接线还有什么问题吗？ Is there anything wrong with wire-connection?

    25. 你看这样接是否可以？ Do you think it okay to connect the wire in this way?

    26. 把这几根线拆下来（全部拆下来）. Please disconnect these pieces of wire.

    27. 我认为线多拆不是最好. I don't think it proper to disconnect the wire frequently.

    28. 接线工艺应该没问题. There isn't anything wrong with the connecting process.

    (二) 谈论绝缘 Talking about insulation

1. 兆欧表准备好了(请看表头读数). The meg-ohmmeter is ready. Please look at the dials (readings).

    2. 现在测量绝缘电阻吗？ May I measure the insulation resistance now?

    3. 1MΩ 以上（绝缘值不低于 1MΩ）. (Megohm) Over $10^6$ ohm. (The insulation value shall be $\geq 10^6$ ohm.)

    4. 绝缘老化了（绝缘不好或绝缘故障）. The insulation is aged (poor). The insulation has broken down.

    5. 绝缘电阻太低. The insulation resistance is too low.

    6. 可能是湿度的问题. Maybe the problem comes from humidity.

    7. 也许是设备的问题. Maybe the problem is from equipment.

    8. 线都检查过了，没有问题. We have checked all the wires and found no problem.

    9. 再检查一下绝缘. Please check the insulation once more.

    10. 绝缘材料有问题. There must be some problem about the insulation material.

    11. 我们会想办法提高绝缘. We'll try our best to improve upon the insulation.

    (三) 谈论调试 Talking about testing

1. 请你检查一下好吗？ Will you please have a check?

    2. 调试（或安装）好了吗？ Have you finished testing (installation)?

    3. 是的，调试（或安装）好了. Yes, the testing (installation) is over.

    4. 已经检查过了，工作正常. We have checked and found it normal (okay).

    5. 我们将按你的建议（要求）去做. We'll follow your suggestion (request).

    6. 这是由于设计（或安装）问题造成的. It is due to the mistake of design (installation).

    7. 已经试验过，情况正常. It has been tested and everything is okay.

    8. 验收报告明天可以给你吗？ Shall we present you the acceptance report tomorrow?

    9. 我们是遵守（X 船级社）得规范和规则做的. We have followed the rules and regulations of the classification society.

    10.（安装）没有问题. No problem (in installation).

    11. 毛病还没有找到. We haven't found out the trouble yet.

12. 等一等，我现在就去找。Just a moment, I'll have a look.
13. 已经准备好了。It's ready.
14. 这样行吗？Is it okay?
15. 现在可以启动了吗？Can I start it now?
16. 我想是这样的（我想不是的）。I think so. (I don't think so.)
17. （你们）准备什么时候试车？When will you begin the testing?
18. 你能告诉我是什么原因吗？Can I tell me why?
19. 还不太清楚，等检查完再说。It's not clear yet. Let's wait for the check report.
20. 那一定是有问题了。There must be something wrong.
21. 让我们看看是否有问题。Let's have a check to see if there is anything wrong.
22. 这样做可以吗？Is this the right way to do it?
23.（试验）时间已经到了。It's time to have the test.(指试验可以开始了); The testing time is up.（指试验结束了）

**(四) 设备调试中专业"术语" Technical terms for equipment testing**

1. 有故障（不正常）。There's some failure.(It's abnormal.)
2. 失灵了。It doesn't work. (It's out of order.)
3. 不能启动。It can't start.
4. 不能跳闸。Fail to trip.
5. 没有指示（指示误差）。There's no sign. (indication error.)
6. 不准确  incorrect.
7. 不动作（动作迟钝）no function.
8. 不平稳(不稳定)  unstable.
9. 振动厉害  serious vibration.
10. 噪声太大  too much noise.
11. 接触不良  poor contact.
12. 断路  open (broken) circuit.
13. 短路  short circuit.
14. 接地  ground.
15. 接错  Connection in a wrong way.
16. 卡死（变形）block (deformation).
17. 间隙太大  too much clearance.
18. 电流太高  too high current.
19. 电压太低  too low voltage.
20. 相序不对  wrong phase/sequence.
21. 频率不对  wrong frequency.
22. 压力太低（太高）too low (high) pressure.
23. 温度太高  too high temperature.
24. 负荷太重  overload (too heavy load).
25. 速度太快（太慢）（突然停下）too fast (slow) speed (sudden stop).
26. 位置不对  wrong position.
27. 数据不准  inaccurate data.

28. 功能不同  different functions.
29. 设备损坏  damaged equipment.
30. 接头松动  loose connection.
31. 绝缘不良  poor insulation.
32. 熔丝熔断  fuse was melted.
33. 元件问题（电阻、电容、集成块）component trouble (e.g. resistance.capacitance.integrated unit)
34. 图纸问题  drawing mistake
35. 操作不当  improper operation

(五) 主机自动化术语 Technical Terms for M.E. Automation
1. 主机  Main Engine (M.E.).
2. 主机遥控  M.E. remote control.
3. 螺旋桨  propeller.
4. 可调螺旋桨  CPP (Controllable pitch propeller).
5. 齿轮箱  gearbox.
6. 轴承  bearing.
7. 推力（中间）轴承  thrust (intermediate) bearing.
8. 凸轮轴  camshaft.
9. 活塞  piston.
10. 主启动阀  main starting valve.
11. 调速器  governor.
12. 汽缸  cylinder.
13. 高压油泵  high- pressure oil pump.
14. 调油杆  oil- adjusting lever.
15. 油排齿条格数  tooth sector.
16. 启动（停止）电磁阀  starting (stopping) electric-magnetic valve.
17. 盘车机  turning gear.
18. 扫气空气  scanvage air.
19. 泵（马达）  pump(motor).
20. 鼓风机  blower.
21. 转速  rpm.
22. 流量  flow.
23. 手动  manual.
24. 自动  automatic.
25. 应急  emergency.
26. 限制  limit.
27. 指示  indicate.
28. 故障  abnormal/trouble.
29. 工况（负荷）  working condition (load).
30. 确认（应答）  confirm (response).
31. 平稳  steady (smooth).
32. 调节  adjust.

33. 复位　reset.
34. 自检　self-check
35. 备用　stand-by
36. 啮合　gear.
37. 脱开　detach.
38. 减速　slow-down.
39. 失败　failure.
40. 零位　nil position.
41. 反馈信号　feed signal.
42. 转换信号　change-over signal
43. 换向信号　reverse signal.
44. 接通　connect.
45. 断开　cut-off.
46. 切断　cut.
47. 正常　normal.
48. 无异常现象　no abnormal.
49. 闭锁　lock.
50. 试验　test & trial.
51. 电源　power supply (source).
52. 交流电源　AC 220V SOURCE.
53. 直流电源　DC 24V SOURCE.

(六) 主机遥控系统 M.E. Remote Control
A. Technical Terms for M.E. Remote Control
1. 主机推进系统　M/E propulsion system.
2. 主机遥控装置　M/E remote control unit.
3. 机旁　local (by engine side).
4. 集控室　ECR (centralized control room).
5. 驾驶室　W/H (wheel-house).
6. 桥楼　bridge.
7. 遥控主车钟　remote control main telegraph.
8. 微速　dead slow.
9. 半速　half.
10. 全速　full.
11. 完车　finish.
12. 辅车钟　aux. telegraph.
13. 应急车钟　emergency telegraph.
14. 车钟记录仪　telegraph recorder.
15. 设定速度　rated speed.
16. 定速　constant speed.
17. 模拟试验　simulation test.
18. 测速装置　speed-measuring unit.

19. 转速传感器  rpm sensor.
20. 启动空气压力表  starting air pressure gauge.

**B. Technical Terms for M.E.Remote Control Testing**

1. 程序（换向/启动/慢转启动/转速/转速自动）控制  program (change-over / starting / slow starting / rpm / rpm automatic) control.
2. 3次自动重复启动  automatic restarting for three times
3. 重启动  restart.
4. 错向报警  wrong-way alarm.
5. 临界转速（最小转速/最大倒车转速/热负荷/手动转速/燃油/扫气压力/手动燃油）限制  critical rpm (Min. rpm / Max. astern rpm / hot load / manual rpm / F.O. / scanvage pressure / manual F.O.) limit.
6. 应急操纵（运行）emergency maneuvering (running).
7. 应急（自动）停车  emergency（automatic）stop.
8. 安全保护装置  safety protection unit.
9. 盘车机未脱开  Turning gear is still geared.
10. 滑油压力低  The pressure of L.O. is too low.
11. 汽缸（活塞）冷却水压力低  The pressure of cooling water for cylinder (piston) is too low.
12. 超速  overspeed.
13. 活塞冷却水流量低  The flow cooling water for piston is too low.
14. 扫气空气（推力轴承）温度高  The temperature of scanvage air (thrust bearing) is too high.
15. 启动时间过长  The starting time is too long.
16. 3次启动失败  starting failure for a third time.
17. 启动（控制）空气压力低  The pressure of starting（control）air is too low.
18. 主启动阀未打开  The main starting valve isn't opened.
19. 机旁操纵（调油）手柄位置  The local handle position for maneuvering.
20. 系统故障   system failure.
21. 内部电源故障  inside power source failure.
22. 故障显示  failure display.
23. 汽缸油断流  cylinder oil non-flow.
24. 越控  skip.
25. 油雾探油装置  oil mist detector.
26. 鼓风机接通（断开） The blower is powered (out down).
27. 调速器  governor.
28. 报警器消音按钮  The silencer push button for alarm unit.
29. 试灯按钮  push button for lighting.
30. 凸轮轴位置检测器  detector for camshaft position.
31. 电气转换  I/P.
32. 故障指示灯  failure indicator.
33. 调光器旋钮  snob for light regulator.
34. 执行机构  actuator.
35. 燃油刻度指示表  fuel oil dial indicator.

**C. Automation of Power Station**
1. 柴油发电机启动失败　D/G start failure.
2. 柴油发电机超速停车　D/G overspeed stop.
3. 柴油发电机滑油低压停车　D/G Lub. oil low press. stop.
4. 柴油发电机淡水高温停车　D/G F.W. high temp. stop.
5. 柴油发电机启动空气低压　D/G starting air low press.
6. 柴油发电机停车电磁阀故障　D/G auto-stop magnetic valve failure.
7. 柴油发电机测速装置故障　D/G speed measurement failure.
8. 柴油发电机空气低压　D/G control air low press.
9. 柴油发电机电源故障　D/G power source failure.
10. 柴油发电机增压器滑油低压　D/G turbocharger Lub. Oil low press.
11. 柴油发电机燃油泄漏柜液位高　D/G F.O. drain tank high level.
12. 柴油发电机预滑油故障　D/G L.O. preheatment failure.
13. 柴油发电机报警闭锁　D/G alarm lock.
14. 柴油发电机功率管理故障　D/G power control failure.
15. 柴油发电机公共报警　D/G common alarm.
16. 柴油发电机燃油模块故障　D/G F.O. module failure.
17. 柴油发电机测速传感器　D/G speed sensor.
18. 柴油发电机预供油泵马达　D/G presupply oil pump motor.
19. 主配电板调速马达　Main switchboard speed-governing motor.
20. 遥控和自动启动（控制）　Remote control and auto start (control)
21. 就地控制　local control.
22. 遥控（手动）停车　stop by remote (hand) control.
23. 发电机运行　D/G operation.
24. 发电机温度及压力显示　Temperature & pressure display of D/G.
25. 发电机燃油进口压力　D/G F.O. inlet press.
26. 发电机高温淡水（滑油）进口压力　D/G high-temp. F.W. (Lub.Oil.) intlet press.
27. 发电机燃油（滑油）进口温度　D/G　F.O.　(L.O.)　inlet temp.
28. 发电机高温淡水出口温度　D/G high-temp. F.W. outlet temp.
29. 发电机 1－3 缸排气温度　Exhaust temp. from the first to the third cylinder.
30. 发电机 R 相（S 相.TS 相）绕组温度　D/G R (S.TS)-phase coil temp.
31. 主空气断路器　main air breaker.
32. 电压表（电流表/功率表/同步表/功率因素表/频率表）．
Voltmeter (Ammeter / powermeter / synchronoscope / power factor meter / frequency meter).
33. 转换开关　change-over switch.
34. 发电机加热器开关　D/G heater switch.
35. 调频转换开关　frequency-regulating switch.
36. 充磁（消音/复位　）按钮　magnetic push button (silencer / reset).
37. 岸电供电（同步）指示灯　shore electricity-supply (synchronous) indicator.
38. 绝缘监视仪　insulation monitor.
39. 熔断器　fuse.

## (七) 谈论发电机调试 Talking about D/G

1. 发电机试车准备就绪。The starting test of D/G is ready.
2. 测试仪表已准备好。The measuring meters are ready.
3. 冷态绝缘电阻测试是否可以开始？Shall we start the testing of cold insulation resistance?
4. 先做报警点试验。Begin with the alarm points testing, please.
5. 这些传感器是开关（模拟）量的。These sensors are of digital (analogue) type.
6. 你看先做哪一个传感器？Which sensor shall we begin with?
7. 可以做超速实效试验。We can make the effect test for overspeed.
8. 这些传感器我们再综合试验室都校正过了。We have calibrated these sensors in lab.
9. 你是否抽空去综合试验室看看？Would you like to have a visit to our lab?
10. 温度（压力）传感器的数值都在允许范围内。
The values of temp (press) sensors are within the allowance.
11. 如果你觉得不满意，我们可以拆下检查。
We can dismantle it and have a check if you are not satisfied.
12. 接线是按图纸施工的，应该没有问题。
 The wire is connected by the drawing. It should be O.K.
13. 现在有点小问题，请你稍等。There is something wrong. Please wait a moment.
14. 这个传感器我们打算换新的。We'll replace this sensor with a new one.
15. 这些问题我们一定解决，你是否可以继续看下去？
We're sure to solve these problems. Would you please go on with the inspection?
16. 数值可以调整。The values can be adjusted.
17. 这个传感器是刚刚换的。This sensor was renewed just now.
18. 传感器的型号是跟图纸一致的。The model of this sensor agrees with the drawing.
19. 传感器安装的位置是符合要求的。The installation positions of sensors are up to the requirement.
20. 传感器和荧光屏上显示的数值是一致的。The value of sensor meets with that on the screen.
21. 报警点的显示有问题，我查查图纸。There is something wrong with the display of alarm points. Let me check the drawing.
22. 传感器的线接错了，现在已经好了。The wire of sensor was connected improperly. We have reconnected it.
23. 现在请再试一试。Please try again.
24. 报警点全部试验过了。We have tested all the alarm points.
25. 有个别的问题我们准备马上修补，你看如何？We'll make the remedy for the few defects soon. What's your idea?
26. 现在是否可以进行发电机动车试验？Shall we begin the starting test for the generator now?
27. 试车设备都检查过了。We have checked all the equipment for testing.
28. 负载桶里的水已加满。The load tank is full of water.
29. 遥控操作没有问题。There is no problem about the remote control operation.
30. 发电机已经启动完毕，一切正常。The generator has been started and every thing is okay.

31. 请你看看主配电板上电压.频率的数值是准确。Please look at the readings of voltage and frequency on the main switchboard to see if they are normal.

32. 现在开始做负载试验。Let's have the load test now.

33. 加负载25%。Add 25% load.

34. 运行时间 10min（15min、2h）。The running time is 10 minutes (15min, two hours).

35. 测量温升×度。Please measure the temperature rise.

36. 发电机的温升没有超过允许值。The temperature rise for D/G is within the allowance

37. 现在做电压特性试验。Let's have the test of voltage characteristic.

38. 发电机负荷充满载至空载（空载至满载）的电压变化率≤±2.5%Nn。The voltage variation rate from full load to no load is within 2.5%Nn.

39. 现在做转速变化试验。Let's have the rpm test now.

40. 稳态（瞬态）频率（±50%FN）。Steady (instantaneous) frequency (±50%FN).

41. 恢复时间（≤7s）。restore time (≤7sec)

42. 突加（减）负载。Sudden load take- on (Instant unload) test

43. 现在做柴油机启动试验。Let's have the starting test of diesel engine.

44. 主空气瓶总压缩空气已经充满。The main air reservoir has been filled with compressed air.

45. 柴油机连续启动 6 次应该没有问题。There should be no problem to start the diesel engine for six times continuously.

46. 现在做并联运行试验。Let's do the parallel running test now.

47. 每种工况各运行 5min。Make it run for 5 minutes under each working condition.

48. 每一并联运行方式运行约 30min。Run for 30 minutes under each parallel condition.

49. 现在做负载转换试验。Let's do the load- shifting test.

50. 现在手动准同步（自动同步）降第 3 台发电机组并网。Please parallel No.3 generator by manual synchro (auto synchro) .

51. 现在降第 1 台发电机组减载至零后退网。Please unload No.1 generator to nil and make it out of service.

52. 你觉得转换负载的稳定性是否有问题？How do you think of the steadiness of shifting load?

53. 现在做绝缘电阻试验。Let's do insulation resistance test now.

54. 三相定子绕组对地绝缘为5mΩ。The ground insulation value for 3- phase stator coil is 5mΩ.

55. 空间加热对地绝缘为 3mΩ。The ground insulation value for heater is 3mΩ.

56. 现在做发电机机旁控制板试验。Let's do the control panel test of generator by engine side.

57. 滑油预供泵（手动.自动）工作正常。The manual & auto control for L.O. presupply pump is in order (okay).

58. 预热装置的电源已经接通。The preheat unit is powered.

59. 柴油机安全保护功能进行模拟试验。Let's do the simulation test for the safety function of D/G

60. 请你检查应急停机电磁阀。Please check the electromagnetic valve for emergency shut-down function.

61. 机组报警具有声光报警功能。The generating set alarm is of audible visual type.

62. 现在做主配电板试验。Let's do the main switchboard test.

63. 发电机保护。D/G protection trip.

A）过载保护　overload trip　B）短路保护　short circuit trip
C）瞬动保护　instant start trip　D）热保护　thermal trip
E）欠电压保护　under voltage trip　F）逆功率保护　reverse power trip

64. 优先脱扣电路试验。Circuit testing of priority trip.

第一(二)级优先脱扣电流设定值。The set value of current for the first-stage(second-stage) priority trip.

65. 现在做主配电板联锁试验。Let's do the locking test of main switchboard.

66. 主配电板与应急配电板自检联锁试验。Locking test between the main switchboard and emergency switchboard.

67. 主配电板与岸电自检联锁试验。Locking test between the main switchboard and shore power.

68. 现在做电站管理系统功能试验。Let's do the function test of power station control system.

69. 现在做应急切断试验。Let's do the emergency cut-down test.

70. 全船风机.空调和油泵已被紧急切断。The blowers, air conditioners and oil pumps on board have been cut down in an emergency.

(八) 监测与报警点表册 Monitoring & Alarm Points List.

**A. MAIN ENGINE (M/E) 主机**

1. M/E HIGH PRESSURE FUEL OIL LEAKAGE. 主机燃油高压管泄漏
2. M/E MAIN LUB.OIL INLET PRESSURE LOW. 主机主滑油进口压力低
3. M/E PISTON COOL OIL OUT. TEMP. 主机汽缸活塞冷却油出口温度
4. M/E THRUST BEARING TEMP HIGH & SLD. 主机推力块高温测量及减速。
5. M/E MAIN LUB OIL INLET TEMP. 主机主滑油进口温度
6. M/E JACKET CFW IN PRESS. 主机缸套冷却淡水进口压力
7. M/E FUEL OIL INLET PRESS. 主机燃油进口压力
8. M/E COOLING WTR. INLET AIR COOLER PRESS. 主机冷却水进空冷却器压力
9. M/E SCAV. AIR PRESS. 主机扫气箱扫气空气压力
10. M/E CONTROL AIR PRESS. 主机控制空气压力
11. M/E STARTING AIR PRESS. 主机启动空气压力
12. M/E SAFETY AIR PRESS LOW. 主机安全空气压力低
13. SEA WATER TEMP. 海水温度
14. SEA WATER PRESS. 海水压力
15. BOILER STEAM PRESS. 锅炉蒸汽压力
16. SERV. AIR RESERVOIR TEMP. 日用空气瓶温度
17. EXH. GAS UPTAKE TEMP. 锅炉烟道排气温度
18. M/E F.W.E BLOCK SIGNAL. 主机完车闭锁信号
19. M/E No.1 CYL. SCAV. AIR BOX FIR. 主机 No.1 汽缸扫气箱失火
20. M/E CRANKCASE OIL MIST DENSITY HIG. 主机曲轴箱油雾浓度高
21. M/E J.C.W. INLET PRESS. LOW. 主机缸套冷却水进口压力低
22. FIRE MANIFOLD S.W. PRESS. 消防总管海水压力
23. M/E NO.1 CYL.J. COOL. WTR OUTLET TEMP. 主机 No.1 汽缸冷却水出口温度

24. M/E NO.1 CYL. EXH GAS OUT TEMP. 主机 No.1 汽缸排烟出口温度
25. M/E EXH GAS BEFORE T/C TEMP. 主机废气进增压器温度
26. M/E THRUST BEARING PAD TEMP. 主机推力轴承块温度
27. M/E L.O. COOLER INTET TEMP. 主机滑油冷凝器进口温度
28. NO.1 MAIN L.O. PUMP ST-BY START. 一号主滑油泵备用启动
29. NO.1 F.O. SUPPLY PUMP ST-BY START. 一号滑油供给泵备用启动
30. NO.1 M/E LTCFW PUMP ST-BY START. 一号主机低温冷却淡水泵备用启动
31. NO.1 M/EJ.CFW PUMP ST-BY START. 一号主机低温冷却淡水泵备用启动
32. NO.1 MAIN S.W PUMP ST-BY START. 一号主机海水泵备用启动
33. NO.1 STERNTUBE L.O. PUMP ST-BY START. 一号尾滑油泵备用启动
34. NO.1 F.O. CIRC. PUMP ST-BY START. 一号燃油循环泵备用启动
35. MSB COMM. ALARM. 主配电板公共报警
36. AC220VUPS ABN (DC-2000). 报警系统 AC220V 不间断电源异常
37. ECC MAIN AC220V DIST. PANEL POWER FAIL. 控台主 AC220V 分电板电源故障
38. AC-4 RCS POWER FAIL. 主机遥控系统电源故障
39. SSU SAFETY SYSTEM POWER FALL. 主机遥控安全系统电源故障
40. UPS FOR AC4/SSU POWER FAIL. 主机遥控不间断电源故障
41. GROUP ALARM RELAY BOX POWER FAIL. 组合报警继电器箱失电

**B. DIESEL GENERATOR (D/G) 柴油发电机**
1. NO.1 D/G SOURCE FAIL. 1 号柴油发电机电源故障
2. NO.1 D/G START AIR PRESS LOW. 1 号柴油发电机启动空气压力低
3. NO.1 D/G SPEED SWITCH FAIL. 1 号柴油发电机测速装置故障
4. NO.1 GEN.R. PHASE WIND TEMP. 1 号柴油发电机 R 相绕组温度
5. D/G F.O. MODULE COMM ALARM. 柴油发电机燃油模块公共报警
6. CENTRAL VACUUM UNIT ABN. 真空装置故障
7. M/E F.O. FLOW METER. 主机燃油流量
8. NO.1 D/G STARTING FAILURE. 1 号柴油发电机启动失败

**C. OTHERS**
1. NO.1 STEERING GEAR NO-VOLTAGE. 1 号舵机失电
2. NO.1 STEERING GEAR OVERLOAD. 1 号舵机失电
3. NO.1 STEERING GEAR PHASE FAIL. 1 号舵机相序故障
4. CO2 RELAY BOX POWER FAIL. CO$_2$ 继电器箱失电
5. MARINE GROWTH PREVENT PLANT ABN. 防海生物装置异常
6. NO.1 AUTOPILOT SOURCE FAIL. 1 号自动舵失电
7. AIR CONDITION COMM ALARM. 空调装置公共报警
8. PROV. REF. PLANT ABN. 伙食冷藏装置异常
9. FIRE DETECTING SYS. POWER FAIL. 火警系统失电
10. BATT. CH. & DISCH. PANEL ABN. 充放电板异常
11. TELEGRAPH SYSTEM COMMON ALARM. 车钟系统公共报警
12. INCINERATOR ABN. 焚烧炉异常
13. EM'CY GEN. ALARM. 应急发电机报警

14. M/E F.O. VISCOSITY HIGH. 主机燃油黏度高
15. M/E L.O. FILTER DIFF PRESS HIGH. 滑油滤器压差高
16. M/E OIL MIST DETECTOR FAIL. 主机油雾浓度探测器故障
17. F.O. PURI. OPERATOR W. TK L. 燃油分油机操作水箱液位低
18. SEWAGE TREATMENT TK LEVEL HIGH. 污水处理柜液位高
19. L.O. TRANS. PUMP ABN. STOP. 滑油油箱泵异常停
20. NO.1 HOT WATER CIRC. PUMP ABN. STOP. 一号热水循环泵异常停
21. CONTROL AIR DRYER ABN. 控制空气干燥器异常
22. NO.1 F.O. PURIFIER UNIT ABN. 一号燃油分油器异常
23. NO.1 L.O. PURIFIER UNIT ABN. 一号滑油分油器异常
24. BILGE SEPARATOR OIL CONTENT HIGH. 舱底水分离器含油量高
25. FORE (P.) BILGE WELL LEVEL HIGH. 前污水井（左）液位高
26. STUFF BOX DRAIN TK LEVEL HIGH. 填料箱泄放柜液位高
27. STERN TUBE L.O. GRAV. TK LEVEL. 艉管滑油重力油柜液位低
28. COMP. BOILER CASCADE TK LEVEL HIGH. 锅炉热井液位高

## 【Training Evaluation】

| 考核内容 | | 所占比例 | 分数 |
|---|---|---|---|
| 知识考核 | | 40% | |
| 会背诵接线、绝缘、调试常用的句子 | | 20 | |
| 准确识读船舶主机自动化术语、主机遥控系统、自动化电站、监测与报警点表册 至少 50 个 | | 20 | |
| 技能考核 | | 60% | |
| 个人考核 | 说出试验和调试术语 20 个以上 | 30 | |
| 小组考核 | 以小组为单位，任选船舶试验和调试某方面，背写出试验和调试术语 30 个以上，填写在附表里 | 30 | |
| 总分 | | | |

附表

| NO. | CHINESE | ENGLISH |
|---|---|---|
| | | |

# Grammar

**(一) 词汇特点**

1. 学生学习专业英语的目的

进行技术交流，分为口头和报告。

2. 专业英语特点

（1）Background(背景) 单词在不同语境中表达的意义不同，比如 art 这个单词，最常见的意思是"艺术"，而在专业英语中常翻译为"技术"。

（2）Grammar(语法) 专业英语的语法结构比较简单，作为经过高中学习的学生来说不是困难的事。

3. 专业英语翻译的基本要求

对专业英语翻译要求有三个层次：即，信、达、雅。所谓"信"，即翻译忠实原文；所谓"达"，即翻译通顺。所谓"雅"，要求翻译在修辞上加以润色，这要求译者有较高的中文造诣。

翻译方法有四种，分别为直译、意译、音译和阐译。原则是直译为主，音译为辅，其余为补。

4. 船舶电气专业英语的遣词、用字

（1）(electrical)marine (电机)包括: motor(电动机)和 generator（发电机）。

（2）电气

| | |
|---|---|
| device | 小型开关电气 |
| apparatus | 工业电气，熔断器等，可替代 appliance |
| switch | 开关功能 |
| equipment | 大型设备 |
| instrument | 仪器仪表（测试） |

（3）从不同方面考虑[电压（voltage）；电流（current）等]

voltage level(电压等级)：low(低)、medium（中）、high（高）、extra(超高)、ultra(特高)。

current: large(大的)、small(小的)

结构:configuration(内部结构)；structure(外部结构)

Speed(速率)；velocity(速度)

（4）船舶电气一些基础单词

① electricity(电)；electrical(电气的)

  e.g. electrical charge 电荷（positive 正的；negative 负的）

② electro-含"电"的词头　e.g：electromagnetic 电磁的

③ component(元件)

| | | | |
|---|---|---|---|
| resistor | 电阻器 | resistance | 电阻 |
| capacitor | 电容器 | capacitance | 电容 |
| inductor | 电感器 | inductance | 电感 |

④ circuit 电路（简单的）； circuitry 电路学（复杂的）
⑤ line 线路（走的线）； wire 导线
⑥ power system

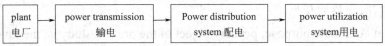

⑦ transformer 变压器

primary/secondary 初/次　　　step up 升压　　step down 降压

⑧ LV.低压：relay 继电气；contactor 接触器

MV.中压：circuit breaker 断路器　　vacuum CB 真空断路器

HV.高压：dis-connector 隔离开关　　earth switch 接地开关

GIS 气体绝缘开关

(二) 专业计算及其符号

1. 计算和计量

缩略语：ect: and others; e.g（等等）；VS（关系）；/ per（每）。

2. 数学符号

| | | |
|---|---|---|
| $A=b$ <br> $a$ equals $b$ | $a\approx b$ <br> $a$ approximately equals $b$ | $a:b$ <br> the ratio of $a$ to $b$ |
| $a>b$: $a$ is greater than $b$ | $a<b$: $a$ is less than $b$ | $a+b$: $a$ add $b$ |
| $a-b$: $a$ minus $b$ | $a\times b$: $a$ times $b$ | $a\div b$: $a$ is divided by $b$ |
| $a^2$: $a$ squared | $a^3$: $a$ cubed | $a^4=a$ to the fourth |
| $a^{-1}$: $a$ to the minus one | $\sqrt{a}$: the square root of $a$ | $\sqrt[3]{a}$: the cube root of $a$ |
| $\sqrt[5]{a^2}$: the fifth root of $a$ square | $a'$: $a$ prime | $a''$: $a$ second prime |
| $a'''$: $a$ triple prime | $dZ/dX$: first derivative of $Z$ with respect to $X$ | $AB//CD$: $AB$ is parallel to $CD$ |
| $AB\perp CD$: $AB$ is perpendicular to $CD$ | 0.51: point five one | 10%: ten percent |

(三) 语法特点

1. 多用陈述句

e.g. All radiant energy has wavelike characteristic.

所有辐射能有像波一样的特性。

2. 多用祈使句

e.g. Note that the word "velocity" requires explanation.

注意单词 velocity 需要解释。

3. 多用长句、复合句、非限制性定语从句

Most computer systems have some way to store information permanently, whether it is on cassette tapes, floppy disks, or hard disk fixed inside the system unit.

大多数计算机系统有一些永久保存信息的方法，无论是在盒式磁带，软盘还是在固定在系统单元的硬盘上。

4. 事实、自然现象规律，多用一般现在时

The computers instructions reside in main memory.

计算机指令存储在主存储器中。

5. 条件句　表示前提、背景（实验条件、模拟条件），推测判断

If we follow those instructions, we will certainly be in good health.

如果我们遵循这些指示，我们肯定会很健康。

6. 句子程式化，"格式化"

E.g.: the chief aim; main purpose; primary object of the present study is; the investigation is ,etc.

E.g.: has (have) been concluded; has(have) been gained; has(have) been obtained; has(have) been reached, etc.

7. 后置定语

（1）adj.及 adj.短语充当后置定语

In radiation, thermal energy is transformed into radiant energy, similar in nature to light.

在辐射中，热能被转化成辐射能，跟光的本质一样。

（2）adv.

The force upward equals the force downward so that the balloon stays at the level.

当上下压力一致时，气球处于水平位置。

（3）ing/ed 分词及分词短语

The results obtained must be checked.

已取得的研究成果必须被检验。

（4）prep.短语

The force due to friction are called frictional force.

由于摩擦产生的力被称为摩擦力。

（5）定语从句

The day will come when coal and oil will be used as raw materials rather than as fuels.

煤和石油作为原材料而不是作为燃料的那天将要到来。

**(四) 阅读和翻译**

1. 长句分析的基本步骤

（1）泛读一遍，了解句子的梗概和大意。

（2）分析句子类型。如果是复合句，找出各个单句。

（3）单句结构分析。

① 确定句型；

② 先找出主、谓、宾、表语等主要成分，后找定、状语等次要成分；

③ 分析各成分之间的关系；

④ 分析各成分的结构；

⑤ 疑难和关键问题分析，最后确定某些待定词汇的意义。

（4）全句翻译。

2. 长句的阅读、分析与翻译

(1) With a CPP-equipped ship, there is roughly a relationship as shown in Fig.1 among the main engine's output, engine speed (rpm), ship's speed and CPP pitch, supposing that the ship's hull conditions (such as draft, fouling of the hull, weather conditions) are constant.

句析：主句是 with…CPP pitch，supposing that 引导条件状语从句。主句里，在 there be 句型中，主语是 a relationship。as shown in Fig. 1 是 a relationship 的定语。among...CPP pitch 是状

语。从句中是简单的主谓结构。翻译时先译状语及状语从句。

全句翻译：对于一艘装备了可控螺距桨的船舶，若假定船的外部条件（如吃水、船体阻力、天气情况）不变，则在主机的输出功率、主机转速（转／分）、船速以及可控螺距桨的螺距之间，如图1所示。

(2) So, with a Fpp-equipped ship, there exists only one relationship among the ship's speed, main engine output and main engine rpm., if the hull conditions are constant, and hence both ship's speed and main engine output can be controlled simultaneously by merely controlling the main engine rpm.

句析：主句是 with...engine rpm.，if 引导条件状语从句，and 引出并列复合句。主句中，主语是 One relationship，谓语是 exists，状语是 with...，among...。并列复合句中，主语是 both...output，谓语是 can be controlled...。翻译时先译状语及状语从句。被动语态宜改为主动语态翻译。

全句翻译：这样，对于一艘装备了 FPP（固定螺距桨）的船舶，如果外部条件不变，则在船速、主机输出功率以及主机转速之间存在着唯一的关系。因此，我们能够仅通过控制主机转速，来同时控制船速和主机输出功率。

(3) This means that there is involved a highly complicated scheme of control if CPP's pitch and main engine rpm. are to be controlled individually, this indicating the need for some form of simplification, and introduced below are some typical proposals for such simplification of control.

句析：主句是 This means，that 引导宾语从句。在宾语从句中，主句是 there is...of control，这是一个 there 位于句首，而真正主语移到句末的一种情况，即主语是(a highly) scheme(...of control)，谓语是 is involved。从句是由 if 引导的条件状语从句。this indicating ...of simplification 为分词独立结构，作状语。and 引出并列复合语句，主语为 proposals，谓语为 are introduced，是倒装句。翻译时被动语态译成主动语态。按中文习惯，名词 need 可以按动词翻译。

全句翻译：这意味着，如果我们独立地去控制可控螺距桨的螺距和主机转速，就将涉及一个非常复杂的控制方案，这表明需要某些简化的方式。下述所介绍的内容是对于这种简化控制的一些典型的建议。

(4) This scheme of keeping the main engine rpm. constant and only controlling the GPP pitch according to the main engine load and the desired ship speed is now widely adopted.

句析；谓语是 is adopted，主语是 scheme。of...介词短语作定语，很长，keeping 和 controlling 为动名词，各带自己的宾语、状语和定语。

全句翻译：此方案目前被广泛地采用，即：保持主机转速恒定不变，而仅根据主机负荷和期望的船速来控制可控螺距桨的螺距。

(5) The relationship for this system among the main engine load, ship speed and pitch is as shown in Fig.2, the change of load caused by variation of the hull conditions being compensatable by pitch adjustment:

句析：主句中谓语是 is shown，中间的 as 为副词作状语。the change of load...being...是分词独立结构，作状语，其中 caused by...conditions 为 change of load 后置定语。

全句翻译：对于这个系统，主机负荷、船速和螺距之间的关系如图2所示。由船体外部条件变化而引起的负荷变化，可通过调整螺距来补偿。

(6) It is, of course, also possible to operate this system with the main engine rpm. kept constant, but described below is the system of setting by handle both load and rpm.

句析：it 是形式主语，实际主语是不定式短语 to operate...。with the main engine rpm.是 with 带主谓关系的复合结构，说明附带情况，作状语。

# Grammar

全句翻译：当然，在保持主机转速恒定的情况下，操纵这个系统也是可以做到的，但下面叙述的是负荷和转速都由手柄给定的系统。

(7) As to the effect of a change in hull conditions on the pattern of the maximum efficiency curve, it is apparent from Fig.3 showing a comparison between full and light load conditions that such a change, which is reflected on ship's speed, has practically no effect on the main engine rpm. /load relationship.

句析：as to...curve 是状语，it 是形式主语，实际主语是 that 引导的主语从句。从句中主语是 such a change，谓语是 has，宾语是 no effect。which...ship's speed 的定语从句中 which 代表 such a change。

全句翻译：至于船体外部条件的变化对最大效率蓝线图形的影响，我们从显示满载和轻载相比较的图 3 中可以明显看出：由船速反映的这一变化对主机转速／负荷关系实际上没有影响。

(8) Since with such a system the pitch is automatically controlled so that the actual load matches the set load, it is then possible to perform unitary control by means of a single control handle.

句析：since..., it is possible...意思是由于……才是可能的。since 引导原因状语从句，从句中又由复合句组成，其中主句的主语是 the pitch，谓语是 is controlled，so that 引导原因从句。全句主句中 it 是形式主语，实际主语是 to perform...。翻译时可在理解全句意思的基础上进行意译。

全句翻译：由于这样一个螺距自动控制系统使实际负荷与给定负荷相匹配，所以才可能用一只控制手柄来完成整体控制。

(9) In this connection, however, to be remembered is that, while in the high load range control of the load is possible through adjustment of the mode of control, it is difficult in the low load range where a change of pitch is less positively reflected on the load.

句析：In this connection 意思是就此而论，在这方面。主句中的谓语倒装。is to be remembered，that 引导出主语从句。while...the mode of control 是由 while 引导的让步状语从句。主句中主语 it 代表 the mode of control，其中 where 又引导出 the low load range 的定语从句。

全句翻译：然而，在这方面应提到的是，虽然在高负荷范围内，以此控制方式的调节进行负荷控制是可能办到的，但在低负荷范围内，由于螺距变化与负荷的关系不大，所以负荷的控制是困难的。

# Appendix  New Words and Expressions

## Unit 1

**Task 1**

| | | | |
|---|---|---|---|
| wheelhouse | ['wiːlhaʊs] | n. | 驾驶室，操舵室 |
| bridge | [ brɪdʒ] | n. | 驾驶室，桥楼 |
| telegraph | ['telɪgrɑːf] | n. | 电报 |
| bulkhead | ['bʌlkhed] | n. | 隔离壁,堵墙,岸壁 |
| charthouse | ['tʃɑːtˌhaʊs] | n. | 海图室 |
| fathometer | [fæˈðɒmɪtə] | n. | 回声探测仪 |
| gyrocompass | ['dʒaɪərəʊˌkʌmpəs] | n. | 陀螺罗经,电罗经 |
| gyroscope | [ˈdʒaɪrəskəʊp] | n. | 陀螺仪 |
| helmsman | ['helmzmən] | n. | 舵手 |
| landmark | ['lændmɑːk] | n. | [航]陆标 |
| pilothouse | ['paɪlətˌhaʊs] | n. | 操舵室 |
| quartermaster | [ˈkwɔːtəmɑːstə(r)] | n. | 舵手 |
| steering | ['stɪərɪŋ] | n. | 转向装置；掌舵；操作；指导 |
|     steering wheel | | | 方向盘；驾驶盘 |
|     steering gear | | | 操舵装置，舵机 |
| platform | ['plætfɔːm] | n. | 台；站台；平台 |
| tachometer | [tæˈkɒmɪtə(r)] | n | 转速计；测速计；旋速计；速度计 |
| bridge wings | | | 驾驶台两侧的翼台 |
|     port bridge wing | | | 左翼（PORT WING） |
|     starboard bridge wing | | | 右翼(经常缩写为 STBD. WING) |
| (bridge control console)BCC | | | 驾控台 |
| Global Positioning System(GPS) Receiver | | | 全球定位系统接收机 |
| Loran-C receiver | | | 罗兰 C, 远程双曲线无线电导航系统接收机 |
| NAVTEX | | | 航行警告电传系统 |

**Task 2**

| | | | |
|---|---|---|---|
| Engine Control Room(ECR) | | | 集控室 |
| Engine Control Console(ECC) | | | 集控台 |
| switch | [ swɪtʃ ] | n.&v. | 开关 转换 |
| propulsion | [ prəˈpʌlʃən ] | n. | 推进 推进力 |
| engine | [ˈendʒɪn ] | n. | 发动机，引擎 |
| main engine(ME) | | n. | 主机 |

*197*

| | | | |
|---|---|---|---|
| generator | [ˈdʒenəˌretə] | n. | 发电机 |
| diesel generator(D.G) | | | 柴油发动机 |
| shaft generator | | | 轴带发电机 |
| turbo generator | | | 涡轮发电机 |
| Unattended Machinery Space（UMS） | | | 无人机舱 |

## Unit 2

**Task 1**

| | | | |
|---|---|---|---|
| electrical-hydraulic | | adj. | 电动液压 |
| auto-tension | | n. | 自动张力 |
| general arrangement | | n. | 总布置图 |
| split type | | | 分体式 |
| manufacturer's standard | | | 制造商标准 |
| polyamide | | n. | 聚酰胺 |
| holding force | [ˈhəʊldɪŋ fɔːs] | n. | 矫顽力，自持力 |
| warping head | [ˈwɔːpɪŋ hed] | n. | 绞缆筒 |
| midship | [ˈmɪdʃɪp] | n. | 船体中央部 |
| | | adj. | 船体中央的；（航海用舵令）正舵 |
| coaming | [ˈkəʊmɪŋ] | n. | 舱口栏板，边材；围板 |
| drain plug | [ˈdreɪnˌplʌg] | | 排污螺塞，放油塞 |
| swivel | [ˈswɪvəl] | n. | 转节；转环；旋轴 |
| windlass | [ˈwɪndləs] | n. | 卷扬机，辘轳，绞盘 |
| hawse pipe | [ˈhɔːzˌpaɪp] | | 锚链孔衬管，锚链筒 |
| shackle | [ˈʃækəl] | n. | [机]钩环；[电]绝缘器 |
| chain locker | | | [船]锚链舱；锚链房；链锁 |
| emergency starting device | | | 应急启动装置 |

**Task 2**

| | | | |
|---|---|---|---|
| displacement | [dɪsˈpleɪsmənt] | n. | 位移，排水量 |
| centrifugal | [ˌsentrɪˈfjuːgl] | adj. | 离心的 |
| rotary | [ˈrəʊtərɪ] | adj. | 旋转的 |
| reciprocating | [rɪˈsɪprəkeɪtɪŋ] | adj. | 往复的 |
| volute | [vəˈljuːt] | adj.n. | 涡形的，蜗壳 |
| turbine | [ˈtɜːbaɪn] | n. | 涡轮，涡轮机 |
| boiler | [ˈbɔɪlə(r)] | n. | 锅炉 |
| distinct | [dɪˈstɪŋkt] | adj. | 截然不同的 |
| furnace | [ˈfɜːnɪs] | n. | 炉子，炉膛 |
| bent | [bent] | adj. | 弯的 |
| drum | [drʌm] | n. | 鼓，锅筒 |
| header | [ˈhedə(r)] | n. | 联箱 |

| generate | ['dʒenəreɪt] | v. | 产生 |
| downcomer | ['daʊnˌkʌmə] | n. | 下降管 |
| donkey | ['dɒŋkɪ] | adj. | 辅助的 |
| installation | [ˌɪnstə'leɪʃn] | n. | 装置 |
| steam ship | [stiːm ʃɪp] | n. | 蒸汽机船 |
| motor ship | ['məʊtə ʃɪp] | n. | 内燃机船 |
| composite | ['kɒmpəzɪt] | adj. | 混合的，复合的 |
| cylinder | ['sɪlɪndə(r)] | n. | 汽缸 |

# Unit 3

**Task 1**

| induction | [ɪn'dʌkʃn] | n. | （电或磁的）感应 |
| synchronous | ['sɪŋkrənəs, 'sɪn-] | adj. | 同步的 |
| asynchronous | [e'sɪŋkrənəs] | adj. | 异步的 |
| squirrel-cage | [sk'wɪrəlk'eɪdʒ] | n. | 鼠笼，鼠笼式 |
| pump | [pʌmp] | n. | 泵 |
| blower | ['bloʊə(r)] | n. | 送风机，通风机 |
| separator | ['sɛpəˌreɪə] | n. | 分离器，分离装置 |
| stator | ['steɪtə] | n. | 定子 |
| rotor | ['roʊtə(r)] | n. | 转子 |
| frame | [freɪm] | n. | 框架，机座 |
| lamination | [ˌlæmə'neɪʃən] | n. | 薄板，薄层，层状体 |
| shaft | [ʃɑːft] | n. | 轴 |
| conductor | [kən'dʌktə] | n. | 导体 |
| nameplate | ['neɪmˌpleɪt] | n. | 铭牌 |
| hydraulic engine | | | 液压机械 |
| auxiliary equipment | | | 辅助设备 |
| stator core | | | 定子铁芯 |
| stator winding | | | 定子绕组 |
| Ingress Protection | | | 防护 |
| insulation material | | | 绝缘材料 |

**Task 2**

| relay | ['riːleɪ] | n. | 继电器 |
| protector | [prə'tektə] | n. | 保护装置，保护器 |
| performance | [pə'fɔːməns] | n. | 性能，工作情况 |
| mechanism | ['mekənɪzəm] | n. | 构造；机理 |
| phase | [feɪz] | n. | 相，相位 |
|     phase sequence | | | 相序 |
| active contact | | | 有源触点 |

199

| | |
|---|---|
| passive contact | 无源触点 |
| relay-contactor | 继电器—接触器 |
| electrical schematic diagram | 电气原理图 |
| element symbol | 元件符号 |
| forward/reversal rotation | 正/反转 |
| thermal relay | 热继电器 |
| low-voltage electrical apparatus | 低压控制电器 |
| (QF)automatic air-break switch | 自动开关 |
| （FU）fuse | 熔断器 |
| （KM）contactor | 接触器 |
| （SB）push button | 按钮 |
| overtravel–limit switch(travel switch) | 行程开关 |
| （KV）voltage relay | 电压继电器 |
| （KI）current relay | 电流继电器 |
| （KT）time relay | 时间继电器 |

## Uint 4

**task 1**

| | | | |
|---|---|---|---|
| generate | [ˈdʒenəreɪt] | v. | 发生，产生 |
| distribute | [dɪˈstrɪbjuːt] | v. | 分配，分给 |
| consume | [kənˈsjuːm] | v. | 消耗，分配 |
| consumer | [kənˈsjuːmə(r)] | n. | 消费者，顾客 |
| parallel | [ˈpærəlɛl] | Adj. &adv. | 并联的,并行的 并联地,并行地 |
| electricity | [ɪlɛkˈtrɪsɪti] | n. | 电力 |
| Uninterruptible Power Supply（UPS） | | | 不间断电源 |
| propel | [prəˈpel] | v. | 推进；驱动；驱使 |
| propeller | [prəˈpelə(r)] | n. | 螺旋桨，推进器 |
| propulsion | [prəˈpʌlʃn] | n. | 推进 |
| prime mover | | n. | 原动机 |
| marine power system | | | 船舶电力系统 |
| power source | | | 电源 |

**Task 2**

| | | | |
|---|---|---|---|
| maintain | [meɪnˈteɪn] | vt. | 保持；维护；维持 |
| maintenance | [ˈmentənəns] | n. | 保持；维护；维持 |
| maturity | [məˈtʃʊərəti] | n. | 成熟；完备 |
| credibility | [ˌkredəˈbɪləti] | n. | 可靠性, 可信性；确实性 |
| spare | [speə] | adj.&n | 多余的，备用的；备件 |

| auxiliary | [ɔːgˈzɪlɪəri] | adj. | 辅助的；备用的 |
| repetitive | [rɪˈpetətɪv] | adj. n. | 重复的（是学过的动词 repeat 的形容词的形式，repeat 的意思是：复述、重复） |
| manual | [ˈmænjuəl] | adj. | 手动的；手制的，手工的；体力的 |
| | | n. | 手册；指南 |
| instruction | [ɪnˈstrʌkʃn] | n. | 授课；[计算机科学]指令 |
| procedure | [prəˈsiːdʒə] | n. | 步骤、程序 |
| forego | [fɔːˈgəu] | vt. | 走在……之前，居先 |
| power station | | | 电站 |
| auxiliary machine | | | 辅机 |
| short circuit | | | 短路 |
| switch on | | | 闭合，接通 |
| switch off | | | 断开 |
| indicator lights | | | 指示灯 |
| manual control buttons | | | 手动控制按钮 |
| reset buttons | | | 复位开关 |
| change-over switch | | | 转换开关 |
| split up | | | 分成……份，分配 |

## Unit 5

**Task 1**

| installation | [ˌɪnstəˈleɪʃn] | n. | 安装；装置 |
| vibration | [vaɪˈbreɪʃn] | n. | 摆动；震动 |
| corrosion | [kəˈrəuʒn] | n. | 腐蚀，侵蚀，锈蚀 |
| mud | [mʌd] | n. | 污物 |
| telecommunication | [ˈtelikəmjuniˈkeɪʃn] | n. | 电信；电通信 |
| petroleum | [piˈtrəuliəm] | n. | 石油 |
| exploitation | [ˌeksplɔɪˈteɪʃn] | n. | 开发；利用； |
| insulation | [ˌɪnsəˈleɪʃn] | n. | 绝缘；绝缘或隔热的材料 |
| conductor | [kənˈdʌktə] | n. | 导体 |
| braid | [breɪd] | n. | 编织物 |
| armour | [ˈɑːmə(r)] | n. | 铠装 |
| cross-section areas | | | 横截面积 |
| open deck | | | 露天甲板 |
| rated voltage | | | 额定电压 |
| fire-resistant | | | 防火 |
| Classification societies | | | 船级社 |
| Regulatory Bodies | | | 监管机构 |

PA/GA 广播/通用报警系统
engine room 机舱
ambient temperature 环境温度

**Task 2**

| | | | |
|---|---|---|---|
| humidity | [hjuːˈmiditi] | n. | 湿度；潮湿 |
| gland | [glænd] | n. | 填料函 |
| ventilation | [ˌventlˈeɪʃn] | n. | 空气流通；通风设备 |
| absorber | [əbˈsɔːbə] | n. | 减震器 |
| screwdriver | [ˈskruːˌdraɪvə] | n. | 螺钉旋具 |

Electrical Installation Standard 电气安装规范
package of equipment 设备的配套
class type approval certificate 船检检验合格证
effective date 有效期限
equipment specification 设备型号规格
insulation resistance 绝缘电阻
ground accessories 接地附件
lighting fixtures 舱室照明灯具
fan and heater 日用电器
flood light 投光灯
defend capability 防护性能
ex-proof equipment 防爆设备

# Unit 6

**Task 1**

| | | | |
|---|---|---|---|
| anchor | [ˈæŋkə] | n. | 锚 |
| detector | [dɪˈtektə] | n. | 探测器,探头 |
| detection | [dɪˈtekʃn] | n. | 侦查,检测 |

UMS(Unattended Machinery Space) 无人机舱

| | | | |
|---|---|---|---|
| monitor | [ˈmɒnɪtə(r)] | n/v. | 监控 |
| audible | [ˈɔːdəbl] | adj. | 听得见的 |
| visual | [ˈvɪʒuəl] | adj. | 视觉的，看得见的； |

audible and visual alarm 声光报警

| | | | |
|---|---|---|---|
| analog | [ˈænəlɔːg] | adj./n. | 模拟的 |
| digital | [ˈdɪdʒɪtl] | adj. | 数字的 |
| exhaust gas | [ɪgˈzɔst gæs] | | 废气 |
| F.O.(Fuel Oil) | [ˈfjuəlˈɔɪl] | | 燃油 |
| L.O. (Lube Oil) | [lubˈɔɪl] | | 滑油 |

F.O.and L.O. system 燃油和滑油系统
false alarm 误报警

extension alarm 延伸警报
upper/lower limit 上/下限

**Task 2**

| | | | |
|---|---|---|---|
| engine telegraph | | | 车钟 |
| automation | [ˌɔtəˈmeʃən] | n. | 自动化（技术），自动操作 |
| button | [ˈbʌtn] | n. | 按钮 |
| instrument | [ˈɪnstrəmənt] | n. | 仪器 |
| connect | [kəˈnekt] | v. | 连接；使…有联系；为…接通电话；插入插座 |

# Unit 7

**Task1**

| | | | |
|---|---|---|---|
| maritime | [ˈmærɪtaɪm] | adj. | 海事的，海运上的 |
| distress | [disˈtres] | n. | 悲痛；危难，不幸； |
| procedure | [prəˈsiːdʒə] | n. | 程序，手续；过程，步骤； |
| protocol | [ˈprəʊtəˌkɔːl] | n. | (数据传递的) 协议； |
| determination | [diˌtəːmiˈneɪʃən] | n. | 确定；测定， |
| coordination | [kəʊˌɔːdnˈeɪʃən] | n. | 协调；和谐 |
| guarantee | [ˌgærənˈtiː] | v. | 保证，担保 |
| radiotelephone | [ˈreidiəuˈtelifəun] | n. | 无线电话 |
| radiotelephony | [ˈreidiəutəˈlefəni] | n. | 无线电话 |
| nautical | [ˈnɔːtɪkəl] | adj. | 海上的，航海的； |
| geostationary | [ˌdʒi(ː)əuˈsteiʃənəri] | adj. | 与地球的相对位置不变的 |
| satellite | [ˈsætəlait] | n. | 卫星 |
| latitude | [ˈlætitjuːd] | n. | 纬度 |
| tonnage | [ˈtʌnɪdʒ] | n. | (衡量船舶大小的排水) 吨位 |
| nautical miles(n mile) | | | 海里 |
| Coast Station | | | 海岸电台 |
| Inmarsat(International Maritime Satellite Telephone Service) | | | 国际海事卫星 |
| geostationary satellite | | | 地球同步卫星 |
| polar region | | | 极地，近极区域 |
| Two-way VHF radiotelephone apparatus | | | 双向甚高频无线电话设备 |
| Radar transponder | | | 雷达应答器 |
| EPIRB (Emergency Position-Indicating Radio Beacon) | | | 应急无线电示位标 |
| EGC (Enhanced Group Call) | | | 增强群呼系统 |

**Task 2**

| | | | |
|---|---|---|---|
| microphone | [ˈmaikrəfəun] | n. | 扩音器，话筒 |
| loudspeaker | [ˈlaudˌspiːkə] | n. | 扬声器；喇叭 |
| duplex | [ˈdjuːpleks] | a. | 有两部分的 |
| radar | [ˈreidə] | n. | 雷达 |

| Aerial/antenna | [ˈeəriəl]/ [ænˈtenə] | n. | 天线 |
| infrastructure | [ˈɪnfrəˌstrʌktʃə] | n. | 基础设施 |
| communication system | | | 通信系统 |
| navigation equipment | | | 航行设备 |
| internal communication system | | | 内部通信系统 |
| talk-back system | | | 对讲电话系统 |
| steering gear room | | | 舵机舱 |
| automatic telephone system | | | 自动电话系统 |
| sound powered telephone | | | 声力电话 |
| UPS (Uninterruptible Power System) | | | 不间断电源 |
| public adress system | | | 广播系统 |
| ARPA(Automatic Radar Plotting Aid) | | | 自动雷达标绘仪 |
| DGPS(Difference Global Positioning System) | | | 差分全球定位系统 |
| echo sounder | | | 回声测深仪 |
| log | | | 计程仪 |
| magnetic standard compass | | | 标准磁罗经 |
| automatic pilot | | | 自动驾驶仪 |
| international shore telephone | | | 国际通岸电话 |
| rescue coordination centers | | | 救援协调中心 |
| SSB (Single Side Band) | | | 单边带 |

## Unit 8

### Task 1

| maintenance | [ˈmeɪntənəns] | n. | 保养；维护；维修 |
| jury-rigged | [ˈdʒʊərɪˌrɪgd] | adj. | 临时或应急配备的 |
| electrolysis | [ɪˌlekˈtrɒləsɪs] | n. | 电解，电蚀；电蚀除瘤[毛发等] |
| vibration | [vaɪˈbreɪʃn] | n. | 摆动；震动 |
| abrasive | [əˈbreɪsɪv] | adj. | 有磨蚀作用的；摩擦的 |
| hose | [həʊz] | n. | 软管，胶皮管 |
| splicing | [ˈsplaɪsɪŋ] | v. | 绞接( splice 的现在分词 ) |
| tangle | [ˈtæŋgl] | vt.& vi. | (使) 缠结，(使)乱作一团 |
| trace | [treɪs] | vt. | 跟踪，追踪；追溯，探索 |
| spaghetti | [spəˈgeti] | n. | 意大利面条；[电]漆布绝缘管 |
| bonding | [ˈbɒndɪŋ] | n. | 黏结；连[搭，焊，胶，粘]接 |
| illustrative | [ˈɪləstrətɪv] | adj.adv. | 解说性的;解说性地 |
| earth potential | | | 地电势 |
| negative potential | | | 负电势，负电位 |

### Task 2

| | | | |
|---|---|---|---|
| personnel | [ˌpɜːsəˈnel] | n. | (总称)人员 |
| voltmeter | [ˈvəʊltˌmiːtə] | n. | 电压表 |
| ammeter | [ˈæmɪtə] | n. | 电流表，安培计 |
| ohmmeter | [ˈəʊmˌmiːtə] | n. | 电阻表，欧姆计 |
| multimeter | [mʌlˈtimitə] | n. | 万用表 |
| wattmeter | [ˈwɒtmiːtə] | n. | 功率表，瓦特计 |
| troubleshooting | [ˈtrʌblʃuːtɪŋ] | n. | 故障查找 |
| logical order | | | 逻辑顺序 |
| verify | [ˈverɪfaɪ] | vt. | 核实 证明 判定 |
| lead-acid | | | 铅酸的 |
| in series | | | 连续地，串联 |
| tool kit | | | 工具包 |

## Unit 9

| | | | |
|---|---|---|---|
| megger | [ˈmegə] | n. | 兆欧表，摇表 |
| meg-ohmmeter | | n. | 兆欧表，摇表 |
| mooring | [ˈmɔːrɪŋ] | n. | 停泊处；系泊用具，系船具；下锚 |
| mooring test | | | 系泊试验 |
| trial | [ˈtraɪəl] | n. | 测试，试验 |
| sea trial | | | 试航 |
| soldering iron | | | 烙铁 |
| performance | [pəˈfɔːməns] | n. | 履行；性能；表现；演出 |
| impedance | [ɪmˈpiːdns] | n. | 阻抗，全电阻；电阻抗 |
| calibrate | [ˈkælɪbreɪt] | vt. | 校准 |
| davit | [ˈdævɪt] | n. | 吊艇架 |
| ladder | [ˈlædə] | n. | 梯子 |
| ohmmeter | [ˈəʊmmiːtə(r)] | n. | 欧姆表 |
| accommodation ladder | | | （船的）舷梯 |
| workmanship | [ˈwɜːkmənʃɪp] | n. | 技艺，工艺 |
| insulation resistance | | | 绝缘电阻 |
| shore-power | | | 岸电 |
| lighting circuits | | | 照明电路 |

## Unit 10

### Task 1

| | | | |
|---|---|---|---|
| breadth | [bredθ] | n. | 船宽 |
| depth | [depθ] | n. | 型深 |
| displacement | [dɪsˈpleɪsmənt] | n. | 排水量 |

| | | | |
|---|---|---|---|
| draft | [drɑːft] | n. | 吃水 |
| Denmark | ['denmɑːk] | n. | 丹麦 |
| alternator | [ˈɔːltəneɪtə(r)] | n. | 交流发电机 |
| manufacturer | [ˌmænjuˈfæktʃərə(r)] | n. | 制造厂 |
| dismount | [dɪsˈmaʊnt] | v. | 拆卸 |
| workshop | [ˈwɜːkʃɒp] | n. | 车间 |
| disassemble | [ˌdɪsəˈsembl] | v. | 解体，分解 |
| cleaner | [ˈkliːnə(r)] | n. | 清洁剂 |
| dried | [draɪd] | v. | 烘干 |
| machine | [məˈʃiːn] | v. | 光车 |
| rust | [rʌst] | n. | 铁锈 |
| potentiometer | [pəˌtenʃiˈɒmɪtə(r)] | n. | 电位器 |
| eliminate | [ɪˈlɪmɪneɪt] | v. | 排除 |
| invalid | [ɪnˈvælɪd] | adj. | 无效的 |
| grease | [griːs] | n. | 润滑脂 |
| lub = lubricating | [ˈluːbrɪkeɪtɪŋ] | n. | 润滑 |
| injector | [ɪnˈdʒektə] | n. | 喷油器 |
| aux. = auxiliary | [ɔːgˈzɪliəri] | adj. | 辅助的 |
| corrosion | [kəˈrəʊzn] | n. | 锈蚀 |
| purifier | [ˈpjʊərɪfaɪə(r)] | n. | 分油机 |
| accessory | [əkˈsesəri] | n. | 属具 |
| relevant | [ˈreləvənt] | adj. | 相应的 |
| critical | [ˈkrɪtɪkl] | adj. | 临界的 |
| servomotor | [ˈsɜːvəʊˈməʊtə] | n. | 伺服电动机 |
| mist | [mɪst] | n. | 雾 |
| sensor | [ˈsensə(r)] | n. | 传感器 |
| ladder | [ˈlædə(r)] | n. | 梯子 |
| staging | [ˈsteɪdʒɪŋ] | n. | 脚手架 |
| labour | [ˈleɪbə(r)] | n. | 劳动力 |
| tender | [ˈtendə(r)] | n. | 报价（投标价） |
| workmanship | [ˈwɜːkmənˌʃɪp] | n. | 工艺 |
| owner | [ˈəʊnə(r)] | n. | 船东 |
| therewith | [ˌðeəˈwɪð] | adv. | 与此；随即 |
| principal specification | | | 要素 |
| Leizhouhai | | | "雷州海" |
| L. O. A. =length overall | | | 总长 |
| G. R. T. = gross weight | | | 总重 |
| one coat of | | | 一层，一度 |
| slip ring | | | 滑环 |

# Appendix  New Words and Expressions

| | |
|---|---|
| driving end | 拖动端，原动机侧 |
| on board | 船上 |
| in order | 就绪 |
| running test without load | 空载试验 |
| hand over to ship | 交船 |
| in triplicate | 一式三份 |
| ACB = air circuit breaker | 空气断路器 |
| reverse power test | 逆功率试验 |
| SCR = silicon controlled rectifier | 可控硅 |
| active power | 有功功率 |
| factor meters | 功率因数表 |
| synchro indicator | 同步指示器，同步表 |
| stand-by | 备用 |
| yard's spares | 船厂提供的备件 |
| M. E. = main engine | 主机 |
| aux. Engine | 辅机，发电机，原动机 |
| steering gear | 舵机 |
| register of shipping | 船舶登记局 |
| windlass motor | 卧式锚机 |
| follow up | 随动 |
| mast house | 桅楼 |
| feed back | 反馈 |
| baking oven | 烘箱 |
| classification society | 船级社 |

## Task 2

| | | | |
|---|---|---|---|
| certificate | [sə'tɪfɪkət] | n. | 证明书；文凭 |
| classification | [ˌklæsɪfɪ'keɪʃn] | n. | 分类；分级；类别 |
| connection | [kə'nekʃn] | n. | 连接；联系，关系；连接点 |
| torque | [tɔːk] | n. | （尤指机器的）扭转力；转动力 |
| overdue | [ˌəʊvə'djuː] | adj. | 过期的；延误的，迟到的；未兑的 |
| amount | [ə'maʊnts] | n. | 总额；金额 |
| rated voltage | | | 额定电压 |
| insulation class | | | 绝缘种类[等级] |
| power factor | | | 功率因数 |
| rated frequency | | | 额定频率 |
| ambient temperature | | | 环境温度；背景温度；周围温度 |

# 参考文献

[1] 中国海事服务中心. 电子电气员英语. 大连：大连海事大学出版社，2012.

[2] 张孔群. 船舶图解大词典. 大连：大连海事大学出版社，2003.

[3] 张晓峰. 通信英语. 第二版. 大连：大连海事大学出版社，2009.

[4] 孙利望. 海事基础英语听说教程. 大连：大连海事大学出版社，2010.

[5] 宋运伟. 船舶电气英语. 哈尔滨：哈尔滨大学出版社，2012.

[6] 刘彤. 船舶电子电气专业英语. 大连：大连海事大学出版社，2012.

[7] 丁晓梅，将更红. 轮机专业英语. 哈尔滨：哈尔滨工程大学出版社，2006.

[8] 余华. 船电专业英语. 哈尔滨：哈尔滨工程大学出版社，2006.

[9] 王天序. 船电专业英语. 大连：大连海事大学出版社，1993.

[10] 陈文涛. 船舶电子电气专业英语. 上海：上海交通大学出版社，2014.

[11] The Sea: Books and Manuscripts on the Art of Navigation, Geography, Naval History, Shipbuilding, Voyages, Shipwrecks, and Mathematics, Including Atlases and Maps. Storrs-Mansfield, CT: Maurizio Martino Publishers, 2003.

[12] Sobel, Dava. Longitude: The True Story of a Lone Genius Who Solved the Greatest Scientific Problem of His Time. New York: Penguin USA, 1996.